European Landscapes of Rock-Art

Rock-art – the ancient images which still scatter the rocky landscapes of Europe – is a singular kind of archaeological evidence. Fixed in place, it does not move about as artefacts and trade objects do. Enigmatic in its meaning, it uniquely offers a direct record of how prehistoric Europeans saw and envisioned their own worlds.

European Landscapes of Rock-Art provides a number of case studies, covering a range of European locations including Ireland, Italy, Scandinavia, Scotland and Spain, which collectively address the chronology and geography of rock-art as well as providing an essential series of methodologies for future debate. Each author provides a synthesis that focuses on landscape as an essential part of rock-art construction. From the paintings and carved images of prehistoric Scandinavia to Second World War graffiti on the German Reichstag, this volume looks beyond the art to the society that made it.

The papers in this volume also challenge the traditional views as to how rock-art is recorded. Throughout, there is an emphasis on formal and on informed methodologies. The authors skilfully discuss subjectivity and its relationship with landscape since personal experience, from prehistoric times to the present day, plays an essential role in the interpretation of the art itself. The emphasis is on location, on the intentionality of the artist, and on the needs of the audience.

This exciting volume is a crucial addition to rock-art literature and landscape archaeology. It will provide new material for a lively and greatly debated subject and as such will be essential for academics, non-academics and commentators on rock-art in general.

George Nash is a part-time lecturer in European prehistory at the Centre of the Historic Environment, University of Bristol, and senior archaeologist with Border Archaeology. **Christopher Chippindale** is a curator in the Cambridge University Museum of Archaeology and Anthropology.

European Landscapes of Rock-Art

Edited by George Nash and
Christopher Chippindale

London and New York

First published 2002
by Routledge
11 New Fetter Lane, London EC4P 4EE

Simultaneously published in the USA and Canada
by Routledge
29 West 35th Street, New York, NY 10001

Routledge is an imprint of the Taylor & Francis Group

Typeset in Garamond by
Keystroke, Jacaranda Lodge, Wolverhampton.
Printed and bound in Great Britain by
TJ International Ltd, Padstow, Cornwall.

British Library Cataloguing in Publication Data
A catalogue record for this book is available
from the British Library

Library of Congress Cataloguing in Publication Data
European landscapes of rock-art / edited by George Nash and
Christopher Chippindale.
     p. cm.
   Includes bibliographical references and index.
   1. Petroglyphs—Europe. 2. Rock paintings—Europe.
   3. Graffiti—Europe. 4. Landscape assessment—Europe.
   5. Europe—Antiquities. I. Nash, George, 1959–
   II. Chippindale, Christopher, 1951–

   GN803 .E87 2001
   709'.01'13094—dc21   2001031993

ISBN 0–415–25734–4 (hbk)
ISBN 0–415–25735–2 (pbk)

for Betty, for Helen and Jim

Contents

Illustrations

Figures

Tables

Contributors

Frederick Baker is a Vienna based documentary filmmaker, whose film for the BBC 'Rebuilding the Reichstag' won the Grand Prix at the international Techfilm 2000 competition in the Czech Republic. He studied archaeology at Cambridge, Tübingen and Sheffield Universities.

Stan Beckensall is a retired headteacher and lecturer. He has directed excavations, researched British rock-art for over thirty years, and has published drama and poetry, some of which has been broadcast.

Christopher Chippindale is a curator in the Cambridge University Museum of Archaeology and Anthropology. He edited *The archaeology of rock-art* (1998, with Paul S.C. Taçon). His own research concerns rock-art in Aboriginal Australia and later prehistoric Europe.

Margarita Díaz-Andreu is a lecturer in the Department of Archaeology, University of Durham. She has published several articles on rock-art of Spain, mainly discussing issues of identity and historiography.

Angelo Fossati is the president of the Footsteps of Man Archaeological Cooperative Society based in Cerveno, Valcamonica. His own research concerns Alpine and European rock art. He edited *Deer in rock art of India and Europe* (1994 with G. Camuri, Y. Mathpal), *Sui sentieri dell'arte rupestre* (1995, with A. Arcà) and *News of the World I* (1996, with P. Bahn).

Michael Frachetti is a Ph.D. candidate in the Department of Anthropology at the University of Pennsylvania. His research has focused on such themes as European rock-art (M.Phil.), medieval Islamic settlement studies in North Africa and currently the prehistory of Central Asian nomadic societies.

George Nash is a part-time lecturer in European prehistory at the Centre of the Historic Environment, University of Bristol, and Senior Archaeologist with Border Archaeology (Herefordshire, England). His main research area is Mesolithic portable and static art of north-western Europe and the Neolithic of western Britain. He organized a series of sessions on rock-art and landscape at the 1997 TAG conference and at the 1998 IFRAO conference.

Avril Purcell is a contract archaeologist working in the Republic of Ireland. Research interests include the early prehistoric period, particularly the Neolithic and early Bronze Age.

Per Ramqvist is Professor in Regional Archaeology at Mid-Sweden University in Örnsköldsvik. He has written books on the early Iron Age sites at Gene (1983) and Högom (1992). His research also concerns rock-art in the Eurasian taiga region.

Kalle Sognnes is a curator at the Museum of Natural History and Archaeology and Professor of Archaeology at the Norwegian University of Science and Technology, Trondheim. His research concerns rock-art in central Norway, on which he has published *Bergkunsten i Stjørdal* (*The rock art in Stjørdal*) in three volumes (1983, 1987, 1990) as well as several smaller papers.

Editors' acknowledgements

The editors thank the contributors for the speedy, good-humoured and efficient way in which they have worked with us, and the team at Routledge. We thank also Mary Baxter, Lindsey Nash and Eva Walderhaug Saetersdal.

Note on radiocarbon dating

Dates given as BC, AD, BP ('Before Present') are in calendar years, however they have been arrived at. Dates given as 'b.p.' are uncalibrated radiocarbon determinations, and are measures of 'radiocarbon years' that do not equate exactly with calendar years.

Chapter 1

Images of enculturing landscapes

A European perspective

George Nash and Christopher Chippindale

Locales and sites

Within archaeology one tends to look at sites as, well . . . sites. The empirical approaches applied to our central notion of the 'site' indeed reinforce an image very much devoid of human meaning. In particular, the concept of recording rock-art focuses first on subjectivity – what is depicted; then on objectivity – the extrinsic value of the site and stratigraphic deposition which lies in front of and underneath the art. Some attention has been given in the past to the landscape of rock-art, albeit from a traditionally stale account of what can be seen. Recently, rock-art and landscape studies have incorporated a text that relies more on personal experience and the cognitive values of the audience – those who witness the act of application or visit the completed panel. We suppose, therefore, that when rock-art was executed, the artist intended it to remain indefinitely; with this was the intentional location of the panel/rock-art surface to the surrounding landscape. By omitting landscape, and, in particular, rock-art as place, one is only looking at subjectivity and ignoring media.

Arguably, landscape and place are as important as the paint or the stone chisel which made the image. Therefore, within this chapter and this book, we try to readdress the importance of landscape/place, to suggest that both can be considered part of the archaeological assemblage alongside the more obvious items: the lithics, pottery, and so on. We highlight the intentionality of landscape and place, suggesting it was as important to the artist as the images she or he was painting or carving. We also place rock-art into a narrative, setting its historical value into a prehistoric context. An emphasis will be placed on hunter-gatherer rock-art that dates from the Mesolithic and is found in both southern Europe (mainly on the Iberian Peninsula) and northern Scandinavia (coastal Norway and Sweden).

Using a range of methodologies, we will also outline an approach which is primarily concerned with the interaction between people, landscape and rock-art, tracing a history of how rock-art may have been incorporated into a series of diverse European landscapes.

Different images, different locales

The landscapes of Europe are so diverse that one could properly devote an entire chapter simply to describing them. Within those landscapes are a number of rock-art enclaves. These are each confined to one of four major zones: Atlantic Europe; the Mediterranean; the Alpine regions of central and southern Europe; and Scandinavia. Each area has its

Figure 1.1 Hunting scene from the Ulldecona rock-shelter (Tarragona), Levantine Spain
After Beltrán (1982: 70)

own intrinsic and idiosyncratic topographic features that make it unique, values which in themselves have influenced the rock-art style and subjectivity. The hunter-gather rock-art around coastal Norway, for example, is dominated not only by elk and reindeer but also by marine mammals and fish. Later farming art from the same region incorporates large numbers of boats of various shapes and sizes. Along the southern European Atlantic coast, and including the Iberian Peninsula, farming art consists of mainly stylized warrior figures and red deer, along with 'abstract' designs such as concentric circles and cup-marks. These images supersede the more representational warrior figures, bulls and red-deer images of the Spanish Levant (Figure 1.1). The subjectivity from all four zones therefore undergoes a stylistic change more than it does changes in subject-matter. And there are enclaves where hunter-gatherer art and farming art are completely different – in style, form and media. These changes, however subtle, span a history of maybe up to 8000 years. If one is also to take into consideration the wealth of cave and exposed Upper Palaeolithic art from the central regions of France, northern Portugal and northern Spain, then the span is even greater – up to 35,000 years.

Rock-art (or any other archaeological site) establishes a place from space (Nash 2000). A place requires that basic human response – experience. The act of initially choosing the place, of using the place and then visiting the place (either frequently or periodically) requires a degree of social and political organization. Chapter 8, by Margarita Díaz-Andreu, explores the sacredness of landscape prior to the execution of rock-art, suggesting that rock-art forms only part of a complex mechanism of social being and place. Choosing a space and turning it into a place, positioning certain figures on certain rock surfaces and using a place over generations require and reinforce an affinity with landscape. We see these mechanisms as the underlying forces that control and manipulate symbolic and religious (cosmological) devices, in this case the art and site location (Figure 1.2). The more one visits a place, the more familiar one becomes with the idiosyncratic nature of the place. When frequently revisiting a rock-art site, one comes to recall the visual

Figure 1.2 Rock-art as a symbolic device: carving (restored) on a late Norman stone doorway at Kilpeck Church, Herefordshire, England

Photograph: G.H. Nash

sequence seen in the rock-art itself – which figure goes where or which panel comes before which. One may also recall the landscape position of the site, relating the panel or rock outcropping to localized features such as other rock outcroppings, nearby rivers and streams, escarpments, pathways and so on. On a micro level, one may recall the nature of the surface and the colour changes of the art under different lighting and weather conditions. These observations may change through time and varying experience.

Experience and analysis

We recall our own experiences when visiting rock-art sites in coastal Levantine Spain, coastal Norway, western Sweden and Valcamonica. Personal experience we see as a valid research methodology, as one extends one's personal visual knowledge beyond the flat and inert surfaces of the available catalogues and gazetteers with their black images on white paper. First in South Africa (Lewis-Williams and Dowson 1990) and now also in North America and Europe (Helskog 1999), rock-art researchers have recently become aware of how much the image may take its place and its form from the surface of the rock. A fissure, crack or slope of the surface is not, then, a distraction or inconvenience to the 'real' image, but part of the reason that image is at a certain place and takes a certain form. A century of ever-more meticulous recording, separating the 'artificial' from the 'natural' and recording the former alone on an ideal plane surface of featureless paper may have been ever-more systematically omitting the key information (Chippindale 2000).

Within the same publications, landscape forms only part of a passive discussion. One tends to ignore (and forget) that our own experiences when visiting sites are just as valid as an archaeological report or narrative text. Experiences differ when the site has been repeatedly visited by the same person, when the site is experienced under different climatic conditions that determine light, temperature and what can be seen, or when sites are interpreted in different ways by different people, be they archaeologists, historians or the modern descendants of indigenous ancestors who carved and used the site many centuries ago (Figure 1.3). These criteria express how one may visualize and experience rock-art and how each group views the art. All this, of course, is rather and rightly subjective; our ideas and experiences may radically differ from those of other archaeologists; they certainly do if we compare them with the experiences of those who visit the sites today with other expectations in mind.

At sites, research methods can include measurements of the angle of slope for each panel, the relationship between the art and the rock surface (horizontal and vertical design fields), the phenomenology of micro landscape (the space immediately around the rock-art) and

Figure 1.3 Ancestral carvings along with modern graffiti at the Buena Vista site in southern Oregon
Photograph: G.H. Nash

of macro landscape (the surrounding landscape) and dominant characters within a rock-art panel design field. These 'objective' measures also rely on subjective experience: judgement and personal perception.

The analytical approach to a site – either through data analysis or assessment of landscape-value and potential – does not convey the experiential awareness that hides oneself as visitor to the site itself. In attempting to understand what might have occurred in the past, a matter of personal interpretation and experience is made by the encoding of the site – what is there, where it is positioned, what is readable, where it is located. Many eighteenth- and nineteenth-century antiquarians were prepared to speculate and propose interpretations based upon their own perceptions of the world – a phenomenology of then, of their present.

Commonly, rock-art sites possess some degree of folk memory and mysticism that, although confusing the overall narrative as the modern research archaeologist sees that, is none the less valid to the overall assessment of the site. Contrary to this, rock-art studies for the most part remain purely descriptive and concerned mainly with motif typology and chronology (Hood 1988: 65). What has been ignored is the human interaction with the monument.

Human experience and place in prehistoric Europe

Phenomenology, or 'being-in-the-world', sets people apart from objects and establishes a 'gap' or 'space', created through using one's senses – seeing, hearing, touching. The phenomenology of visiting a place – say, a building, landscape vista or, in this case, a rock-art site – involves setting oneself apart from the objectivity – creating experience. Similarly, as Bourdieu (1977: 4) has suggested, on a human level landscape, or the phenomenology of landscape, is created as a lived experience so that the mode of knowledge, through one's senses, is inherent in all acts. This is a precondition to constructing landscape and, in the words of Bourdieu, constitutes 'a social world as a system of objective relations independent of individual consciousness and wills'. The construction of landscape becomes a critique; a collection of chapters is chronologically and geographically ordered. We, as individuals, add more to these chapters, creating this sense of space, belonging, ancestry when visiting a single monument over time. This act above all sets ourselves, the occasional visitor, away from an individual whose ancestors used the site time and time again; or from the artist who may have visited a site seasonally to add, to superimpose or to remove motifs from a panel.

One could regard the reinterpretation of any rock-art site as a simple process – I saw, I recorded, I superficially discussed. If one was to rely on site-recording from the standard sources in the seminal works and the site monographs, ignoring personal experience, the process of recording and writing about rock-art and landscape would be mere description. Beyond description, our own experiences allow us to make a valid attempt to discuss why sites were chosen, why certain motifs and figures were used, and how rock-art may have been witnessed.

Compared with the more 'straightforward' physical objects, the bones and the stones of dirt archaeology, rock-art seems an elusive field within archaeology. One can recognize pictures of boats or of halberds – but how can we know they are pictures of those physical things? And if they are, how are we to know what boats or halberds meant in their own time? Here rock-art takes us to the heart of current research concerns in later prehistoric

Europe. The singular features of later European prehistory have been recognized for centuries, since the early antiquarians grasped the antiquity of the great stone monuments of the British Isles and western continental Europe, the megaliths which seemed and still seem enigmatic. What was their purpose? What social role did they play?

With nearly two centuries of prehistoric research to draw on, the farming societies of the Neolithic and metal ages in Europe seem more odd rather than less. These were subsistence farmers, their means of subsistence depending on the varied ecologies of temperate Europe; yet it is clear that they were not controlled by those ecologies. Fine-grained excavation and analysis show singular feature after singular feature, to the point that even the simple and robust categories of objective description and functional logic fail. 'Rubbish' was not rubbish, unwanted debris and residues. 'Disposal of the dead' was not the putting-away of the body, nor 'burial' the placing of the corpse into the earth and beyond living society.

For a century, our models for these prehistoric European societies have been the societies of early modern or medieval Europe: take a marginal peasant farmer, in the Scots islands or the marginal high country of Alpine Europe; remove the later elements – the Christianity, the feudalism, the objects bought from the market, the things made of smelted iron; and we have the makings of prehistoric Europeans of the fifth or fourth millennium BC. Not so, for the 'strange' and 'singular' elements are not optional but fundamental and ubiquitous.

So where are our models and analogies to come from? Exotic societies in other places have been drawn upon if they are formally consistent in some ways: the technologically Neolithic societies of highland New Guinea have in that way given us a model for the first generation of European farmers who also felled their forests with stone axes and fire. But those comparisons are with societies in climates and environments far removed from those of temperate lands in the northern hemisphere. And most of them lack the distinctive features so striking in Europe: highland New Guinea has no Stonehenge or Carnac, no megalithic gallery graves, no *terremare* settlements, no Maltese temples, no 'Iceman'. So we are rightly reminded that the story of later prehistoric Europe is a unique one, paralleled to slight extent in temperate Asia and temperate North America, but nowhere exactly matched.

This should and must push us back on to the specifics of the ancient European experience, as prehistoric Europeans experienced it. That should and must send us to the rock-art; enigmatic and puzzling it may be, yet it has the supreme merit of giving us a record of those ancient worlds as those ancient people saw and experienced them. It is the record of prehistoric experience as prehistoric people themselves chose directly to record it.

Constructing landscapes

Landscape is very much a social construct which is developed within each and everyone's minds. One landscape may have a thousand meanings when viewed by a thousand people. If landscape is constructed within our minds, how can landscape be humanized? Turning a space into place is fundamental in constructing landscapes (Bradley 1997, 1998, 2000; Nash 2001: 1–17; Heyd 2001: 20). Julian Thomas (1994), commenting on Renfrew's celebrated study of 'Megaliths, territories and populations' (1976), considers monument-building as 'signalling group identity'. But who controls the location of monuments

Figure 1.4 Exercising territoriality through sectarianism: painted mural on the Shankill Road, Belfast, Northern Ireland

Photograph: L.J. Nash

within a landscape? Space, according to Foucault (1984: 252), 'is fundamental to any exercise of power'. If one is to look at contemporary forms of rock-art such as that found, say, in Northern Ireland or the graffiti on the walls of the Reichstag, space becomes an important component, especially if one is using rock-art as a landscape-maker (i.e. a wall or fence (Figure 1.4)). For many years the religious divide in Northern Ireland has used rock-art to express the entrenched positions across the sectarian divide. The style between both sets of frescoes can be considered similar but the way in which certain icons are used by both sides creates a series of recognizable signatures. Here, the image establishes territoriality, social identity and religion.

This form of statement is not new. A more blatant social and political statement is seen with the graffiti found on the walls of the Reichstag. Fred Baker (Chapter 2) reinforces a notion of power and control. In many respects, these statements are personal; more importantly, they are not cohesive. What one person says about a European war, the Second World War, is contradicted by others. Here, the graffiti reveal *the* artist. Through careful dissemination, one finds out what this person was thinking, where he/she came from – what regiment and what part of the Soviet Union. This art, probably more than any other discussed in this book, reflects a personal attitude towards executing rock-art.

This study of modern Europe is fundamental in helping our understanding of why someone should want to draw, paint or write on a static surface. The interpretative value of, say, a piece of static art commissioned 20,000 years ago, or even 4000 years ago, is reduced, fearfully so, for the researcher can never know the complete interpretative value of the site. However, with this contemporary rock-art, we see a Soviet soldier's thoughts of how the war was going scribbled on a wall, and not just any wall, but the Reichstag wall – a symbol of a defeated Germany; a symbol of hatred and revulsion to the conquering Red Army. The graffiti are not just personal statements but reuses of symbol space.

Those who decide where to locate a 'place' – in the case of the studies in this book, rock-art – exercise power. Painting or carving on to a rock surface could be a secondary process within a legitimized (power) regime, the actual place chosen by a group or clan leader and the art ritually or symbolically performed there. As the decision to locate and to paint is undertaken by certain ranks within society, landscape can in this way represent order, social stratification, control. It can also represent chaos, turmoil and social disorder. In forming a cognitive or mental map, places become names, and names determine meaning. These names become things, objects and places which in particular one can see inscribed on to smooth rock outcrops. In Chapter 5 Angelo Fossati shows the importance of incorporating landscape features located within the Valcamonica on to menhirs. This brings the landscape into a microcosm, creating a series of recognizable images that one considers were important to the artist who created the rock-art images, and, more importantly, the people who witnessed the commission and those who used it afterwards.

Bradley (1998, 2000) has adopted the idea of space, place and landscape as part of a historical and geographical discourse. Indelibly linked with this idea are the human emotions of power, time, memory, social interaction and politics. Landscape, although natural in its physical construction, does rely culturally on the mechanics of the mind. As Weedon (1987: 32) states: 'it is language in the form of conflicting discourse which constitutes us as conscious thinking subjects and enables us to give meaning to the world and to act to transform it'. By using a philosophical approach to landscape, it and the deliberate siting of rock-art become interesting and meaningful phenomena. In one way, landscape represents the wider outside, the known world. Yet rock-art, visually does not seem directly to represent this world; the images are of repeated subjects – animals often – but where are the pictures of the land? There are very few identifiable images of landscape in any form: typically animals are shown, but no recognizable element of the space in which those animals stand.

The only recognized group of maps in prehistoric Europe are those in the central European Alps. However, is the landscape hidden or omitted? Only a few components of this world are portrayed; and the things that are portrayed are surely those considered important. This omission of the real world is explored by George Nash (Chapter 9) and Kalle Sognnes (Chapter 10). Both researchers, using northern Scandinavian examples, acknowledge the value of rock-art and its landscape position, either acting as territorial markers or marking migration routes. Here, each figure may represent part of a wider landscape. The spatial arrangement on each panel may be more than just haphazard. Each figure, bear, elk, reindeer, seal, whale and occasional anthropomorphic figure, creates an ordered visual narrative whereby the reader moves across the panel like he or she would move across the landscape.

Concerning regional variation, Per Ramqvist (Chapter 7) discusses rock-art style and distribution from the Fenno-Scandinavia region. Here, similar approaches to the distribution of style over a wider landscape are applied. By using these approaches, one draws on the notion that landscapes can be read; they make a language.

Lévi-Strauss (1963: 56) has stated that language is a social phenomenon; it acts as a form of linguistic behaviour which relies on unconscious thought. Without believing that landscape should follow structuralist rules, we see that features within a landscape do act as signs and these signs control social and political behaviour. During the

Neolithic, the construction of monuments and the formation of territory are actions not based merely on political behaviour; they were symbolically and socially constructed with landscape in mind. As Bradley reminds us, monuments evoke memories (1993: 2); landscape, too, creates a sense of time and belonging. This accumulation is not created overnight but over generations. This concept would certainly account for the retouching and repainting of figures on, say, the Spanish Levantine rock-shelters. Bourdieu (1977: 4) suggests that, on a human level, landscape or the phenomenology of landscape is created as a lived experience. The German rock-art researcher Herbert Kühn (1955: 126) was living his experiences when visiting the Spanish Levantine sites of Les Dogues, Cuevas del El Civil, Cuevas de la Arana and Minateda not with just the rock-art, but with the journey to each site; each of us does that every time we go to a site. Kühn recalls:

> After a good four hours of tramping, that is to say about eleven o'clock, we drew near to the Valltorta Ravine. There is a wide glen whose banks fall steeply down to a stream. Bushes and scrub cover the sides from the top to the bottom but cannot hide the large stones and boulders. If one chanced to step upon or against a stone it went tumbling, rumbling down right into the brook below. The ravine twisted and turned. Sometimes it was a quite narrow canyon and then again the gorge would widen out somewhat. The cliffs contain a number of natural recesses, little rock-shelters, from three to six feet deep. Many of them present no pictures, but then again others are crowded with paintings and drawings.

In order to establish a symbolic landscape as a meaningful entity, components need to be ritualized, and ritual requires a focus (Figure 1.5). Hood (1988: 65) has described rock-art as a sociological and ideological product which is actively manipulated within social strategies. The focus for this activity is not merely a passive arena for adaptation. For generations, hunter-gatherer rock-art sites may have acted as foci perpetuating a cult of ancestry. In the areas where we find art religion would have helped to forge and maintain a sense of place and territorial identity for prehistoric people. As part of this process of fixing communal identity, it is probable that rock-art incorporated earlier beliefs associated with traditional hunter-gatherer subsistence practices and landscape knowledge, beliefs which ascribed symbolic value to certain prominent landscape features – mountains, river valleys, estuaries and the sea (Bradley 2000; Nash 2000). These features may, since earliest times, have harboured food sources essential to the survival of communities inhabiting the post-glacial landscape. Equally, the landscape, and especially the mountains, may have acted as a symbolic taboo, forbidden places perceived by indigenous communities as dangerous. In our own culture the passion for mountains is a novelty of recent centuries; before the romantic era, the mountains of Europe were more perceived as dangerous and sinister places.

Significant landscape features may also have served as signposts in the landscape, guiding hunters and foragers on seasonal journeys around the loosely defined territories which they exploited. Bradley (1993) suggests that paths were important to hunter-gatherers, who identified their territories by these linear features linking particular places which may later have been ritually and symbolically utilized to site the earliest rock-art. Within these foraging territories, symbolically important landscape features may have generated myths connected with times of plenty and with the origins of the groups. Aborigines inhabiting the Northern Territory of Australia wove topographical features

Figure 1.5 From social to symbolic space: religious graffiti on a house in St Helier, Jersey

Photograph: G.H. Nash

of their landscape, together with rocks possessing human characteristics, and various animals and sea-creatures, into a complex creation (Dreamtime) myth (Flood 2000). The myth is believed to refer to major routes by which people historically moved into the area. Myths such as these, of how things came to be, enable communities to establish a sense of belonging within a landscape.

If such explanatory stories circulated in core areas during early prehistory, they may have been perpetuated through traditions of oral story-telling, dance and ritual, to be taken up with renewed vigour in the Neolithic and Bronze Age periods, when the old hunter-gatherer way of life began to disappear and when farming art and monumentality emerged (Bowra 1962). This may have been a period of disorientation and of 'recourse to place as a source of authority and stability' (Massey 1994: 15). Certainly, towards the end of the Mesolithic, there are indications that the loose territories which had existed for much of the period were contracting and becoming in some senses bounded (Hood 1988; Zvelebil 1986a, 1986b).

In southern Scandinavia during the later Mesolithic, or Ertebølle, phase, our knowledge of the material seems sufficiently clear to tell the story: mobility seems to decrease, there is a geographical shift towards coastal sites, and artefact styles begin to be used as symbolic markers defining boundaries (Andersen 1980; Nash 1998). We think this was probably due to increasing social and political complexity, as prime hunting-gathering territories were consolidated and as land ownership, wealth and the control of human and natural resources became more controlled. Competition between the emergent territorial units can also be envisaged. This process may well have been linked, though not directly, to the lurch towards a farming economy in parts of Europe from the sixth

Figure 1.6 Turning a space into a permanent place: the large reindeer carving at Bola, Nord-Trøndelag, central Norway

Photograph: G.H. Nash

millennium BC onwards (Whittle 1985), an influx of new ideas and opportunities for Mesolithic communities being a spin-off from these developments. In this social and political ferment, one can see ritual as playing a stabilizing role, emphasizing tradition in the form of permanent monuments – especially the rock-art (Figure 1.6). These embodied and traditional mythological interpretations of the animals depicted and of the environment may have represented a timeless community rooted in the locality, an enduring reminder of identity and a focal point for ritual performance.

Western and northern European rock-art

Along the fjords of central coastal Norway, the shift from hunting art to farming art appears more subtle (Sognnes 1998). For both types of art, panels are highly visible; but they also, from a distance, appear to be hidden within the landscape. Nevertheless, each carving panel may have possessed a cognitive impact. This pattern in positioning suggests secret ritual knowledge, possibly controlled by high-status individuals or groups. These groups, if they controlled both the specialist knowledge and rituals associated with the carvings, and access to the panels themselves, would thereby also have monopolized the community's links with its ancestors. In symbolizing a community of ancestors, therefore, the rock-art also acted as symbols of power in the present, as well as territorial markers for the group as a whole. A similar spatial pattern, albeit from the Bronze Age, may be witnessed within the narrow mountain passes and traditional communication routes of the Iveragh Peninsula, County Kerry, south-west Ireland. Here, Avril Purcell (Chapter 4) suggests that each rock-art panel was a deliberate and intentional act.

Within northern Scandinavia, the fjords leading to steep-sided river-valleys may have served as transportation channels, while the larger ones were additionally important migration routes for fish; that factor also appears to have governed the designs on particular panels (Gjessing 1932, 1936; Hallström 1938). Salmon and halibut depicted on the coastal panels of Finnhågen (Nordland) and Kvernevika (Nord-Trøndelag) not only suggest the presence of fish close by but also portray a symbolic allegiance with the artist. Fjords clearly were important landscape features socially and economically during the Mesolithic. Extensive scatters of flint and shale tools have been discovered at a number of inner and outer fjord sites (Nygaard 1989), many close to the carved panels.

The imposition of animals over other animals at sites such as Evenhus (Figure 1.7) and Bardal (Figure 1.8), both in Nord-Trøndelag, reinforces the notion that rock-art is produced over long periods of time, so it may have embodied older beliefs alongside new ones. The siting of rock-carving panels may have already long been set in relation to symbolically important places in the seasonal movements of earlier Mesolithic hunter-gatherers. In other words, by carving on to natural rock surfaces, communities were creating a history, an identity with the landscape using the ancestors. Mountains and upland environs above the rock panels seem to have been important focal points for hunter-gatherer artists, as they were for their early Mesolithic and, in the case of southern and central Europe, for their Palaeolithic forebears.

The execution of rock-art may have enhanced and supported long-term hunting strategies (Children and Nash 1997: 1). These in turn would have been based upon the need to organize and control much-needed food resources within a confined (or defined) hunting territory, especially towards later prehistory. These practices may have formed part of a broad spectrum of activities integrated within a seasonal pattern of movement, taking in upland, lowland and coastal areas prior to the introduction of farming and its associated ideas. While mobile hunting and gathering continued as the basic lifestyle of Mesolithic people, this would suggest efforts were being made to control the environment, rather than relying wholly upon what nature provided.

Figure 1.7 Elks, boats and whales: Evenhus V, Nord-Trøndelag, central Norway
After Hallström (1938)

Figure 1.8 Plethora of elk and reindeer activity at the main Bardal panel, Nord-Trøndelag, central Norway

After Hallström (1938)

The conventional economic definition of hunter-gatherers, as people who do not interfere with or control landscape as agriculturalists do, makes it easy to overlook two key similarities. Hunter-gatherer societies *do* interfere with and control their environments in other ways, such as by burning (see Jones (1968, 1995) for how burning in Australia has shaped the landscape of the continent which seems, on the surface, to be most 'natural' in its character). And hunter-gatherers often have an intense symbolic relationship with the landscape in which they must do the right things so that the animals shall move to their proper places, the fish at their due season return up the rivers, and the spirits of the land be generous to the people as they should be. In following the usual opposition set between hunting-gathering and farming, we may mislead ourselves. In Europe the preconditions for a farming economy already existed along the coastal fringes long before evidence for the cultivation of wheat and barley, and the rearing of cattle, sheep and pigs appeared in the archaeological record.

Understanding human experience of place in prehistoric Europe

These truths bring us to a central issue in prehistoric Europe – and the central issue of research into prehistoric Europe. Rock-art is at the heart both of the problem and of how best we tackle it: hence the present volume.

The early era of European rock-art is in the Palaeolithic: it clearly belongs to a world for which we have no close human experience. There is no ethnography to tell us directly about human lifestyles and attitudes under the icy conditions of the later Pleistocene in what is now temperate Europe. Importantly, however, there have been European people in recent centuries living largely or entirely on a subsistence basis that is not agricultural and under climatic conditions like those of the Ice Age further south. These are the northern peoples of Scandinavia and Russia, close by the Arctic Ocean, whose singular lifestyles have much in common, in a 'circum-polar province', with the northern peoples of Asia and of America (Appelt *et al.* 2000) – the latter, we think, deriving from north Asian people who colonized that previously empty continent at the end of the glaciation. If these northern people did indeed descend from the populations who were in central and southern Europe in the Ice Age, retreating to the far north as the icy conditions they were used to themselves retreated, then the singular features of their recent culture (see, e.g., Jacobson 1993), notably shamanism (Price forthcoming), may arise through some kind of persistence from the Ice Age peoples. Certainly, there are intriguing insights to be had into north European rock-art if those are approached with some of the cultural attitudes known from the northern people of ethnohistoric times and of today (Helskog 1999).

Even if there is some reasonably direct cultural descent from the Ice Age people of now-temperate Europe to those of the far north today, we can be sure it has been tempered and transformed by 10,000 subsequent years of human society. Importantly, study of the rock-art of Australia, a region of the world where the idea of an 'unchanging aboriginal' still persists, now gives a reliable dating. With that reasonably robust chronology we can begin to discern a rather different picture (Chippindale and Taçon 1993, 1998). That sequence shows how profound the changes in imagery, and we think in its meaning, have been over a similar time-period in a region without profound climatic change and with superficially stable hunter-gatherer lifestyles. While the imagery of what is now called the 'Dreamtime' runs back some 4000–5000 years in tropical north Australia (Taçon *et al.* 1996), at about that time there is some kind of decisive break and there survive from before it remarkable rock-art images of a different character (Chippindale *et al.* 2000).

Although we have no direct ethnography for the European Palaeolithic, there is a research habit – as old, it sometimes seems, as the systematic study of Palaeolithic archaeology – of looking to and depending on ethnography for Palaeolithic insight (e.g. Hayden 1979). At one time sketching a rather fuzzy picture of a generalized primitive, this approach now has been strengthened into a clearer proposition. Essentially, this underlines the strong similarities in the social and economic structures between such varied hunter-gatherer societies as we seem to have good report of, including some strong similarities in their art and iconography (Ouzman 1998), and thereby seeks a rationale in the later Palaeolithic consistent with those broader regularities. The best known of recent studies in this spirit is Clottes and Lewis-Williams's (1998) application of a shamanistic model to the later Palaeolithic art of the European caves, by analogy with the shamanic element in the recent rock-art of southern Africa.

By comparison, we seem to have slighter directly relevant ethnography for the Europe of the early farmers – hence the dependence noted above on a vision, hazy again, of the Neolithic as being like the societies of classical or even medieval Europe minus whatever can be identified as their later accretions. If one looks for analogy in a comparable climatic zone on another continent, there are the temperate lands of central and southern North America. In that part of the world, strikingly, and despite contact-period ethnography and subsequent ethnohistory, there is a sharply similar pattern and a matching research question. The elaborate societies of lowland North America in the Mississippian river valleys (Muller 1997) present intriguing and recalcitrant features (Lewis and Stout 1998), a great investment in earthworks of uncertain functional utility (Brown 1995), distinctive funerary customs (Black 1979), and an elaboration of iconography with distinct and repeated traits – the whole not simply to be grasped either by extrapolation from contact-period ethnohistory (Milanich 1991) or by a functionalist approach from the uncompromising material evidence. The transatlantic analogy to the recalcitrant phase in European prehistory is itself recalcitrant in the same spirit.

This truth for the archaeology of Neolithic and metal-age temperate Europe is emphasized when it comes to the rock-art. Strikingly, rock-art in Europe does not much coexist with writing and the opportunity of direct historical records. Noticeably, in Valcamonica – the greatest single concentration of rock-art in later Europe – the abundant Iron Age rock-art which dominates the major surfaces (e.g. Arcá et al. 1995) appears to stop abruptly when the expanding Roman domain swallows up this Alpine valley. There is not an absolute full stop, for a slight and sometimes enigmatic medieval tradition (e.g. Sansoni and Gavaldo 1997) is strong in Austria (Burgstaller 1972) not far to the north, but certainly no striking continuity of a kind by which to enable one to take any sort of 'direct historical approach' from the historic periods smoothly back into prehistory. And the striking features of the Alpine rock-art of the metal ages – with its strong compositions of standardized type, its close relation to monumental stone sculptures of

Figure 1.9 A 'mundane' farming scene from the rock-art of Alpine Europe: oxen with plough, Mont Bego, Alpes-Maritimes, France

Drawing: Christopher Chippindale

anthropomorphic figures, its emphasis on the halberd, most enigmatic of metal object-types of the era – all push it away from ideas of a mundane world in which the meaning of things will easily be deduced from their functional role in a utilitarian world of simple farming experiences (Figure 1.9).

Mentioned above (when this point was being made for the generality of the European Neolithic) were striking features of the British Neolithic. In tune with that, the rock-art of post-glacial Britain (Beckensall 1999 and this volume, Chapter 3), much of which is now cautiously placed in a broadly late Neolithic era is recalcitrant and opaque: its geometrically simple shapes of cups, rings and lines surely mask or represent a depth rather than a shallowness of meaning. The more striking rock-carving of that era, the megalithic art of Ireland and Atlantic Europe generally (Shee Twohig 1981), is not strictly rock-art, for it is cut on mobile slabs built into structures; again, the imagery is reticent, elaborately geometrical but not self-evidently representational, and the places themselves – although they contain human bones and bodies – are not simply functional places, tombs for the efficient disposal of the dead.

One special opportunity, then, is given by images which are themselves part of the grand and enigmatic monuments, and there are some intriguing proposals being made. Whittle (2000) wonders whether a distinctive motif seen (rarely) on Breton menhirs is in fact an image of a whale; he sees whales as a compelling representation of a natural creature, a creature whose symbolism one can see might be central to myth at the time of the Neolithic–Mesolithic transition. But the Breton motif is hard to read – previously it had been identified as an axe or an axe-plough. Fortunately, many of the images in European rock-art are more transparent, at least at the surface level: we think we may know what they are pictures of, even though we are less sure what those subjects mean.

Informed methods and formal methods in studying the rock-art of prehistoric Europe, and in the present volume

In short, then, the rock-art of later prehistoric Europe encapsulates the paradox of its period: a singular world which is to be understood by some grasp of the ancient meaning of things, a singular world to which we have no easy access beyond the material remains in which archaeology traditionally has found it hard to see meaning.

Introducing an earlier volume of rock-art studies, Taçon and Chippindale (1998) found it useful to define *informed methods* and *formal methods* in rock-art studies.

By *informed methods* we mean 'those that depend on some source of insight passed on directly or indirectly from those who made and used the rock-art – through ethnography, through ethnohistory, through historical record, or through modern under-standing known with good cause to perpetuate ancient knowledge; then, one can hope to explore the pictures from the inside, as it were'. For nearly all later rock-art in Europe, it seems, we have slight or no access through informed methods.

Complementing the informed methods are *formal methods*, those that depend on no inside knowledge, but which work when one can come to the stuff 'cold': 'The infor-mation available is then restricted to that which is immanent in the images themselves, or which we can discern from their relations to each other and to the landscape, or by relation to whatever archaeological context is available.' For later rock-art in Europe, it seems, it is the formal methods we are to use, and it is case studies of that approach which we offer here.

References

Andersen, S.H. 1980. Ertebølle art: new finds of patterned Ertebølle artefacts from East Jutland, *KUML* 4: 6–60.

Appelt, M., J. Berglund and H.-C. Gulløv (eds). 2000. *Identities and cultural contacts in the Arctic*. Copenhagen: Danish Polar Centre.

Arcá, A., A. Fossati, E. Marchi and E. Tononi/Cooperativa Archeologica 'Le Orme dell'Uomo'. 1995. *Rupe Magna: la roccia incisa più grande delle Alpi*. Sondrio: Ministero dei Beni Culturali e Ambientali, Soprintendenza Archeologica della Lombardi, Consorzio per il Parco delle Incisioni Rupestri di Grosio.

Beckensall, S. 1999. *British prehistoric rock art*. Stroud: Tempus.

Beltrán, A. 1982. *Rock art of the Spanish Levant*. Cambridge: Cambridge University Press.

Black, T.K. III. 1979. *The biological and social analyses of a Mississippian cemetery from southeast Missouri: the Turner site, 23BU21A*. Ann Arbor: Museum of Anthropology, University of Michigan. Anthropological papers 68.

Bourdieu, P. 1977. *Outline of a theory of practice*. Cambridge: Cambridge University Press.

Bowra, C.M. 1962. *Primitive song*. London: Weidenfeld & Nicolson.

Bradley, R. 1993. *Altering the earth: the origins of monuments in Britain and continental Europe*. Edinburgh: Society of Antiquaries of Scotland. Monograph Series 8.

Bradley, R. 1997. *Signing the land: rock art and the prehistory of Atlantic Europe*. London: Routledge.

Bradley, R. 1998. *The significance of monuments: on the shaping of human experience in Neolithic and Bronze Age Europe*. London: Routledge.

Bradley, Richard. 2000. *The significance of natural places*. London: Routledge.

Brown, J.A. 1995. *The Spiro Ceremonial Center: the archaeology of Arkansas Valley Caddoan culture in eastern Oklahoma*. Ann Arbor: Museum of Anthropology, University of Michigan. Memoirs of the Museum of Anthropology 29.

Burgstaller, E. 1972. *Felsbilder in Österreich*. Linz: Landesinstitut für Heinmatpflege und Volksbildung.

Children, G. and G. Nash. 1997. Establishing a discourse: the language of landscape, in G. Nash (ed.), *Semiotics of landscape: the archaeology of mind*: 1–5. Oxford: British Archaeological Reports. International Series 661.

Chippindale, C. 2000. Capta and data: on the true nature of achaeological information, *American Antiquity* 65(4): 605–612.

Chippindale, C., B. Smith and P.S.C. Taçon. 2000. Visions of Dynamic power: archaic rock-paintings, altered states of consciousness and 'clever men' in western Arnhem Land (NT), Australia, *Cambridge Archaeological Journal* 10(1): 63–101.

Chippindale, C. and P.S.C. Taçon. 1993. Two old painted panels from Kakadu: variation and sequence in Arnhem Land rock art, in J. Steinbring *et al.* (eds), *Time and space: dating and spatial considerations in rock art research (papers of Symposia F and E, AURA Congress Cairns 1992)*: 32–56. Melbourne: Australian Rock Art Research Association. Occasional AURA Publication 8.

Chippindale, C. and P.S.C. Taçon. 1998. The many ways of dating Arnhem Land rock-art, north Australia, in Christopher Chippindale and Paul S.C. Taçon (eds), *The archaeology of rock-art*: 90–111. Cambridge: Cambridge University Press.

Clottes, J. and J.D. Lewis-Williams. 1998. *The shamans of prehistory: trance and magic in the painted caves*. New York: Harry N. Abrams.

Flood, J. 2000. *Archaeology of the Dreamtime: the story of prehistoric Australia and its people*. 3rd edition. Sydney: HarperCollins. [1st edition, 1983.]

Foucault, M. 1984. *The history of sexuality*, 1. Harmondsworth: Penguin.

Gjessing, G. 1932. *Arktiske helleristninger i Nord-Norge*. Oslo: H. Aschehoug (W. Nygaard). The Institute for Comparative Research in Human Culture, Series B 21.

Gjessing, G. 1936. *Nordenfjelske ristninger og malinger av den arktiske gruppe*. Oslo: H. Aschehoug (W. Nygaard). The Institute for Comparative Research in Human Culture, Series B 30.

Hallström, G. 1938. *Monumental art of northern Europe from the Stone Age, I: The Norwegian localities.* Stockholm: Almqvist and Wiksell.

Hayden, B. (ed.). 1979. *Palaeolithic reflections: lithic technology and ethnographic excavations among Australian Aborigines.* Canberra: Australian Institute of Aboriginal Studies.

Helskog, K. 1999. The shore connection: cognitive landscapes and communication with rock carvings in northernmost Europe, *Norwegian Archaeological Review* 32(2): 73–94.

Heyd, T. 2000. Rock-art: art status, aesthetic appreciation, and contemporary significance, in G.H. Nash (ed.), *Signifying place and space: world perspectives of landscape and rock-art*: 17–24. Oxford: British Archaeological Reports. International Series S902.

Hood, B.C. 1988. Sacred pictures, sacred rocks: ideological and social space in the North Norwegian Stone Age, *Norwegian Archaeological Review* 21(2): 65–84.

Jacobson, E. 1993. *The deer goddess of ancient Siberia: a study in the ecology of belief.* Leiden: Brill. Studies of History of Religions 55.

Jones, R. 1968. Fire-stick farming, *Australian Natural History* 16(7): 224–228.

Jones, R. 1995. Mindjangork: legacy of the firestick, in D.B. Rose (ed.), *Country in flames: proceedings of the 1994 symposium on biodiversity and fire in North Australia*: 11–17. Darwin: North Australian Research Unit. Biodiversity Series 3.

Kühn, H. 1955. *On the track of prehistoric man.* London: Hutchinson.

Lévi-Strauss, C. 1963. *Structural anthropology.* London: Weidenfeld & Nicolson.

Lewis, R.B. and C. Stout 1998. *Mississippian towns and sacred spaces: searching for an architectural grammar.* Tuscaloosa: University of Alabama Press.

Lewis-Williams, J. David and Thomas A. Dowson. 1990. Through the veil: San rock paintings and the rock face, *South African Archaeological Bulletin* 45: 5–16.

Massey, D. 1994. *Space, place and gender.* Cambridge: Polity Press.

Milanich, J.T. (ed.). 1991. *Earliest Hispanic/Native American interactions in the American Southeast.* New York: Garland. Spanish Borderlands Sourcebook 12.

Muller, J. 1997. *Mississippian political economy.* New York: Plenum Press.

Nash, G.H. 1998. *Status, exchange and mobility: portable art in the Scandinavian Mesolithic.* Oxford: British Archaeological Reports. International Series S710.

Nash, G.H. (ed.). 2000. *Signifying place and space: world perspectives of landscape and rock-art.* Oxford: British Archaeological Reports. International Series S902.

Nash, G.H. 2001. Conceptualising a landscape: discovering and viewing on Bronze Age rock-art of the Campo Lameiro Valley, southern Galicia, Spain, in K. Sognnes (ed.), *VITAK.* Trondheim: University of Trondheim.

Nygaard, S.E. 1989. The Stone Age of northern Scandinavia: a review, *Journal of World Prehistory* 3: 71–116.

Ouzman, S. 1998. Toward a mindscape of landscape: rock-art as expression of world-understanding, in C. Chippindale and P.S.C. Taçon (eds), *The archaeology of rock-art*: 30–41. Cambridge: Cambridge University Press.

Price, N. Forthcoming. The archaeology of shamanism: beyond rock-art, in G. Blundell, C. Chippindale and B. Smith (eds), *Knowing and seeing: understanding rock-art with and without ethnography.*

Sansoni, U. and S. Gavaldo. 1997. L'arte rupestre di Campanine di Cimbergo (Valcamonica), *TRACCE* 9 [http://www.rupestre.net/tracce/].

Shee Twohig, E. 1981. *The megalithic art of western Europe.* Oxford: Clarendon Press.

Sognnes, K. 1998. Symbols in a changing world: rock-art and the transition from hunting to farming in mid Norway, in Christopher Chippindale and Paul S.C. Taçon (eds), *The archaeology of rock-art*: 146–162. Cambridge: Cambridge University Press.

Taçon, P.S.C. and C. Chippindale. 1998. Introduction: an archaeology of rock-art through informed methods and formal methods, in C. Chippindale and P.S.C. Taçon (eds), *The archaeology of rock-art*: 1–10. Cambridge: Cambridge University Press.

Taçon, P.S.C., M. Wilson and C. Chippindale. 1996. Birth of the Rainbow Serpent in Arnhem Land rock art and oral history, *Archaeology in Oceania* 31: 103–124.

Thomas, J. 1994. The hermeneutics of megalithic space. Unpublished manuscript.

Weedon, C. 1988. *Feminist practice and poststructuralist theory*. Oxford: Blackwell.

Whittle, A. 1985. *Neolithic Europe: a survey*. Cambridge: Cambridge University Press.

Whittle, A. 2000. 'Very like a whale': menhirs, motifs and myths in the Mesolithic–Neolithic transition of northwest Europe, *Cambridge Archaeological Journal* 10(2): 243–259.

Zvelebil, M. 1986a. Mesolithic prelude and Neolithic revolution, in M. Zvelebil (ed.), *Hunters in transition: Mesolithic societies of temperate Eurasia and their transition to farming*: 5–15. Cambridge: Cambridge University Press.

Zvelebil, M. 1986b. Mesolithic societies and the transition to farming: problems of time, scale and organisation, in M. Zvelebil (ed.), *Hunters in transition: Mesolithic societies of temperate Eurasia and their transition to farming*: 167–188. Cambridge: Cambridge University Press.

Chapter 2

The Red Army graffiti in the Reichstag, Berlin

Politics of rock-art in a contemporary European urban landscape

Frederick Baker

The Reichstag graffiti: then and now

The rock is sandstone, the art is Russian, the landscape is German. After their victory in May 1945, hundreds of Red Army soldiers covered the walls of the Reichstag – Germany's once and future parliament – with Cyrillic writing. The Reichstag is the place where politics, archaeology and architecture meet. The Red Army graffiti were rediscovered by the British architects Foster and Partners in the course of renovating the building for its rebirth as the parliament of the newly united Germany in 1999 (Kleine 1999). After reunification in 1990, the members of the German parliament in Bonn had decided to move back to Berlin and reuse the Reichstag building, which had been designed as the first German parliament by Paul Wallot in the 1880s (Cullen 1995).

In contrast to much of the rock-art in this volume, the Reichstag graffiti (Figure 2.1) are easy to date; most of its inscriptions date themselves. The earliest date from 2 May 1945 – the day the fighting stopped in Berlin. In the case of the Reichstag it is not the content but the form that makes this into rock-art. Not one piece of the graffiti is pictorial, or even a pictogram. Everything is written, and every word is in Russian, in Cyrillic letters. It is this – for Western eyes – foreign lettering that turns the graffiti into art. The Cyrillic, combined with the chaotic manner in which the words are written on the walls, gives the visual impression of an abstract expressionist painting, a Jackson Pollock or Willelm de Kooning. This visual analogy was celebrated and even encouraged by the CIA (Stonor Saunders 1999), as an image of Western democracy and freedom, when it was found among other things on the Berlin Wall during the 1980s (Baker 1993). When it comes to the Red Army graffiti in the Reichstag, a very different view is taken.

Wolfgang Zeitelmann of the right-wing Bavarian political party the CSU told me, 'I think that is an illness of our age, that we keep scribbles, as if they were holy. I don't care what Russian veterans think about it. This is a German parliament and I don't see why it has to be covered in smears' (Baker 1999). The word Zeitelmann used was *Schmierei*, which in English would be something between a squiggle and a doodle. It is what a schoolteacher calls bad handwriting that is not going to receive a gold star. It is very much closer to Mary Douglas's definition of dirt as 'matter out of place'. In contrast, for the architect, Lord Foster, the discovery of the graffiti was a great event, fitting wonderfully into his avowed 'archaeological' approach to the building. His

Figure 2.1 Writing in Russian on the Reichstag, 1945

Photographs: Bildarchiv Preußischer Kulturbesitz and Novosti (London): (a) by an unnamed photographer; (b) by A. Morozov; and (c) by L. Korobova aim was to 'expose all the layers, not just these [the Red Army graffiti] but also the nineteenth-century mouldings and the present, which is by far the dominant' (Baker 1999). Foster's idea was that the building should become a museum of its own history.

Zeitelmann has threatened to daub over the graffiti with black paint, which he claims would then be his own graffiti. Only a few metres of writing should be left, according to him. Against this, Foster argues, deciding where he should start and with what criteria he should choose to cut or keep would amount to censorship.

The Russian graffiti

While the total of 202 graffiti now existing may seem large, the reverse is the case. Any photos of the Reichstag in the three years after the war will show how densely the Reichstag then was covered with writing. What has remained cannot be more than 5–10 per cent of what was originally put there.

The Russians meant their words to be read by their fellows. The audience was not the Germans. The same is true of the writers of the spray-paint street graffiti: those 'tags' can only be properly deciphered by the insiders who know what those 'squiggles' stand for. A key aspect is the issue of taboo and transgression. For the street-writers the spraying must be illegal; it must be a transgression (Van Treeck 1995, 1998a, 1998b; Walsh 1996). The Reichstag writers at the end of the war knew they where writing on a once-sacred, non-sanctioned zone. This is clear from some of the comments:

> We Russians were here and always beat the Germans
>
> A cock down the Fascists' throat not Russia!
>
> serves them right sons of bitches.
>
> They certainly paid for Leningrad!

This aspect is, however, the minority of the graffiti. Of circa 200 preserved graffiti only 7 can be classed as direct insults. Expressions of joy form the next category with 9 graffiti, some of them personal expressions: 'Modshetian was here on the day of victory over the Germans.' And there are more directly political ones, clearly written by or with the secret police in mind.

> Glory to the Stalinist Falcons who took part in the battle for Berlin.

What if the walls had the name 'Ivan Denisovich' on them? Then the name would be sacrosanct. The truth is that many of these names might as well have been those of Ivan Denisovich; in real life these soldiers suffered the deprivations that Solzhenitsyn's fictional soldier suffered when he returned with the Red Army. Many of those who got to see even the smashed-up remains of the West were incarcerated by Stalin, for fear they tell the folks back home too much about the standard of living there, and so sow the seeds of discontent. That makes some graffiti the more chilling and the more relevant, when they remind us this was one tyrant defeating another:

> Long Live Stalin, his army and his soldiers! Death to the Germans R.M. Boiko, Kiev

Another category, of twenty-two graffiti, is the simple travelogue:

Route of march Teheran–Novosibirsk–Baku–Berlin.

Moscow–Stalingrad–Berlin.

These show how the Reichstag became part of a victory tourism, visited after the battle was won. This anonymous person had to fight all the way to the River Elbe before coming back to Berlin and adding his journey to the thousands around him: 'Caucasus–Sotshi–Warsaw–Berlin–Elbe.' These journeys underline the status of this site as a piece of world, not just local, history. They also suggest that it might have been the location for the telling of a story, a narrative of a journey, a personal Red Army song-line.

The largest group of graffiti comprises the simple signatures or statements: 'Laptev was here. Ivan Georgiewitch.' These totalled 168. This has the closest links to very old forms of rock-art, outlines of a hand or foot. It is a simple 'I am', a statement that one is present and alive. This becomes all the more important and moving when it is remembered that these were written in the context of a war. When one thinks these corridors were all filled with 300,000 visitors to the Nazis' anti-Bolshevik exhibition held in the Reichstag in 1937 (Cullen 1995: 249), the dialectical interlinked nature of history becomes particularly clear. The graffiti are an answer to Hitler's lunge for Moscow in 1941, an attack the Nazis prepared the Berliners for with the Reichstag exhibition of 1937. That is underlined by the six names prefaced by 'the defenders of Moscow'.

The palimpsest landscape of the Reichstag – landscapes of power: landscape of victory; first Prussian, then Nazi, then Russian, then in a divided Germany, then in a Germany reunited

In 1999, on the eve of the German parliament moving back to Berlin, Jürgen Leinemann of *Der Spiegel* wrote, 'The political class in Bonn will have to come to terms with the fact that with the creation of the Berlin republic, they are – symbolically at least – stepping into the shoes of the German Reich' (Leinemann 1999: 92).

As the central place in a central city of European modern history, the Reichstag has been a participant and witness to key events: the unification of Germany, for which it was built as the national assembly building; the rise of the National Socialists, and their ambition of a thousand-year Reich; the Allied victory of 1945 and the fall of Berlin to the Soviet forces, the event from which the Red Army graffiti derive; the division of Berlin as a central point of tension for the fifty years of the Cold War – the Berlin Wall was not five metres from the Reichstag; the collapse of the Soviet empire, and the reinstalling of the national assembly – the Bundestag – in the Reichstag, as renewed in Foster's design. Each event has reworked the urban landscape of and around the Reichstag.

Foster's understanding of 'layered-ness' at the Reichstag extends to the landscape that sets the context for the graffiti. The landscape is one of war, and then of victory.

The first 'layer' is the park laid out in front of the building (Figure 2.2). The park functioned as public space; it had originally been a military parade-ground. There were two main statues: one was of Bismarck, founding father of the united Germany; the second of a winged goddess of victory, symbolizing the defeat of Denmark, of Austria and most importantly of France in 1871, the event that marked the birth of Bismarck's Reich (Cullen 1995: 26). The ensemble provided a spatial plan of the ambition, of the nature of the positive values of the Prussian-led German state.

Figure 2.2 The Reichstag, as built in the later nineteenth century

Photograph: from *Das Reichstagsgebäude in Berlin* (1897)

How is one to 'read' the site and grasp the importance of this landscape in which the graffiti are now preserved? The meaning of the graffiti of the Reichstag is just as contested as in any aboriginal site, and its contextual landscape is just as complex. These statues can be seen as totems, to be read as physical embodiments of Germany's own creation myth. The same can be said of the architecture itself. The four towers of the Reichstag were said to symbolize Prussia, Würtemberg, Bavaria and Saxony, the four founding kingdoms of the new German state. The sculptures in the lobbies (that in 1945 were to become irresistible objects of graffiti: Figure 2.1) were figures of German history like Otto the Great lending their authority to a national temple in the secularized religion that is nationalism and democracy. The planned dedication to the German people – '*Dem deutschen Volke*' – that adorns the building's front was born of war. The Kaiser, who hated and feared the building as a symbol of middle-class democracy, made the concession in 1916 that the inscription could be placed there with the proviso that its letters be made from the metal of captured French guns. It was a Christmas present to boost German morale.

The second landscape is that of the Third Reich, of victory over democracy. The Nazis hated the Reichstag, seeing it as an ineffectual talking shop. They used the military parade-ground to greet visiting Italian Fascists, and the building to house anti-Bolshevik (in 1937) and anti-Semitic (in 1939) exhibitions (Hahn in Welfing 1999: 52). The symbols of victory from the Second Reich were removed to prepare the way for the landscape of the victory of the Third Reich, Speer's huge domed hall that would house assemblies of the future subjects of 'Germania' (Le Tissier 1997). The angel of victory

Figure 2.3 The Reichstag ruined, after the fall of Berlin in 1945 and in the desolation of Berlin in rubble

was moved to the '*Grosser Stern*', where it still stands in a position made famous by Wim Wenders in his film *Wings of Desire* (Wenders and Handke 1989). Bismarck was also removed; the statue now stands on the edge of the Tiergarten. The Reichstag itself would have been destroyed if Speer had had his way; intervening, Hitler commanded it be kept because 'National Socialists fought in it' (Hitler quoted in Welfing 1999: 56).

The third landscape was again one of victory (Figure 2.3), but this time Russian victory (Burlakow 1994; Read and Fischer 1998). The storming and raising of the Red Flag over the Reichstag became a central iconic event. This was in part Soviet propaganda, but it also grew from a popular reading of the material culture. In one of the preserved pieces of graffiti a certain 'Captain Kokliushkin, and First Lietenant Krassnikov, J.' wrote, 'We made it to the Reichstag, Hitler's lair! 15.5.45.' They got it wrong; Hitler despised the democracy the building stood for. But the mistake was easy to make: the building is such an emphatic statement of the national identity, a nationalism Hitler had harnessed to his political project. It is one of the paradoxes of the Reichstag that it was as important to the Soviets as it had not been to the Nazis. In 1945 the building was full of medical records, the Reichstag Library, Albert Speer's architectural models for 'Germania', and a maternity ward (Baker 2000). I once asked Jewgeni Khaldei, the Red Army photographer who took the famous photo of the Red Flag over the Reichstag (Volland and Krimmer 1994), why the Russians invested the building the Nazis despised with so much importance. Apart from the memory of the Reichstag fire in 1933 and the famously unsuccessful trial against the Communist Dimitroff, Khaldei came up with a very material answer: 'The Reichstag was the closest thing in Berlin to the Moscow Kremlin.' To the ordinary Russian, to write on the walls of a kremlin would be an ultimate taboo; to write on the Reichstag was the ultimate statement of victory.

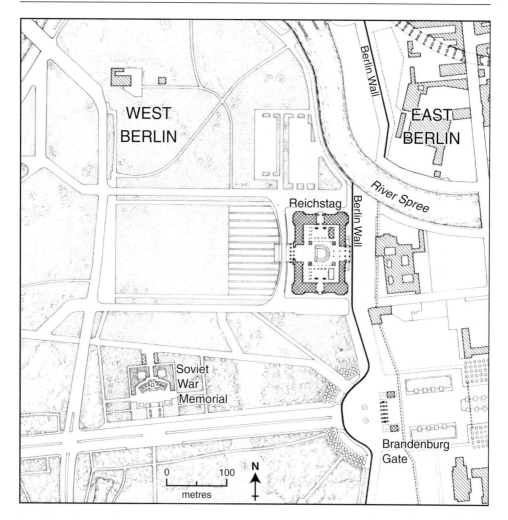

Figure 2.4 The Reichstag and its neighbours in the later Cold War years, 1961–1989. To the south-west is the Soviet war memorial, placed on the axis of the masterplan for Nazi Berlin that had been devised by Hitler's state architect Albert Speer. Immediately to the east was the Berlin Wall. Cutting through the old heart of the city, it ran from the Potsdamer Platz immediately past the Reichstag to cross the River Spree a little north of the building. To the south-east, just on the East German side of the wall, is the Brandenburg Gate, ceremonial entranceway into the city, and the surviving portion of a previous Berlin city wall, the Customs Wall, demolished in 1867

Map: Owen Tucker

Another component in turning this area into a landscape of Russian victory (Figure 2.4) was the erection of a barrow, or mass grave, within sight of the front steps of the Reichstag on the road leading to the Brandenburg Gate. Though not the largest Russian military memorial in Berlin (Figure 2.5), this was the first; it was made of red marble taken from Hitler's real lair, the *Reichskanzelei* (Reichschancellory). The lists of the prominent dead (Figure 2.6a) line the marble flanks of the monument, which is surmounted

a

b

Figure 2.5 The Soviet war memorial, with the Reichstag behind. The photograph was taken after reunification and rebuilding of the Reichstag, with the new dome and with the German national flag flying

Photograph: Barrie Baker

Figure 2.6 Details of the Soviet war memorial, part of a list of names of soldiers who fell in April 1945 (a), and the inscription in Russian below the statue of a Soviet sentry (b). The inscription is given in German and English, as well as Russian. The English reads: 'Eternal glory to heroes who fell in the struggle against the German Fascist invaders for the freedom and independence of the Soviet Union'

Photographs: Barrie Baker

Figure 2.7 The Reichstag and the Berlin Wall during the Cold War. In the later years of a divided Berlin, the Reichstag (left) was a few metres into West Berlin. This photograph dates from the first era of the Berlin Wall, 1961–1964, when it was a structure of rough-cast concrete blocks topped with barbed wire

by a huge stern Soviet sentry (Figure 2.6b), would have been all the more visible after the war, because all the trees in the surrounding park were cut down for firewood. This memorial is the sequel to the goddess of victory and Bismarck, as totem of the park.

So adjacent in central Berlin are the two sets of Russian names. The one set, the personal graffiti written on the Reichstag in myriad different hands, were written by living individuals. The other set, a list of only the important dead, is carved on the Soviet memorial in a typographic uniformity within the symbolic bracket provided by Stalinist art. There totalitarianism is united – Stalinist lettering on Nazi marble! Each Reichstag graffito is a small spark of individual expression, the more important for having been produced under the conditions of a communist dictatorship.

Even before Berlin fell in 1945, the tensions were evident between Russia and the Western states which together made the Allied powers. Those tensions of the Cold War crystallized in a symbolic rhetoric of confrontation in Berlin, divided from 1961 by the Berlin Wall (Figure 2.7). The Russians handed the Reichstag building over to the Germans in June 1945. Under the four-power agreement dividing Berlin into British, French, Russian and US sectors, the building fell into the British sector of the city which was divided along old borough boundaries. When Stephen Spender visited the Reichstag in the autumn of 1945, he noted that the building was 'covered in an alien patina like the relicts of all final catastrophes . . . you approach with the same amazement, the same tense fantasy as the Colosseum in Rome' (quoted by Hahn in Welfing 1999: 59). From 1961, when the boundary between the Russian and the British sectors became the Berlin Wall, the Reichstag still drew tourists like Spender, but this time it was the fine view of

Figure 2.8 The Reichstag and the Berlin Wall soon after German reunification in 1989. In its final form, the Berlin Wall was a smooth-faced wall of cast-concrete segments topped with a curved asbestos–cement pipe. The West German side was famously covered with spray-painted graffiti, the East German side kept in neat order by the border police. As this photograph taken from the east soon after German reunification shows, the east side of the wall was immediately also covered in graffiti. Segments of the pipe topping to the wall have been removed, and there are holes hacked through it

the wall just below the Reichstag's east windows that provided a 'must do' for all state visitors to West Berlin: from Queen Elizabeth to Thatcher and Reagan. This is a fourth urban landscape, one of superpower confrontation and manoeuvring, one of menace and some physical violence. With the city divided, the Soviet war memorial fell in West Berlin, and the Soviet insistence that their soldiers travel from East Berlin into the Western sector to attend it was one of many gestures of skirmish in Berlin between the Cold War combatants.

The fall of the Berlin Wall in November 1989, a symbolic event of the collapse of Soviet power (Figure 2.8), provides a fifth distinct urban landscape for the Reichstag. The Potsdamer Platz to the south, pre-war famously the busiest square in Europe and in the years of the wall a frontline waste ground, sprang again to life, and is now the busiest building site in Europe. In this fifth landscape for the Reichstag, the glass and steel towers of the new Potsdamer Platz are the historic citadels of new powers, of Daimler-Chrysler, Siemens and Sony, where the rhetoric of capitalist prosperity declared who had won the next war, the Cold War 1945–1989 that had been the third European war of the century. The Bundestag, the parliament of the Federal Republic (West Germany) from 1949, had been in Bonn, a small and modest city on the Rhine south of Cologne, its placing there symbolic of a country which had lost a European war, and would now be quieter in

Figure 2.9 The Reichstag as restored by Foster, with the new glass and steel cupola

Photograph: Dennis Gilbert/View

its demeanour. With reunification in 1990, the Bundestag became the parliament of all Germany. Where should it be? Should it stay in Bonn? Should Berlin be the capital again? And if Berlin was the capital, should the parliament return to the Reichstag, or install itself in a new building without a freight of history? The politicians chose to return to Berlin and the Reichstag.

From the refitting of the Reichstag to receive the deputies arose a set of choices: how was the history of the building to be noticed and addressed? The best known of the responses made by the architects, a British rather than a German practice, was to rebuild the dome over the Reichstag, not recreating the old design but in a new version (Figure 2.9). Its glass funnel under which the deputies sit in the debating chamber has been taken as a symbol of openness: the politicians will not decide matters in a closed and dark hall, but under the light (Baker 1999). Another choice was how to respond to the graffiti.

Meanings of the Reichstag graffiti

Interestingly, the West German response in the 1950s and 1960s had been to add to the emaciation of the Reichstag which the Soviets had started. In 1954 the West German government ripped all the statues off the roof, dynamited the remains of the dome, and imposed Paul Baumgarten's modernist architecture inside (Bartetzko in Welfing 1999). Foster's archaeological approach has exposed the ruthlessness with which the West German authorities gouged out its nineteenth-century national pomp. The huge holes made in that refitting (Fig. 2.11), which make the graffiti seem minute in comparison, provide a physical manifestation of West German extremism in wishing to exorcize the past and flee into a fresh, modern future. It was at this stage when the vast majority of the graffiti were cleaned off, or whole walls on which graffiti had been written were taken away. Helmuth Engel (2000: 118) remembers that the extensive structural changes in the building caused by the demolition today 'make it almost impossible to comprehend just how much of the building was covered with inscriptions, but it can be said with some certainty that the whole structure was covered, to above the height of a man (in some places even to ceiling height) with Cyrillic writing.' It was as if they wanted to suggest the size of the victory with the distances covered in the struggle.

It was Paul Baumgarten, the West German architect who won the 1960 competition to revise the Reichstag, who both destroyed and saved the graffiti. While on the one hand he criticized the government's destruction of so much ornamentation, on the other he removed whole walls inside the building, destroying much graffiti in the process. However, it was one of Baumgarten's measures to 'modernize' the aesthetic of the corridors which saved the graffiti that Foster found.

There were inscriptions in white made with chalk, and in black made with burned wood. The graffiti that remains now only survived because it was cheaper to put up plain white plasterboard over the walls in the corridors than to clean them off. This stripping of the building was seen as improving the architecture into a modernist style, but it was a flight from the past. Baumgarten's Reichstag may have housed a permanent exhibition, 'Questions on German history' (Deutscher Bundestag 1984); yet it literally covered up the Reichstag's own evidence for that history. At the dawn of the century one of the founders of modernism, the architect Adolf Loos, made the observation in Vienna, 'Modern materials are always those which are most economical. It is a common error nowadays to believe that only concrete and iron are modern' (Kulka 1979: 18). Paradoxically, the old graffiti-clad walls of the Reichstag are more 'modern' than Baumgarten's white plasterboard. Norman Foster proudly calls himself a modernist, but his approach to the building shows a far more subtle and imaginative application of modernist principles to historic buildings (Foster 1999: 182):

> We started with a building whose mutilated symbolism meant very little to the contemporary Germans. The most straightforward approach would have been to gut the Reichstag and to insert a modern building in the place of the odd mix of late nineteenth century and the 1960s fabric which then existed. Yet this would have been in a sense too easy. We believed that history could not simply be swept away.

This idea links to the archaeological tradition supported by the Active Museum of Berlin, which dug up the remains of the Gestapo headquarters down the road from the Reichstag, with the battle cry, 'The wound must stay open' (Baker 1987, 1990). A guiding tenet of modernism, as laid down by Le Corbusier, is the idea that the architect should remain true to the nature of the building material used. If the walls are old, then they should show that age. If they are covered in graffiti, then those graffiti should be expressed and made visible.

Much of the writing was faded when found. It was a conscious decision by Foster and the conservationists to have the graffiti not just preserved but also restored (Figures 2.10 and 2.11). Foster's archaeological or layered approach to the building derives from the logical extension of this principle: as well as making the old look its age, so should the later interventions be absolutely clear.

The clear division of new and old, twinned with the clear physical expression of the two, gives the Foster Reichstag a dynamic quality in which new and old compete: a tension makes the building dynamic, as opposed to the false harmony of many postmodernist architectural pastiches. The graffiti have been placed in a new landscape, the landscape of democratic dialogue between the different forms, materials and functions, which used the aesthetics of ruins and the chaotic as visual brakes against hubris. The material culture speaks to the modesty necessary for peace and democracy. This is a positive example of the postmodern idea of fragmentation.

Leinemann (1999: 103–104) says of the transformed Reichstag:

> The Berlin Reichstag is not a model of the *Titanic*. The scorch-marks, the inscriptions by the Russian victors of 1945 are all genuine . . .

> When places, people and things really meet each other, then historical memory is intensified, traces are uncovered that run counter to the glossy staging of a coherent sheen . . .

> In the Reichstag, where Norman Foster has carefully uncovered the layers and conserved them, the words of the Green Vice-president of the parliament Antje Vollmer are made particularly clear. 'Many have tried to draw the face of this nation in Berlin. The remains of their incisions show how powerful they were but no one managed to finish the picture.'

Figure 2.10 Conserving the Reichstag graffiti during the Foster restoration

Photograph: Rudi Meisel/VISUM

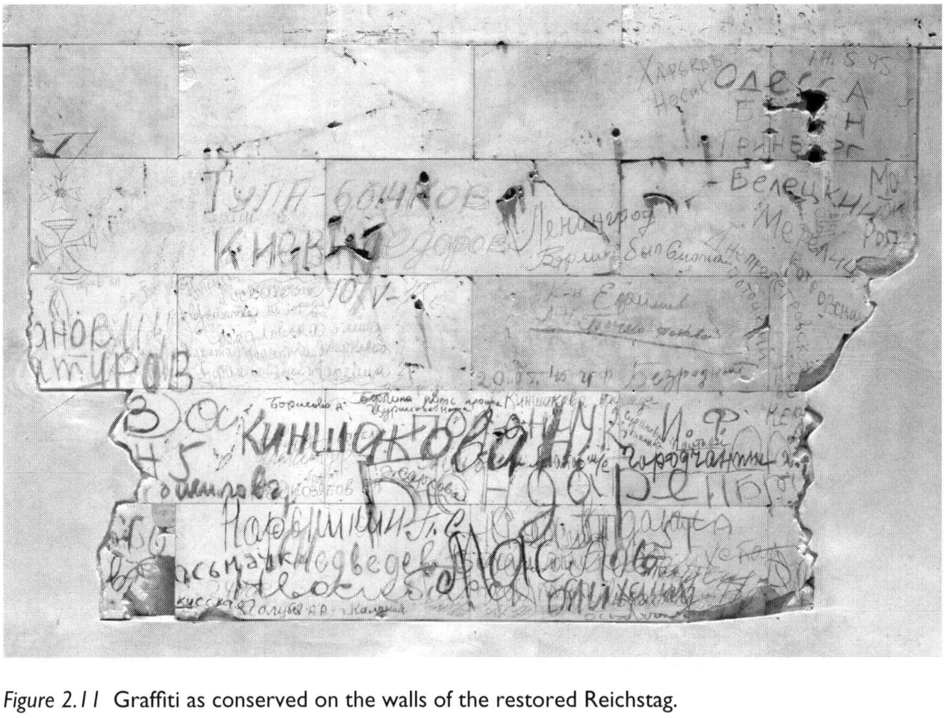

a

Figure 2.11 Graffiti as conserved on the walls of the restored Reichstag.

b

c

Figure 2.11 (continued) By their patchiness, the graffiti surviving show the hazards of the building's treatment since 1945. The graffiti by the doorway show another trace of the building's history, with the stone broken where the elaborate mouldings were hacked off by Baumgarten's refit after the war

Photographs: Nigel Young, Foster and Partners

Architects as archaeologists

The transforming of the Reichstag began with an artist's event, the wrapping in 1995 of the entire Reichstag building in silver fabric sheeting by the artists Christo and Jeanne-Claude. Christo has wrapped buildings before – and one of the Paris bridges across the Seine – and made landscape pieces: his early 'running fence' went for miles up and across the landscape of coastal California, and he has fringed tropical atolls with pink wrappings. His Reichstag wrapping was a larger gesture, for it enclosed the blackened and battered old building immediately before it was remade anew (Baal-Teshuva 1993).

The wrapping by Christo started the game of covering and uncovering the Reichstag, a game of architecture and archaeology. Norman Foster recalls (Foster 1999: 183–4):

> I remember particularly, on the last day of the wrapping – July 6th – walking through the building with my wife Elena, and Christo and Jeanne-Claude, seeing the silvery light filtering through the fabric saying good-bye, to the old building's past. At the end of that two week event the fabric began to come down and the crane moved in to start demolishing the roof. The transition was as sudden as that. I felt that the Christo wrapping had been cathartic; it seemed to unburden the building of its more tragic associations and prepare it for the next phase of its career . . . As we peeled away the layers of history and removed Baumgarten's interior, the bones of Wallot's Reichstag gradually came to light, along with striking, even bizarre, imprints of past events, such as the graffiti chalked on the walls by victorious Soviet [Soldiers] in 1945. I was struck by how affecting this graffiti was; each message a simple reminder of a painful human story, otherwise long forgotten . . . The Reichstag bears the imprint of time and events in a way that is more powerful than any exhibition could hope to be: preserving the scars allows it to function as a living museum of German History. This decision led to the quite extraordinary sight of specialist conservators working with almost watchmakerly precision to protect fragile remains, while the demolition crews with huge machines of destruction made inroads around them (Figure 2.10).

These two 'archs' – architecture and archaeology – are Janus-headed, not identical twins but very much related. Both have to do with matter, space, time. But while architecture looks to projecting into the future, archaeology searches for the face of mankind in the past. Like Walter Benjamin's angel of history, archaeology is condemned to look into the past; architecture is the angel who builds jetties into the future. And the architect knows that the sands of time will eventually destroy the monument, whose only hope of resurrection will then be through the knowledge and the tenacity of the archaeologist.

Walter Benjamin, *Thesis IX*

Benjamin (1992: 249) writes:

> A Paul Klee* painting, *Angelus novus*, shows an angel as though about to move away from something he is fixedly contemplating. His eyes are staring, his mouth is open, his wings are spread. This is how one pictures the angel of history: his face turned

* One remembers that Paul Klee taught at the Bauhaus, centre of the modernist architecture the Nazis abhorred, and was among the many painters the Nazis damned as decadent.

towards the past. Where we perceive a chain of events, he sees one single catastrophe which keeps piling wreckage upon wreckage and hurls it in front of his feet. The angel would like to stay, to awaken the dead, to make whole what has been smashed. But a storm is blowing from paradise: it has got caught in his wings with such violence that the angel can no longer close them. This storm irresistibly propels him to the future to which his back is turned, while the pile of debris before him grows skyward. The storm is what we call progress.

The archaeologist is like the angel looking down, but the architect is strapped to his back and ever looking upwards, dreaming and building the utopias that with time fall and become the wreckage that interests the archaeologist. Both archaeologist and architect live in the present, but they look in different directions. In the case of the Reichstag an architect has chosen to recycle one of the pieces from the tower of wrecks that Benjamin describes as growing skywards.

Both have their limits, the architect those of engineering and materials that limit the dreams of future worlds. For the archaeologist it is the limit of what has been left by the destruction of time. Both are projections into a canvas bounded by the limits of technology, material and time. One says how it was, the other how it may be. Both are alchemists in the sense that they open up matter and space, turning them into homes, streets, civilizations. Once the building is complete and the public takes over, the architect can no longer control whether the thing he has built really 'works' as was intended. The same with archaeologists, who cannot control how their interpretations will work. There is always the next generation, the next piece of evidence that could suggest the interpretation is wrong. There is also a sense that archaeologists build the past – except that instead of adding, they take away.

Archaeological debate

Archaeology is a practice, but not all practitioners are archaeologists. Ian Hodder (1999) has had an aim to open up the bounds of archaeology; his work at Çatalhüyük has interestingly grappled with the complex and often contradictory pressures that are involved in doing archaeology. While the importance of Hodder's work lies in the fact that he is inside the discipline, earlier attempts have come from outside.

Take, for example, the ideas and practice of the Active Museum in Berlin (Baker 1990). They were influences on the opening of the concept of the boundaries of archaeology, as I proposed in 1988 in 'Museums without walls' (Baker 1988). The case of the Reichstag graffiti is an interesting extension of these issues, except now the archaeological landscape is literally inside the corridors of power. There are echoes the conflict between a 'world heritage' and the heritage of a local community in the framework that Hodder outlines (1999: 204). Except in this case the local community is not a Turkish village but the political élite of one of the most powerful countries in the world. This example I see as pushing back the boundaries of what we mean by community; as Vaclav Havel told me, 'Politicians are a club of people who have a common tribal interest and instincts, which it is very difficult for outsiders like myself not to get drawn into' (Baker and Garton-Ash 1999).

The Reichstag affair also opens up the point that it is not archaeologists who have a monopoly on archaeological activity. For a hi-tech architect, Norman Foster, archaeology can become a part of his design language, an extension of his being true to the form, to the material. In this sense the layers of the Reichstag extend the work of Foster's old partner Richard Rogers at the Pompidou Centre in Paris or Foster's own Hong Kong and Shanghai Bank. At the Pompidou, the piping normally hidden inside was put on the outside, with pride in the nature of the building as machine. The Reichstag as an old building should not hide signs of its age.

Hodder talks about virtual sites, centres and communities. The work of the architects reminds me of another virtual archaeological community, those who use archaeology as metaphor, those who dig – investigative journalists, poets (Heaney 1969), war-crime investigators, and – the oldest of all – Freud and the psychoanalysts. The discovery of the great Hallstatt sites and of the European Bronze Age was taking place in the Alps during the last years of the Austro-Hungarian Empire, at just the time when a professor of medicine at Vienna University, Dr Sigmund Freud, was making discoveries just as, if not more, important. Instead of the amnesia that Paul Baumgarten's architecture offered, Norman Foster has put the head of German power on the couch. Foster has confronted the German republic with the memories in its subconscious, represented by the Red Army graffiti. For the Germans they are an abstract chaos of squiggles into which – as with Freud's famous abstract-pattern cards – the deputies read their hopes and fears that lie below the smooth surface of the new German capital. For the Russians the Cyrillic squiggles are a reminder of home and a dream of past glory: journeys made into a foreign land.

References

Baal-Teshuva, J. 1993. *Christo und Jean-Claude: der Reichstag und urbane Projekte*. Munich: Prestel.

Baker, F. 1987. History that hurts: excavating 1933–45, *Archaeological Review from Cambridge* 7(1): 93–101.

Baker F. 1988. Museums without walls. Unpublished M.Phil. thesis, Department of Archaeology, University of Cambridge.

Baker, F. 1990. Archaeology, Habermas and the pathologies of modernity, in F. Baker and J. Thomas (eds), *Writing the past in the present*: 54–63. Lampeter: St David's University College Press.

Baker, F. 1993. The Berlin Wall: production, preservation and consumption of a 20th-century monument, *Antiquity* 67: 709–733.

Baker, F. 1999. 'Rebuilding the Reichstag'. *Omnibus*, BBC 1, 7 June.

Baker, F. 2000. Mythos Reichstag, in N. Foster *et al.*, *Rebuilding the Reichstag*. London: Weidenfeld and Nicolson.

Baker, F. and T. Garton Ash. 1999. 'Magic lantern'. *Freedom's battle* BBC 2, 14 November.

Benjamin, W. 1992. *Illuminations*. London: Fontana.

Burlakow, M.P. 1994. *Sowjetische Truppen in Deutschland 1945–1994*. Moscow: Junge Garde-Verlag.

Cullen, M. 1995. *Der Reichstag im Spannungsfeld der deutschen Geschichte*. Berlin: be.bra Verlag.

Deutscher Bundestag. 1984. *Questions on German history*. Bonn: German Bundestag Press.

Engel, H. 2000. The marks of history, in N. Foster *et al.*, *Rebuilding the Reichstag*. London: Weidenfeld and Nicolson.

Foster, N. *et al.* 2000. *The Reichstag*. London: Weidenfeld and Nicolson.

Heaney, S. 1969. *The death of a naturalist*. London: Faber and Faber.

Hodder, I. 1999. *The archaeological process: an introduction*. Oxford: Blackwell.

Foster, N. 1999. Ein optimistisches zeicher für ein modernes Deutschland, in *Welfing*.

Kleine, H. 1999. Theatre of democracy: reinventing Berlin's Reichstag, *Architecture Today* 98: 48–59.

Kulka, H. 1979. *Adolf Loos*. Vienna: Locker Verlag. [First published 1931.]

Leinemann, J. 1999. *Gratwandereungen, Machtkämpfe, Visionen Deustsche Momente*. Wien: Picus Reportagen.

Le Tissier, T. 1997. *Berlin – then and now*. London: Battle of Britain Publishers.

Read, A. and D. Fischer. 1998. *The fall of Berlin*. London: Pimlico.

Stonor Saunders, F. 1999. *Who paid the piper?* London: Granta.

Tilley, C. 1994. *A phenomenology of landscape: places, paths and monuments*. Oxford: Berg.

Van Treeck, B. 1995. *Writer Lexikon: American graffiti*. Moers: Edition Aragon.

Van Treeck, B. 1998a. *Graffiti art 9: Graffiti und Wändern und Mauern*. Berlin: Schwarzkopf & Schwartzkopf.

Van Treeck, B. 1998b. *Graffiti Lexikon: Legale und Illegale Malerei im Stadtbild*. Berlin: Schwarzkopf & Schwartzkopf.

Volland, E. and H. Krimmer (eds). 1994. *Von Moskau nach Berlin: Bilder des Russischen Fotografen Jewgeni Chaldej*. Berlin: Nicolai.

Walsh, M. 1996. *Graffito*. Berkeley: North Atlantic Books.

Wenders, W. and P. Handke. 1989. *Der Himmel über Berlin: ein Filmbuch*. Frankfurt am Main: Suhrkamp.

Welfing, H. (ed.). 1999. *Dem Deutschen Volke: der Bundestag im Berliner Reichstagsgebaeude*. Berlin: Bouvier.

Chapter 3

British prehistoric rock-art in the landscape

Stan Beckensall

Figure 3.1 England, Scotland and Wales, showing the main areas of rock-art

An overview of British prehistoric rock-art

Once thought of as a purely Bronze Age phenomenon, British rock-art is now generally regarded as late Neolithic, with a use over at least 1000 years continuing into the early Bronze Age. Its position in the landscape on 'living' and earthfast rock, mainly horizontal surfaces, opens it up to the sky. It is not found on the most fertile areas that would have been most attractive for arable farming, but in the upland, marginal areas of thinner, poorer soils that supported wild and domesticated animals – a food source that continued to be of prime importance even when arable farming intensified. Much of it 'signs the land' at the best viewpoints, often on ridges overlooking fertile valleys and plains. One

a

b

Figure 3.2 Rock surfaces and their rock-art: a: Argyll, Ballygowan; b: Northumberland, Weetwood

imagines pastoral nomads moving through well-known and well-marked territory, able to see the migration of game from an advantageous height.

We are considering panels of rock that were decorated with symbols and motifs by impacting the rock surface with a hard stone tool. The individual pick-marks are very clear on some examples. For this reason it is unusual to find decoration on hard rocks, such as igneous and metamorphic; instead, panels of softer rock, such as the fell sandstones of Northumberland or the greywacke of Scotland, are preferred. Almost every marking is abstract in form (Figure 3.2). The most common symbol is the cup mark, and linear and ringed grooves are also plentiful.

From such simple beginnings as a cup and groove, people who chipped their patterns were familiar with many common motifs, but others expressed some individuality. If you like, they shared the same language, but some were more articulate than others. Rosettes, radiates, multiple concentric rings, crowded and well-spaced motifs are just a few variations on the theme. Spirals, much rarer, have their own mystery. What is stunning is that almost all British rock-art is abstract. This opens it up to people reading into it what they will, and leads to some unsubstantiated conjectures. Ronald Morris, a solicitor, listed 104 speculated meanings that he had encountered and gave them marks out of ten! (Morris 1979)

Some markings were not exposed for long. Some motifs cannot be seen until you are almost on top of them, and people must have known where to look. We can sometimes predict where we might look for 'new' ones. Their locations may coincide with strikingly visible natural features, such as cliffs, but they do not give themselves away easily. And who knows what message they conveyed to which group of prehistoric people? How did people know where to find them?

Some of the rock surfaces are large, like those at Achnabreck in Argyll, and some are small pieces of earthfast rock carried by ice, such as those on Barningham Moor, County Durham.

Open-air motifs blend sympathetically with the landscape, and use surface irregularities on the rock in their design. The spacing of motifs on the surface is important, for they may be widely separated, linked very closely, run into each other, cover the surface, or leave unmarked patches and borders. It is rare to find evidence of superimposition, which would help to hint at some sort of chronology.

There is a way of looking at the designs. No matter what features of the landscape the sites may overlook, the people who made the designs used the slope of the rock, cracks and natural indentations to create a design which is meant to be viewed from the bottom of the slope.

If all rock-art were in the open air like this, we would find it very difficult or impossible to date. It can be linked to a semi-mobile way of life, that's all. The motifs also appear on a small number of monuments, but even then they cannot be dated.

Long Meg (NY 510372*), a tall pillar of red sandstone outside the portal entrance to a massive circle of volcanic standing stones in Cumbria, is covered in motifs (Beckensall 1992a). Whether this legendary witch, turned to stone for dancing with her daughters on the Sabbath, lay flat or was part of a cliff is unknown, but the raising of this huge stone creates a totally different impression from a horizontal outcrop. Motifs may have

---

* The map references in the text refer to the British National Grid, the Ordnance Survey.

been added when the monument was erected, or much later; or Long Meg may have been brought to the site covered in decoration centuries old. The monolith is part of a much more extensive and complex site.

A spiral and lozenge shapes have recently been recorded at Castlerigg on standing stones of the stone circle (NY 292236) (Frodsham 1996). Rather plainer designs occur on standing stones in the Kilmartin Valley (RCAHMS 1988). These examples are interesting, but at what stage the motifs became part of the monuments is not known. That they are *there* means that the motifs were clearly regarded as important to whatever rituals were enacted there.

What has always attracted researchers' attention is the presence of motifs on stones in a few early Bronze Age cairns. On close examination, however, it has been found that the motifs on many of the decorated cist slabs were eroded before the slabs were inserted, and some were broken off larger surfaces. An example is an early Bronze Age cist at Balbirnie (NO 285030) in Fife, Scotland (Figure 3.3). In the Neolithic tombs of Ireland's Boyne Valley, however, some decorated slabs were purpose-made, and others had been reused. What we now make of the reuse of decorated surfaces taken from open-air art is that its purpose had changed: the marked rocks were buried, often face-down, no longer to be seen, but still a meaningful symbol.

Whatever the meaning of these abstract designs, they eventually went out of use. It may be that their Neolithic symbolism was irrelevant to, and perhaps hopelessly

Figure 3.3 Fife-decorated cist slab: Balbirnie. The site on excavation, showing the carvings facing inwards in the cist

Photograph: R.W.B. Morris archive. Reproduced by permission of Scottish Heritage incompatible with, that cosmology of the Bronze Age which gave rise to the interment of important individuals in single graves, or to the burial of several such individuals in the same mound. The fact that some early Bronze Age cists contain reused panels of formerly open-air rock-art, however, may represent the last vestiges of a belief system, at a time of change and probably of crisis in many ways, which still recognized the power of the old symbolism.

It is beginning to be recognized that some decorated slabs were produced specially for the monuments in which they were discovered. In these cases, however, the decoration had been used in a way that suggests its meaning had changed – or was in the process of change. It was again buried, often face-down, and no longer to be seen. An example is the recently excavated cist at Witton Gilbert (Beckensall and Laurie 1998), near Durham city, where the cover was purpose-built and decorated on two sides, with the more elaborate cups and rings on the underside. Not only that, but also two freshly decorated stones were placed inside the cist.

Similarly, in the material used to build stone cairns, some stones are now being found with freshly decorated cups and rings mostly face-downwards, like wreaths brought to a funeral. One such double-kerbed mound at Fowberry (NU019278) (Beckensall 1991), Northumberland, was built on profusely decorated outcrop rock. There are other round cairns on decorated surfaces in the same county that reinforce the significance of these places. Thus the motifs can continue to be used, perhaps for as long as hundreds of years, but in a different way and with a different meaning.

Northumberland has rock-shelters with motifs, but Food Vessel and Beaker burials in two of them could be later than the making of the motifs. Establishing a chronology for the motifs is very difficult.

I doubt whether we will ever know precisely what the symbols mean, whether some of the people who made the motifs were clear about their origins, or why the markings have so much in common with those, for example, in Galicia or California. We may speculate that the motifs may also have been tattooed on the skin, painted on wood, or woven into material, but these do not endure like stone.

The images were meant to last. They appear on outcrop and earthfasts in the landscape, but some are on 'portable' rocks (i.e. blocks small enough to be moved).

The landscape

From regional surveys we can imagine a landscape 4000–5000 years ago in areas that had rock-art in an almost pristine wilderness. Some changes had been made: a clearing, a well-defined path, signs of a camp, or a burned area where vegetation could regenerate. In marginal areas like these there is evidence that the earlier Mesolithic hunters and gatherers had chosen the same areas for their camps and blade-making as did the motif-makers. This stands out particularly clearly in County Durham (Beckensall and Laurie 1998). Agriculture brought with it a more static society based on farms and land enclosures, but hunting and herding continued to play big parts in their economy. Deer, represented, for example, among the motifs of Valcamonica in northern Italy, are post-Neolithic in date and are much more widespread and common than images of domestic animals.

We tend to separate secular from ritual activity in modern society, but the distinction may not have applied to earlier societies. It is not surprising, therefore, to find that motifs may mark special places in the Neolithic landscape relevant to hunting areas, and that the same motifs are put into graves and on standing stones. Their use reflects a different way of thinking about them.

In some ways decorated panels enhance the landscape. Unlike what was around them, they were organized, compact, spread across rocks specially chosen for the purpose; an encounter with some of them would have been very impressive. However, leaves and other things would have covered some of them in a short time; for their use to be anything more than temporary, one has to assume that the surfaces were kept clean. Perhaps the paths to them were so well used that this became an automatic process. We don't know. Assuming they could have been put there in a period that might amount to 2000 years, the process becomes even more difficult to understand.

Exposure for long periods could erode some motifs and deepen others, especially those on a slight slope.

Establishing a framework of study

Interest in motifs has not sufficiently taken into account the details of their setting. That many panels of rock-art are at prominent viewpoints has been recognized, but it is only through the recent work of Richard Bradley and his Reading University students (Bradley 1997) that an attempt has been made to place this within a coherent statistical framework.

What distances can be seen from marked rocks? In what directions? How close do you have to be before you can see the marked rocks?

Is there a reason why some rocks were chosen for marking and not others? Studying this involves taking a sample of all outcrop rocks in the area and comparing them. Are the sites of marked rocks inter-visible? Is there any rule that determines where different designs are sited? For example, are complex designs (with many concentric circles) set in different places in the landscape from simple patterns (such as cups or single rings)? If so, as motifs are a means of communication, are they designed for different audiences?

This work has involved dividing a landscape into grids that include marked and unmarked rocks, measuring distances from rocks and the angle of sight, and making sense of the results. This has been done for many sites in different regions in Britain, taking into account information already available. One element of the research programme, when I was present, was to set down the students in a limited area of known rock-art to see if they could predict where the markings might be. They were able to do so quite accurately.

Although all regions where there is rock-art must be seen as different, Richard Bradley has put forward a number of common factors. Where there are monuments, the rock-art leads to them in a carefully constructed way, with the complex motifs at the highest parts. Simple motifs tend to be lower down on the margins, where local people went about their daily business. Bradley thinks that the complex motifs are therefore addressed to people coming from some distance to the monument sites. His landscape surveys show that the complex motifs are often at 'entrances' in the natural terrain, reached by a sequence of others. He sees 'thresholds', which may have conspicuous rocks or rock outcrops overlooking the river valleys, at places where valleys run into an area of ritual. This proposition can be tested on a regional basis, and what now follows looks at some examples.

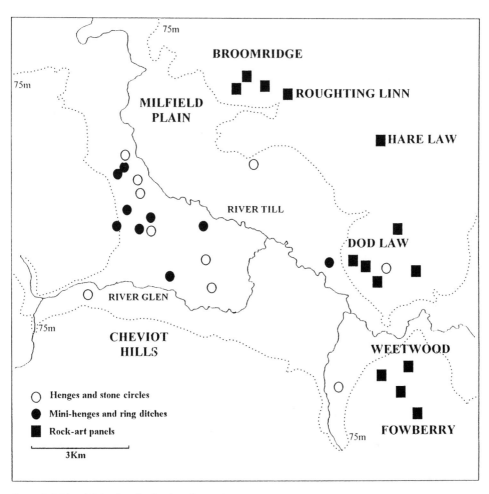

Figure 3.4 North Northumberland rock-art sites

North Northumberland

All known rock-art panels in this region of north-east England, adjacent to the Scottish border, have been recorded by the author (Beckensall 1991). Reading University has recently surveyed some areas (Bradley 1997). Many of the panels have been known for nearly 200 years.

Open-air rock-art in Northumberland (Figure 3.4) has a wide distribution and follows an interesting pattern. In the Wooler area, where the River Till flows towards the Tweed along a flat plain consisting of sediments laid down by a large glacial lake, the plain is reached through gaps in the sandstone scarps to the south and east. The River Glen flows in from the west past the Cheviots, which are composed of igneous rocks. The Till begins its life as the River Breamish, rising in the Cheviots, flowing down the Ingram Valley, then north past sandstone ridges on either side, which include major rock-art sites at Hunterheugh (Beanley Moor), Old Bewick, Amerside Law Moor, and Weetwood and

Fowberry on the opposite bank. The river skirts Chatton Park Hill, and at Horton and Buttony makes a right-angled turn to break through the sandstone scarp at Weetwood Bridge, before flowing north past Gled Law and Dod Law towards Milfield and Ford. The plain is of crucial importance, because recently it has been shown to contain not only Saxon buildings, but henges, cemeteries, linear ditches and pit alignments of the prehistoric period.

The sites just mentioned have elaborate panels of rock-art sited on scarps that are clearly visible from each other, and lead the way towards gaps into the Milfield Plain.

Goatscrag and Roughting Linn

This area illustrates how the siting of rock-art works. One of the 'entrances' to the Milfield Plain is along the valley of the Broomridgedean Burn. The burn has cut into the sandstone; it is flanked by a steep sandstone scarp known as Broomridge, which has panels of rock-art (Figure 3.5), four figures of deer, burials under a rock overhang, evidence of destroyed burial cairns at the west end, and the largest outcrop of marked rock in England (Beckensall 1991).

The ridge has its own distinctive natural focal point in outcrops of sandstone that are eroded into dramatic shapes visible for many kilometres; they lie below that part of the ridge from which burial cairns were cleared away for recent agriculture. The survival rate of rock has been affected by the use of some outcrops for the quarrying of millstones, some of which, in various stages of removal, are still visible. Surface traces in the thin soils have been disturbed by rig-and-furrow ploughing. The ridge has marked outcrops that overlook the Broomridgedean Burn Valley, with its access to the Milfield Plain via a sunken lane; the other side has views of the North Sea and Ford Moss.

From west to east, there are three panels of rock-art on outcrop. The first (NT 9736 3718), now covered over, faces away from the scarp edge. The motifs consist of a central cup with three irregular rings, a concentric arc, and a long curvilinear groove that surrounds most of this.

The next rock, c. 100 metres east (NT 9719 3778), has many different types of motifs on a large outcrop (where there are later millstone quarries). One figure has a central cup with seven concentric rings that on close examination don't quite meet. There are three other motifs of the cup and ring type on the same patch of rock. Further west are incomplete concentric rings, a rosette, cup clusters with two cups joined and one with a sharp duct leading out (all with well-defined pick-marks). There are other single scattered cups and some natural ones.

Two hundred metres further east, and away from the scarp edge on a raised natural rock platform, partly eaten away by quarrying, is a slab of rock (NT 9703 3708) with the design arranged to point towards the south valley. It was one of the first decorated surfaces to be recognized and recorded in the nineteenth century. As Figure 3.5b shows, its decoration is based upon variations of cup-and-ring motifs. There are a diametric groove, arcs, cups and rings, motifs joined together by grooves; at the north end are large rings.

Goatscrag Hill rises above the rest of the ridge; on one edge (NT 976 371) are sets of two cups joined together by a curved groove, like horseshoes. Underneath the rock overhang were Early Bronze Age cremation burials in pots buried below the present floor level. Four figures of deer are pecked into the vertical iron-stained wall of the rock

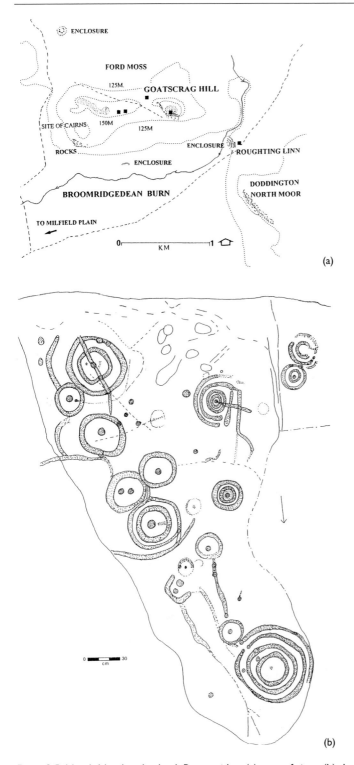

ENCLOSURE

FORD MOSS

125M.   GOATSCRAG HILL

150M

SITE OF CAIRNS

125M

ROCKS

ENCLOSURE   ROUGHTING LINN

ENCLOSURE

DODDINGTON
NORTH MOOR

BROOMRIDGEDEAN BURN

TO MILFIELD PLAIN

0   KM   1

(a)

0   30
cm

(b)

Figure 3.5 North Northumberland, Broomridge: (a) map of sites; (b) drawing of panel

overhang. Three are static, and one has its legs bent in movement. They appear to be prehistoric, but are not definitely so.

The crag drops away to the stream, which meets a second stream; together, they have cut through the sandstone to form a promontory. The Broomridgedean Burn tumbles over the edge of this as a waterfall called Roughting Linn, a place-name which means that here the water bellows like a bull into the pond. This promontory has massive, multiple earth and stone walls separated by ditches, enclosing the promontory in an arc. It has never been excavated, so we cannot assume anything more than that it is prehistoric.

Beyond this by only a few metres is a large whaleback of sandstone (NT 983 367), uncovered by William Greenwell in the mid-nineteenth century. Half of it on the west has been quarried away, and a large slice has been cut out of it crosswise, but the rest has such a variety of motifs that it is justifiably acknowledged as one of the finest rock-art panels in the world. Richard Bradley (1997) drew attention to its similarity in appearance to a long barrow or chambered tomb, and pointed out that the deep, ringed motifs run around the edge like the decoration on Irish passage grave kerbs. The more delicate, plant-like motifs are arranged further into the rock, above the others.

This natural outcrop occupies an important place in the landscape at the threshold between the route to the Milfield Plain and access to the coastal plain of the North Sea. Recent clearing of Harelaw Crags (NU 013 335–012 335) in a small wood has added more complex motifs to those recorded (Beckensall 2000b). Harelaw Crags link Roughting Linn to the high ground overlooking another threshold to the Milfield Plain, near the village of Doddington. Between Roughting Linn and the sea, there are other examples of rock-art, but they are portable stones that range in size from cobbles to small slabs, the original position of which is not known.

Millstone Burn/Snook Bank

This second area of Northumberland marks the gap and communication route between low-lying, level ground to the south and hills to the north. The burn is so named because millstones have been quarried in the area, and Snook Bank is the ridge where the beasts were shackled. The Roman road, the Devil's Causeway, follows the same valley on its route from Hadrian's Wall north. Other cup-and-ring marks in the area follow a north-east to south-west course towards Alnwick and Rothbury on high ground. On the Millstone Burn side, west, the marked rocks (NU 1189 0521–1142 0528) (Beckensall 1992) are outcrop and earthfast boulders with views across the valley south; the highest on the ridgetop look towards the Cheviots. The Snook Bank sites (NU 1293 0520–126 056), to which we have added in our recording very recently, lie on top of steep outcrops that overlook a plain to the south, and others are hidden in cleared ground with rough pasture that contains cairns and marshy hollows.

Most of the rock-art is on exposed outcrop or in thin soil that supports some heather, grass and bent; it is only used for grazing. The sandstone ridge, pierced by the burn, contrasts with the large area of lowland that opens out at its foot to the south.

The area with this large sample of marked rocks was examined in Richard Bradley's (1997) survey. He noted that the most distant views extended in two directions along the axis of the valley.

The motifs on these rocks do not include the largest systems of concentric circles, but there is a great variety of motifs, some unique to this area.

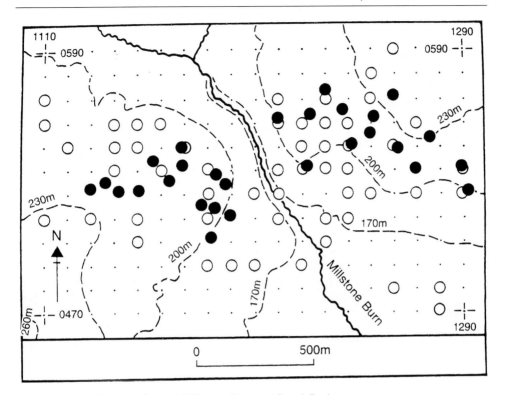

Figure 3.6 North Northumberland: Millstone Burn and Snook Bank

Key: •: rock-art; open circles: control samples for the comparative study of locations with and without rock-art
Map: Bradley (1997: 85)

To be added to the published sites (Beckensall 2000a) are five panels of rock-art at Snook Bank, and another panel on a path to Caller Crag at Wellhope (NU 115061)

Lordenshaw (NZ 0512 9912–0060 0045) (Beckensall 1992)

An outstanding ridge of sandstone flanked by stream valleys that are tributaries of the River Coquet is dominated by a large enclosure, usually referred to as a hillfort. This continued in use as a settlement in Romano-British times. Within the fort are faint cup marks; on the slopes leading away from the ridge to the east are varied motifs that include very large cups, one at the head of a long and wide serpentine channel. Also on the whitened outcrops are long grooves linked in some cases to cups, and cups and rings, basins, and clusters of midget cups. The ridge leads down to the junction of the Whitton Burn to the River Coquet, including cairns and more marked rocks, ending at the valley bottom with large cups on outcrop.

To the west, the art nearest the hillfort begins on a large outcrop, now much quarried away, with some fine motifs, overlooking the Coquet Valley to the Cheviots, and looking up to the Simonside Hills. Near by is a disturbed cairn with two marked boulders. Below, further west on a parallel outcrop, is another set of motifs including the famous 'Horseshoe rock' (NZ 0502 9918) on the edge of a cairn. Some sites chosen for cairn-building were already 'sanctified' where the outcrop was marked.

Figure 3.7 North Northumberland: Lordenshaw. Rock-art in its landscape context

The relationship between cairns and motifs is close; this ridge is an important ritual site where the rock-art has very extensive views of the landscape below and all around it. This natural, dominant position of the ridge is not the highest part of this landscape; immediately to the south are the Simonside Hills, with no rock-art. It has been used later as a deer park, for some arable farming, and for temporary herders' huts.

There are many examples in Northumberland of motifs occurring in cists, on the cobbles that cairns are made of, and on the rocks on which cairns stand. The currency of the motifs lasts into the early Bronze Age, and they are used in a different way from open-air rock motifs. Some rock-shelters also have motifs (Beckensall 1991, 1992a), and simple cup marks appear on standing stones (Beckensall 1992b). Spirals occur in one cremation pit at Lilburn (NU 013256) (Beckensall 1991). A cup-marked cobble has been found in a henge pit (Beckensall 1983).

Interesting though these discoveries are, they appear in only a very small proportion of monuments such as cairns.

County Durham, Swaledale and Wensleydale

Not long ago, this important area was relatively unknown. It has now been thoroughly researched and published (Beckensall and Laurie 1998). It has neither the large multiple concentric circles of Northumberland and Argyll, nor extensive outcrops suitable for this, but it has a great range of motifs and a fascinating distribution pattern.

The areas favoured by Mesolithic people – when hunter-gatherers left slight traces in the landscape of their flint and chert chippings during their incursions from more permanent sites on the coast – coincide in some cases with the same areas favoured by Neolithic pastoralists and hunters at a time when arable farming was being established in the more fertile areas such as the river valleys and terraces. Rock-art overlooks those lowland sites; the motifs survive because the thin moorland soils are not suitable for anything more than mineral exploitation, rough pasture, grouse rearing and army ranges.

The markings are not found at intermediate heights at any distance from the rivers. One may assume that before they were made the people using the land would have plentiful game to hunt for food and skins, and fish, especially migratory salmon. There would have been little alteration to the pristine wilderness.

Much of the rock used for marking had been moved there originally by ice sheets; it is in the form of small flat earthfasts and boulders. In Teesdale, most of the marked rocks occur in open clusters or groups of individual sites above 250 metres OD* on the highest slopes that form the southern edge of the Tees valley. The sites are listed as High Hagg, Feldom and Gayles Moor, Barningham Moor, Cotherstone Moor, and above Deepdale. Most recently found are in a line east of Eggleston, a bleak area that has produced some surprises, including a rare Beaker burial in a cist, and other unexplored cairns and enclosures. Others occur above 300 metres OD, at Bracken Heads, Blake Hill, Howgill and Marwood.

In Swaledale, the markings are confined to rough pasture and heather moor just below or above 300 metres OD in the vicinity of Marske Beck, a principal north-bank tributary of the Swale. The patchy distribution provides a link between the developing and increasingly successful farming communities of the late Neolithic, Bronze Age and Iron Age. Swaledale and Wensleydale begin to fill in the archaeological record when the first pastoralists arrived with henges, round barrows and cursus monuments in the Vale of Mowbray and the Vale of Eden.

An abundance of rocks suitable for marking, the altitude and remoteness of the areas make it likely that these areas always had a preponderance of such sites. There is rock-art at a lower elevation that shows that it may have had a wider distribution, but all the evidence there is from portable rocks, some from burial contexts.

Other burial associations are on the high moors, in cairns. The only other firm context is on Ellerton Moor at Juniper Gill, where a cupped standing stone marks a pass or saddle between Swaledale and lower Wensleydale. The most important site is a recent excavation at Fulforth Farm, Witton Gilbert (NZ 230 465), near Durham city, where there were a double-sided purpose-made cist cover and two pristine marked rocks in the cist.

The most extensive sites are at Barningham Moor and Gayles Moor. The former (Beckensall and Laurie 1998) has very wide views from almost every spot northward over the valleys. Nearly 100 rocks have motifs, many with simple cups, and the more elaborate lie in the vicinity of springs and streams rising from Osmonds Gill and Eel Hill. They cluster near Osmonds Gill, Washbeck Green and Scale Knoll.

Cups alone can produce interesting designs without being enclosed by rings. We see them linked together like strings of beads, or in zigzag and other patterns, joined in pairs, clustered in large numbers. In some cases they are so large that they become basins. The smallest cups form three lines of three.

---

* 'OD' – above Ordnance Datum, i.e. sea level.

The ringed motifs do not exceed four rings, one fine example being on a flat slab in Osmonds Gill.

Some ringed figures appear on boulders and slabs that have been placed vertically. Some low enclosures contain rock-art that predates them, and the most elaborate enclosures are to the east below How Tallon, with stone foundations, facing north. The use of some of these is for dwellings, but the stone-dump enclosure constructions are for herding. Apart from the enclosure context, marked stones are also found in and on cairns. The large, excavated cairn called How Tallon – the pottery and other artefacts dating it to *c*. 2000 BC – contained marked cobbles. Other cairns remain unexcavated, with decorated slabs and small boulders embedded in their surfaces.

There is a small seven-stone circle above Osmonds Gill, near to a cairn with a decorated boulder; their presence, another cairn and a unique panel of rock-art on Eel Hill help to emphasize that Osmonds Gill is a special place in the landscape. The junction of Osmonds Gill and Cross Gill, both formed by ice, has produced a spring source of great character. A line of stones across it suggests that it would have been ideal for herding. The place has a powerful feel to it, shut in and deep; it is marked and overlooked by decorated rocks. Water that begins underground, and that can be heard before it is seen, flows to the site of a burned mound towards the north.

Tim Laurie has investigated the burned-mound phenomenon, of which 74 have been recognized in Wensleydale, Swaledale and Teesdale. He concludes that they were not associated with permanent occupation, but as picnic saunas, alfresco dilettante-group feasting-places with wild boar on the menu, and saunas where flagellants applied birch branches after hot baths in steaming tents. Some excavated in Northumberland have given early Bronze Age dates.

Since Beckensall and Laurie (1998) was published, more rock-art has been found farther west, on Scargill Moor. The search continues.

West and north Yorkshire

Two hundred and ninety-seven marked rocks were originally recorded in this region and published by the Ilkley Archaeology Group (Hedges 1986); the same group has since recorded a comparable number in other areas from Nidderdale in the north to the main bulk of the rock-art in west Yorkshire: Washburndale, Wharfedale and Airedale. A total of 637 marked rocks are now known in the whole region. Six hundred or 94 per cent of all the rocks listed, lie in these watersheds: north Aire (191), north Wharfe (152), south Wharfe (192) and south Washburn (65).

Almost all the marked rocks lie in the broad band of the Millstone Grit series to the east of the Pennines anticline. The moorlands generally slope from west to east, and hard bands form the edges of shallow terraces in the hillsides. There is a widespread scatter of varying gritstones and sandstones, some formed by landslip and others moved by ice. Markings are found on these bedrocks, boulders and erratics.

Examples are given below.

Rombalds Moor

The area, of gritstone, is today moorland with mainly heather, peat and bog. To the north is a scarp above Addingham, Ilkley and Burley; about half the marked rocks lie along

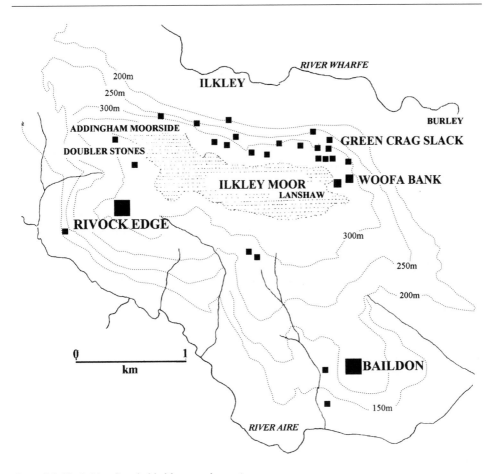

Figure 3.8 Yorkshire: Rombalds Moor rock-art sites

the scarp, above and below it, with extensive viewpoints north-east and north-west over the Wharfe Valley. Above the scarp is a series of plateaux on the north-east; the most important, containing Green Crag Slack and Woofa Bank, has over a third of all the rock-art on the moor. They have 96 of the 271 rocks on Rombalds Moor.

To the south-west is another concentration, at Rivock Edge, on another plateau, from which the land slopes to the River Aire. The land has been reforested, but about thirty marked surfaces are known. Forestation means that several are now impossible to see or even to relocate.

Although the outcrops form the scarps, there are some boulders and other earthfasts brought down by glaciers, as in the Teesdale–Swaledale area. Some of their mostly horizontal surfaces are decorated. The boulders vary in size, with some large ones decorated at Rivock Edge. The shape of the rocks has, in many cases, determined the kind of decoration pecked on the surfaces. As in other parts of the country, some natural features have been incorporated or enhanced to become part of the design.

The greatest concentration of marked rocks at Green Crag Slack (SE 135457) coincided with a visible important 'enclosure' wall. An excavated area had walling that was not at all prominent until it was dug; it had not previously been identified as a wall. Both 'enclosures' are associated with marked rocks, although only a few of the total number on the slack. Stone artefacts and pottery from the late Neolithic and early Bronze Age were excavated. The flint artefacts are of high quality, and the raw material came from the North Sea coast. These finds are associated with Grooved Ware pottery, elsewhere often found in special ritual contexts. Radiocarbon dating from one of these concentrations gives a late Neolithic date.

Recognized settlement sites have not come to light on Rombalds Moor, but there is a significant number and concentration of flints, from the Mesolithic, Neolithic and early Bronze Age from wide parts of the moor, particularly along its northern margins and terraces. One collector alone (Robin Hardistry, personal communication) has 8000 flints from the local moors, mostly from Rombalds Moor.

The siting of the rock-art is not confined to good viewpoints. Most upland sites have extensive views, if there are no trees, but the smaller marked rocks and decorations often lie well back from any scarp. The absence of settlement sites suggests that the area was used for pastoral and hunting activities. No marked rocks are known near the stone circles or the really large cairns, which occupy different areas. There are a few minor markings in small cairn-fields. The three recognized cairn-fields on Rombalds Moor are Stead Crag, Woofa Bank and the smallest on Hawksworth Moor in the south-east sector looking over Airedale from the north.

In the wider landscape setting, the researchers attribute the absence of marked rocks below 300 metres OD to agriculture and quarrying; they point out that there are some in pastures below Addingham Moorside, Rivock Edge, Morton Moor, Baildon Moor and Burley Moor and observe that 411 out of the region's 637 sites (64 per cent) lie within 250–360 metres OD.

The patterns on the rocks show regional variations. There is an extensive use of cups; linear and curved grooves are incorporated; although some striking results are produced by the makers, there is no widespread use of multiple concentric rings of the type seen in Northumberland and Scotland. There are similarities between the way this and other British rock-art is made and used; the big uniting factor is that it is all abstract. Many rock-art sites command extensive viewpoints, with the arc of scarp from Addingham Moorside to Burley Moor overlooking Wharfedale particularly striking for the positioning of art in the landscape.

The River Wharfe watershed

Marked rocks are found in the greatest numbers on the sides of the moderate uplands that border the middle sections of the river valleys. Whereas the survey of Rombalds Moor covered less than 150 square kilometres, the study of the concentration around mid-Wharfedale and of smaller groups in adjacent regions covers 2500 square kilometres. The marked rocks are in a band eight kilometres long and one kilometre wide. In the region as a whole, the great majority of marked rocks lie between 200 and 300 metres OD. (There are records of several at low levels in the Aire Valley, now destroyed or lost.)

Clearance for agriculture and other developments distorts the distribution picture; those that survive are usually in places where people do not want to develop the land.

Snowden Carr, with 49 rocks, between 220 and 260 metres OD, is perhaps best known for 'The Tree of Life Rock' (Figure 3.9) (SE 177.9 5123) and 'The Death's Head Rock' (SE

Figure 3.9 Yorkshire: Tree of Life, Snowden Carr

Photograph by Edward Vickerman

1797 5116), which lie close to each other and among other marked rocks. These rocks are not 'complex' in the sense used of multiple concentric circles of other areas, but the more limited symbolism of cups and grooves is put to equally good use. At the first, a central stem and its offshoot-grooves incorporate cups to form a plant-like effect. The other has four cups linked and enclosed by grooves, appearing improbably to some people as a skull.

There is a settlement and cairns in the same area. Among the many marked rocks are cups, curving and linear grooves, and mostly single rings.

A series of clusters of marked rocks on the moorland stretches north above Wharfedale from the Washburn on the east to Langbar Moor and Middleton Moor on the west. Fieldwork continues to find new rocks in this marginal land. Modern settlements tend to concentrate on the major river valleys. The survey shows again that a pastoral–hunter economy is likely to have been the most successful in the high moorland, taking into account changes in climate and vegetation.

The importance of having the many new sites documented cannot be overstressed, and one hopes that this may be done with a publication of a quality equal to that produced in 1986 by the Ilkley Archaeology Group, who have provided all this unpublished information.

Strath Tay

Rock-art in Strath Tay is in a limited area twenty kilometres from the confluence of the River Tay to the River Tummel at the eastern end of Loch Tay (Bradley 1997; Stewart

1958). The valley is very fertile. Round barrows, stone and timber settings, and stone circles occupy the terraces. Cup-marked rocks are found on the major terraces; the more complex motifs are on higher ground, where the land today is above modern cultivation. The marginal land overlooks the valley from higher up the slopes. There is a clear distinction between the ways in which 'simple' and 'complex' rock-art is situated.

Galloway

This has one of the highest concentrations of rock-art in Britain, but has very little of it in monuments. The distribution of rocks with motifs does not occupy the whole of the coastline, but is restricted to a forty-kilometre band along the coast that extends fifteen kilometres inland.

The map (Figure 3.10) shows how the art clusters around peninsulas that are the estuaries of major rivers. The coast is fertile; it is used today mainly for pasture, and in the past may have been fringed by marshland. The coast is easily accessible from the hinterland.

The proximity of the sea to many of the marked rocks has made it obvious why so many have extensive sea views. Those who see history as invasions or movement of settlers into the area from elsewhere point to the location of suitable landing places along this coast for such incursions, but it could just as easily work the other way: local people fished or launched their own explorations from here.

Away from the coast around Cairnholy the land becomes steeper and opens up into large tracts of moorland. In other parts, away from the sea, the land is broken up into basins,

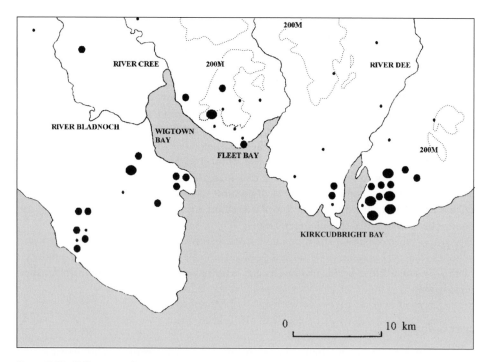

Figure 3.10 Galloway rock-art sites

and divided by rock outcrops and dykes (walls), and there are small pools and lakes. Most rock-art is in shallow valleys on or around the coast.

Whereas megalithic structures such as the two Cairnholy cairns are close to the sea, round cairns are to be found on isolated hills.

Some sites do not have 'wide views', and there must be reasons other than that for their siting. In other parts of Britain, although most rock-art is sited at the best viewpoints, some can mark an important water source, for example, or a limited area where there may be a watering hole. The High Banks site has no view, but was close to a source of water. Torrs and Blairbuy are also near to water sources. The coincidence of rock-art and spring or other water sources emerged during the County Durham survey.

The Reading University survey area looked at unmarked as well as marked rocks to see if there was a special reason for choosing one rock surface rather than another. The survey was not concerned with finding more rock-art, but with the logic of its distribution. Over 400 marked rocks have been recorded in Galloway, although some may no longer be found. Prominent on them are cup and ring motifs, and there are more spirals in the landscape than anywhere else in Britain. The spirals are not so varied as motifs of a site like Morwick, Northumberland (NU 233044), but are impressively well spread. Only one monument, the Cairnholy cairn, had decorated stone in it.

The rocks are mostly greywacke, metamorphic slate, soft enough to peck designs with a hard stone pick. These pick-marks are visible in many of the motifs. The vast majority is on outcrop, on about 300 panels. About 100 outcrop panels have cups only. This is easily accounted for: the most accessible rock is used, and the picture contrasts with County Durham, for example, where there is little outcrop but scattered glacially carried slabs. Half the sites are at 10–70 metres OD, and 36 per cent are at 90–120 metres OD. The hill-country sites are generally on the lower slopes.

A general characteristic of the landscape is that it is undulating, with extensive outcrop ridges and small hillocks. There is an abundance of open views, mainly because decorated rocks are close to the sea, overlooking it. There is some boggy ground. In hilly country some of the streams cut deeply. There is some modern arable, much pasture, and rough land characterized by gorse and bracken. Some important sites are in danger areas, used as military ranges. With these general observations as background, each area of rock-art has to be seen in its specific setting; designs, although sharing similar symbols, must be examined to see if there are individual characteristics. For example, spirals are relatively plentiful and concentrated, some areas have unique decorations, and others have rare motifs such as 'keyholes' and 'rosettes'.

All the sites have been well documented, notably by Morris (1979), Van Hoek (1995) and Bradley (1997).

Argyll

This area has concentrations of rock-art (Figure 3.11) ranging from simple to complex motifs. South Argyll has most of its motifs on boulders, whereas the Kilmartin area, mid-Argyll, has more on outcrops (Bradley 1993, 1997; Morris 1977; RCAHMS 1988).

Kilmartin is quite remarkable, not only for the quality of its rock-art, for its burials and ritual monuments, but also for the way in which motifs are placed in the landscape. The area is an important through-route from the sea, and this ease of land-based access probably accounts for the area's economic importance and for its status as a ritual centre.

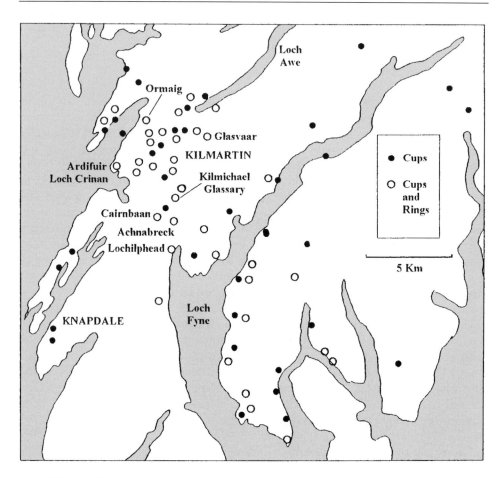

Figure 3.11 Argyll rock-art sites

Until quite recently low land was covered with peat, and it preserved the monuments that peat-cutters exposed.

The rock motifs occupy a significant place in the landscape, marking the places that give access to this large plain. In many ways it is like the situation in north Northumberland. The outcrop rocks are not prominent features; they are near-horizontal and can only be seen close by. High above and around the plain they are a base for a rich variety of motifs. To go from one site to another means walking above the plain, which is, like the entrances to it, what the decorated wide viewpoints overlook.

The outcrops are sedimentary sandstone, shale and limestone that have been meta-morphosed by heat and pressure caused by earth movements. They have turned into quartzite, schist and marble. Ice sheets moved south-west, leaving boulder clay and raised beaches. It is possible that about 5000 years ago, the periods of the cups and rings, the climate was warmer and drier before deterioration set in and peat began to form. There have been 200 years of peat-digging to expose the monuments that we see today.

It is difficult to see how people earned their living there except by farming, pastoralism and hunting; there is little evidence of where they used to live, although the terraces on either side of the plain seem to be likely candidates. Perhaps the impressive monuments have distracted attention from more modest traces of activities in the past. These margins of the now-flat valley are where the rock-art is. The rocks themselves must have protruded from the soil or had a very thin vegetation cover. The area with the monuments is surrounded by clusters of rock-art, generally at a higher level, where there are also occasional standing stones and cairns.

Achnabreck (NR 55906, 857906, 856905) is the largest decorated outcrop in Britain (Figure 3.12). Until recently it was in the middle of a wood, which has now been cut down so that not only the motifs but the valleys leading to Lochgilphead and to the modern Crinan Canal are visible. This is a crucial threshold site for access to the Moine Mhor and sea. Were there trees when these motifs were chipped into the rock? If so, this might not work as a viewpoint. Were there distinctive well-worn paths leading to it? Was it a route-way? If there were no trees, then the rock outcrop itself might be seen from afar.

Photographs and accurate drawings do justice to this extraordinary site. The variety of motifs, the ways in which they are spaced and linked, the way in which they use natural cracks and surface irregularities and put out grooves to follow the downward slopes are very impressive. The position of the sun, the wetness or dryness of the rock have much to do with how we view it today.

The highest part of the outcrop has attracted speculation; some see in the making of the motifs different hands at work and different periods, as suggested by the super-imposition of a few figures. I have reservations about this theory.

Figure 3.12 Argyll, Achnabreck: part of the panel surface

The sheer size of some of the concentric rings, their spacing, the way some of them incorporate cups not just into their centres but into the spaces between rings give a distinct quality to the use of symbol in design.

If one moves from this splendid outcrop to the car-park and road, the valley that opens up to the west follows the Crinan Canal to the sea. Two ridges overlook this, the more southerly being the site of a cairn burial that contained rock-art and the other at Cairnbaan having two outcrop panels of rock-art within 100 metres of each other (NR 839910, 838910). These pose interesting questions about their relationship, for they have different kinds of motifs and different viewpoints. The low ground here around one rock is quite sodden, and one wonders if the rock outcrop may be at a spring source. The other slopes more, and the area around it is usually dry.

A second representative rock is at Kilmichael Glassary (NR 857934, 858935), which lies in another entrance into the Kilmartin Valley. It is an untidy site, lying above the valley among houses, with a metal fence protecting some of the markings. The emphasis is on cups, many deep and linked to others by short grooves. They are arranged to follow the crack lines in the rock; near the lowest slope some have long, thin ducts coming from cups, and there are curvilinear grooves that enclose groups of motifs.

Monuments

Burials and standing stones, including the Temple Wood stone circle (NR 826978), have long been recognized as having a variety of motifs. The recent excavation of the Temple Wood circles shows that the site has a time-scale of up to 2000 years; the presence at other sites of simple cup marks, complex spirals and flat pitted axes reinforces the use of motifs over a long period. Unlike rock-art in the landscape, that in burials was not meant to be seen, and marks a difference in perception of how it should be used. As in other areas, it was earth-oriented rather than arranged to look up at the sky.

Landscape and monuments

The main emphasis so far has been on art in the landscape, where its position indicates its use by people who were mobile pastoralists and hunters rather than settled farmers. As such, they left little of their presence, as they would have used temporary shelters in their camps. People who practised arable farming became more settled as they established fields, walls and fences. Their circular-based huts become more obvious to us. The transition to this more settled way of life was gradual; the hunting and pastoral territories would continue to be used extensively. Population gradually increased, and the pressure on land intensified. The practice of arable farming would have brought a different way of using the land, and people would have begun to see landscape in a different way. Rock-art was in the open air, looking up to the sky, marking special places in the landscape that included in some regions the entrances to ritual centres. Such panels cannot yet be dated; art used in a firmer context and associated with ritual structures allows us to come closer to a time-scale.

There are two main groups of monuments in which rock-art is found: on standing stones and stone circles, and in burial cairns, either as parts of cists or as an integral part of the mound material. In Northumberland there are rock-shelters where decoration is used, and there are some house sites in Britain where rock-art is buried.

The presence of rock-art in these contexts represents a very small proportion of monuments, and there is a danger of drawing general conclusions from a few sites. From many of the examples, however, it is possible to say that a change takes place in the way rock-art is used; its incorporation in some ritual sites shows that it is taken out of the open air and buried with the dead. It retains a ritual/religious significance within these sites and reminds us not to make a sharp distinction between the religious and the secular.

Standing stones and circles of stone

Cumbria has almost all its rock-art in monuments (Beckensall 1992a).

Long Meg (NY 571 372) is a 3.66-metre pillar of Eden Valley red sandstone that stands outside the stone circle of her 'daughters', all reputedly turned to stone for dancing on the Sabbath (Figure 3.13). The ice-borne volcanic rocks of the circle vary considerably in size; at the north-east arc their alignment flattens because they respect a buried ditch of a huge enclosure that takes in the present farm buildings. The ditch, which cannot be seen at the site, was discovered and recorded from the air with infrared photography. Another circular buried ditch lies to the south-east, and to the north-west

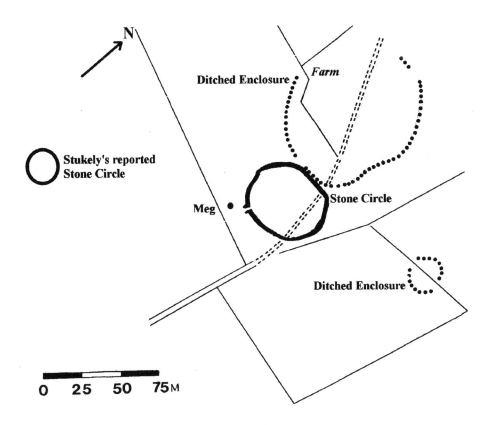

Figure 3.13 Cumbria: Long Meg in its relationship with other monuments

is the site of a stone circle recorded by Stukeley in the eighteenth century, now destroyed and invisible.

Inside the main stone circle, burial cairns were reported; this has not been tested by excavation. In some similar stone circles such burials are usually later than the circle itself, and arranged in the early Bronze Age for individual rather than communal burial. The sandstone pillar is covered on only one face with linear grooves, concentric arcs, spirals and cups and grooves, not all finished, and there is some recent graffiti. There is a possibility that some marks on two of the stones of the north arc may be artificial. Despite the problem posed by natural markings on some metamorphic rock, there are two ill-formed spirals discernible on a fallen rock of the north arc.

From the west the first stone to be seen is Long Meg, which has a 360° view around it. Seen from the centre of the circle, over the two western portal stones (and not through the portal itself), it is aligned on the axis of the midwinter sunset. Both the visible and buried circles occupy gently sloping land away from it, and there is a drop of about six metres to the edge of the stone circle. The motifs speak of the outstanding importance of the monolith, but as yet we do not know of its relationship in time to the stone circle. Most probably it was quarried from a cliff face in the Eden Valley near by. Some of the motifs may have already been on it when the slab was brought to the site; as it lay horizontally, more motifs could have been added. It may have preceded the stone circle, or could be related to some earlier, buried structure. We don't know. It could have been added after the stones were erected.

Before . . . during . . . after?

As no part of this site has been dated by modern excavation, we are left with a vague, vast time span. But what is clear is its importance to, or its predominance over, other stones there – bigger, more colourful and decorated.

Burial sites

The presence of rock-art in burial cairns, especially in cists, has led to the false assumption that it is of the same period as the burial. Some of the marked rock was reused, and thus earlier. Its use is deliberate; the motifs represent the more complex designs, and the decorated panels are placed face-down within the cists. Their significance was understood, but they were used in a different way.

Fulforth Farm, Witton Gilbert

The site of two burial pits was excavated using modern methods. One rectilinear pit was divided into two. One half was packed with cobbles and cremations, with a polished stone axe placed blade upward at one corner. The other was arranged like a cist, and this part was covered by a slab decorated on two sides. The complex designs of cups and rings and a zigzag were picked into a surface prepared by light pecking, and faced into the burial. The top surface was covered with small cups, some linked.

A slab with pristine pick-marked motifs of cups and single rings and a zigzag had been hammered into an upright position in the cist. On the floor a small boulder had been tamped down into the base; it was decorated on two sides with deep, linked cups on the top side and the beginnings of a cup on the other. The cist contained two rough flint blades and a piece of charcoal. The date was late Neolithic/Early Bronze Age.

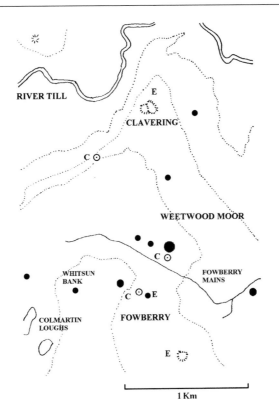

Figure 3.14 Northumberland rock-art sites in their archaeological landscape: Weetwood and Fowberry

Key: ●: rock-art surface; C: cairn with rock-art; E: enclosure

The second boat-shaped pit contained a plano-convex knife at the bottom, aligned on the long axis, an implement usually found in an early Bronze Age context in northern England. Thus the site was used for burial around 2000 BC, with the rocks marked for it (Beckensall and Laurie 1998).

Weetwood and Fowberry

An important site where art in the landscape is in the same place as monumental art is at Fowberry and Weetwood (Beckensall 1991; Bradley 1997; Figure 3.14). The sites are located on a sandstone massif that is bounded on the east by the River Till, on the north by the Milfield Plain, on the west by the valley of the Wooler Water, and to the south by a continuation of the sandstone. Part has been forested, some is arable, and the rest is pasture and moorland. At Coldmartin there are two 'loughs' which act as water-holes; this vital area is overlooked by a decorated outcrop (NU 0103 2803). There are enclosures, probably of the Iron Age, including a fortified one at Clavering overlooking the place where the River Till enters the Milfield Plain.

Thin soils scarcely hide panels of rock-art, many of which were recorded over a century ago. There have been reports of burial cairns and some inexpert digging of them in the past.

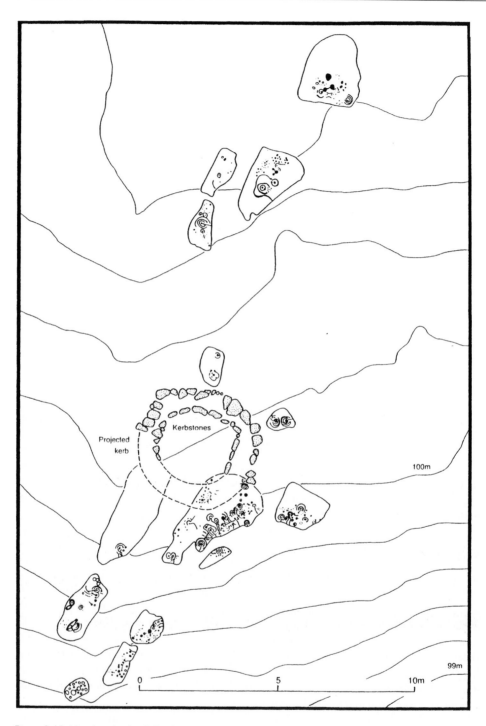

Figure 3.15 Northumberland: Fowberry cairn. Kerb cairn with associated rock-art
Plan: Bradley (1997: 144)

The motifs arranged on outcrops are interesting, but even more interesting is the way in which motifs appear both in the open air and in cairns. Two cairns have given a great deal of information out of all proportion to their size, despite both having been disturbed, because they were excavated using modern methods.

Fowberry Cairn (NU 0197 2784) is a small doubled-kerbed round cairn built on outcrop rock covered with motifs, including cups, grooves, cups and rings, and a rectangle, with some interesting variation on themes (Figure 3.15). There was very little soil between cairn and outcrop, just enough to contain a scraper, and had there been a burial it must have been a body covered with stone, without a cist. The site was disturbed by quarrying, like the rest of the area, and by tree growth, but most of the cairn was intact. It was built of two kerbs of cobbles, four of which were cupped. The outer kerb made use of erratic granite boulders that made a colour change. Between the kerbs was a packing of small stones, and the centre was filled with small cobbles. Twenty stones from the mound and its spread were marked, including a countersunk cup, and double penannulars with radiates ('complex' by any standards). They were all in fresh condition, with pick-marks clear. The main quarrying activity fortunately did not disturb much of the mound; to the north of it the outcrop had been dug out in steps until there was no more suitable rock. There may have been other cairns removed as the surface was prepared for quarrying.

The Weetwood cairn (NU 0215 2810) was discovered after the Fowberry cairn when the heather was removed and the land ploughed to make rough pasture. The mound had been three-quarters bulldozed.

Figure 3.16 Northumberland: decorated rock outcrop (including 1834 additions) overlooking Coldmartin Loughs

The cairn lies just below a gently sloping high outcrop that has many decorated surfaces. It was an oval, kerbless mound with one large boulder in its circumference that is decorated with concentric rings and three radial grooves. This same motif also occurs on outcrop on Whitsun Bank Site 2 (NU 018 279). The boulder originally faced into the mound, so it was not meant to be seen, and its complex decoration was appropriate for its size and position. Thirty-seven decorated cobbles were recovered from the cairn, those *in situ* being face-down, mostly on the ground surface. There were signs of disturbance prior to bulldozing, which may reflect the interest in barrow-digging in the last century in this area. The decorated cobbles, with those from Fowberry, are now in Berwick Museum, but the large boulder, with its decoration facing outward, remains with the reinstated cairn.

What do these two cairns and their outcrop rock-art tell us? The decoration at the time of the mound-building had taken on a different meaning, for it was no longer meant to be seen. If these were burial cairns, the decorated cobbles may have been brought in during the building like wreaths at a funeral. It was an intimate matter between the living and the dead. The 'offerings' varied in complexity of design; all were as fresh as the day they were made. Many were unfinished, as if the act of making the marks, however tentative, was sufficient for the ritual purpose. These decorated stones had not just happened to be lying around, waiting for someone to use them as building material.

There are cairns with marked stones in them that do not lie in areas so heavily decorated as Weetwood and Fowberry. The whole area must have been of great ritual importance, and the open-air rock-art commands wide vistas. The Fowberry cairn is particularly well placed at a viewpoint, more so than the Weetwood cairn.

Other cairns are built on already-decorated outcrop in Northumberland, like the Fowberry example (Beckensall 1991, 1992a).

All the above sites are comparatively recent discoveries, within the past thirty years. Hopefully, this process of discovery will go on.

Rock-shelters

Northumberland has another unique feature in the placing of decoration on and in rock overhangs. A fine example, Corby's Crags (Figure 3.17) (NU 1280 0965), was excavated by the author. The rock-shelter overlooks Edlingham Castle and an Iron Age enclosure at one of the best viewpoints in the county. On the top surface is a large basin and surrounding groove with a duct. The dome of rock has been a boundary in recent centuries, with steps carved out of it, but the secrets of the shelter below were revealed twenty years ago. The shelter had been used by Mesolithic hunters. A cremation in a Food Vessel covered with a triangular stone had been buried in the soil of the floor, with a pecked groove on the base rock directed at it. Bell-pit workers or shepherds then cut an armchair with their metal tools and ledges to hold their bottles and food (we found their glass, pottery, clay pipe and an old penknife). This continued use of a site is not unusual; in a nearby wood are prehistoric rock motifs on the same outcrop as three runes!

We cannot say that the rock-art and the pot (2000 BC) belong together, but it is likely.

Figure 3.17 Northumberland: rock-art on a rock-shelter at Corby's Crags. Basin, groove and duct on the roof of the rock-shelter

From topographic understanding to new models

The collected research, sketched above, on British rock-art sites shows a pattern of where they commonly occur. Surprisingly, one might think, in a country so populated as England, there are still new sites to be discovered; perhaps the rate of discovery has increased now there are several of us actively searching. We see, for example, a perceptual imbalance in the occurrence of sites in northern England, where there are decisively more on the eastern side, in Durham and Northumberland, than on the western side, in Cumbria, where is little art, and what there is can be found on monuments rather than rock outcrops. Is this a real pattern from prehistory? If so, is it some kind of cultural choice, that in one region people chose to make more rock-art, and in different places? Or does it follow from some other factor, such as there being in the west less rock outcropping that prehistoric people thought suitable for marking?

New discoveries in October and November 1999 change this. The statement above that Cumbria's motifs are almost exclusively on monuments is no longer true, since some of the most dramatic and important art in the landscape has been discovered in two major valleys in the Lake District. This illustrates that there may be many more to be discovered, and those discoveries will change our grasp of what British rock-art amounts to.

The Golden Beck flows into Ullswater; along its narrow valley are three sites. These are on linear and massive outcrops that overlook what might have been swamp at the source of a major lake (Figure 3.18). They command views in all directions along the valley on the major pathways above the flood levels.

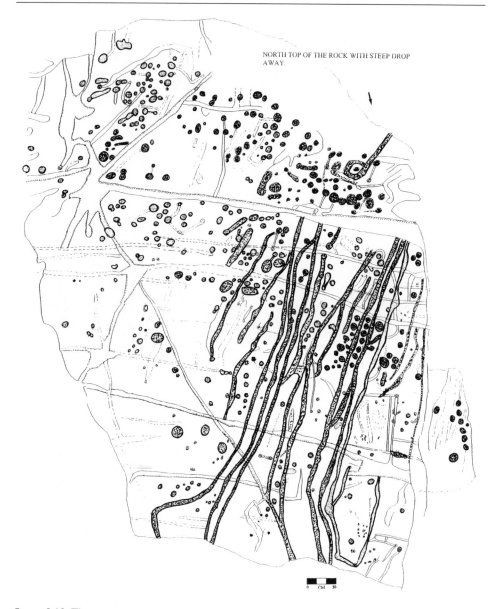

NORTH TOP OF THE ROCK WITH STEEP DROP
AWAY.

0   CM   30

Figure 3.18 The main outcrop at Green Rigg, Patterdale. Cup marks and channels over a large
'saddleback' outcrop. About 5 by 5.5 metres

Drawing: Stan Beckensall

Crookabeck (NY401157) has a decorated dome of outcrop, possibly with a cairn, that
continues the same line towards the Kirkstone Pass, and may have been an island in the
marsh. Beckstones (NY403150) is the most southerly cup-marked outcrop.

The motifs are hundred of cups, ovals, rectangles with rounded corners, three cups
with single rings, and massive grooves or channels pecked into the rock, mostly parallel
to each other.

Figure 3.19 Chapel Stile, Langdale. Unusually for a British rock-art site, this is on a vertical face. The drawing shows the full extent of the art, except for the strip towards the right (above the scale in the drawing) where the rock is hidden by a field wall abutting it. The photograph is taken obliquely from the right-hand end

Drawing and photograph: Stan Beckensall

A massive block of andesite tuff, broken off the mountain and coming to rest in the Great Langdale Valley leading from the Neolithic axe factories to Lake Windermere, has its east-facing vertical face covered with motifs (Figure 3.19). They include concentric rings and three parallel grooves that run into a chevron before joining a figure with eleven rings (the largest number in Britain). The site name is Chapel Stile (NY31400582). It was found after a systematic search by Paul and Barbara Brown, who were testing the theory that such markings would be at viewpoints on major route-ways through the valleys. So right! And all this in a few weeks in the autumn of 1999.

There are now local people who are determined to find more.

Acknowledgements

My thanks to the discoverers of the new Cumbrian sites who are now my friends: Tim and Pat Cook, Jan and Tony Ambler and Mary Bell; they and Paul and Barbara Brown have agreed to my mentioning the sites.

References

Those marked with an asterisk are general surveys.

*Beckensall, S. 1983. *Northumberland's prehistoric rock carvings*. Rothbury (privately printed).

*Beckensall, S. 1991. *Prehistoric rock motifs of Northumberland*, 1. Hexham (privately printed).

*Beckensall, S. 1992a. *Prehistoric rock motifs of Northumberland*, 2. Hexham (privately printed).

*Beckensall, S. 1992b. *Cumbrian prehistoric rock art*. Hexham (privately printed).

Beckensall, S. 1995. Recent discovery and recording of prehistoric rock motifs in the North, *Northern Archaeology* 12: 9–34.

Beckensall, S. 1999. *British prehistoric rock-art*. Stroud: Tempus.

Beckensall, S. 2001. *Prehistoric rock art of Northumberland*. Stroud: Tempus.

Beckensall, S. and P. Frodsham. 1998. Questions of chronology: the case for Bronze Age rock art in northern England, *Northern Archaeology* 15/16: 51–70.

*Beckensall, S. and T. Laurie. 1998. *Prehistoric rock art of County Durham, Swaledale and Wensleydale*. Durham: County Durham Books.

*Bradley, R. 1993. *Altering the earth: the origins of monuments in Britain and continental Europe*. Edinburgh: Society of Antiquaries of Scotland.

Bradley, R. 1996. Learning from places – topographical analysis of northern British rock art, *Northern Archaeology* 13/14: 87–99.

*Bradley, R. 1997. *Signing the land: rock art and the prehistory of Atlantic Europe*. London: Routledge.

*Bradley, R. 1998. *The significance of monuments: on the shaping of human experience in Neolithic and Bronze Age Europe*. London: Routledge.

Frodsham, P. 1996. Spirals in time: Morwick Mill and the spiral motif in the British Neolithic, *Northern Archaeology* 13/14: 101–138.

*Hedges, J. D. (ed.). 1986. *The carved rocks on Rombalds Moor: a gazetteer of the prehistoric rock carvings on Rombalds Moor, West Yorkshire*. Wakefield: Ilkley Archaeological Group/West Yorkshire Archaeology Service.

*Morris, R.W.B. 1977. *The prehistoric rock art of Argyll*. Poole: Dolphin Press.

*Morris, R.W.B. 1979. *The prehistoric rock art of Galloway and the Isle of Man*. Poole: Blandford Press.

*Morris, R.W.B. 1989. The prehistoric rock art of Great Britain: a survey of all sites bearing motifs more complex than simple cup-marks, *Proceedings of the Prehistoric Society* 55: 45–88.

*RCAHMS. 1988. *Argyll*, 6. Edinburgh: HMSO.

Stewart, M. 1958. Strath Tay in the second millennium BC, *Proceedings of the Society of Antiquaries of Scotland* 92: 71–84.

*Van Hoek, M.A.M. 1995. *Morris' prehistoric rock art of Galloway*. Oisterwijk (privately printed).

Waddington, C. 1996. Putting rock art to use: a model of early Neolithic transhumance in north Northumberland, *Northern Archaeology* 13/14: 147–177.

Waddington, C. 1998. Cup and ring marks in context, *Cambridge Archaeological Journal* 8(1): 29–54.

Chapter 4

The rock-art landscape of the Iveragh Peninsula, County Kerry, south-west Ireland

Avril Purcell

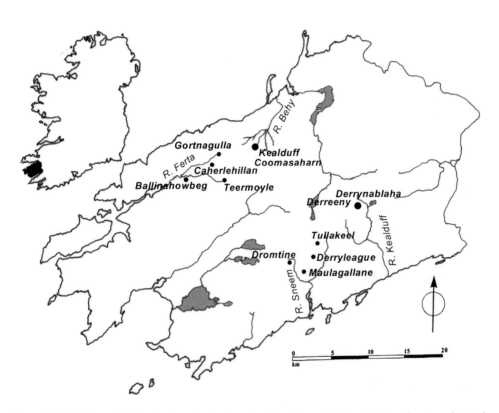

Figure 4.1 The Iveragh Peninsula showing the location of each townland in which rock art was located that was included in the study

Iveragh and its rock-art

Iveragh is a large peninsula in south-west Ireland, extending approximately seventy kilometres (forty miles) into the Atlantic Ocean (Figure 4.1). To the north is the Dingle Peninsula and to the south the Beara Peninsula, separated from Iveragh by Dingle Bay and the Kenmare River respectively. The landscape of Iveragh is dominated by an impressive mountain range, the Macguillycuddy's Reeks, which run primarily in an east-north-east to west-south-west direction. Between these high mountains are deep U-shaped valleys and glacial lakes where the numerous rivers of the peninsula rise (Nevill 1963). This is a landscape dominated by high, rugged mountains and an abundance of lakes and rivers. Mobility on the peninsula is heavily influenced by this landscape. The primary road around the peninsula today is largely coastal, the well-known 'Ring of Kerry'; only two minor roads traverse the interior of the peninsula (O'Sullivan and

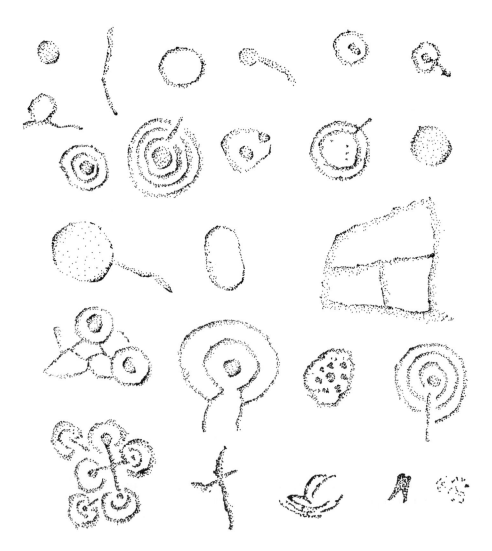

Figure 4.2 The twenty-four motifs represented on carvings within the study area. Top row: cup mark; line; ring; cup and line; cup and ring; cup, ring and line; (below left) ring and line. Second row: cup and two or more rings; cup line and two or more rings; motif with satellite cup; two or more rings and a line; basin. Third row: basin and line; oval; grid. Fourth row: web; keyhole motif; rosette motif; coiled or broken spiral motif. Fifth row: cruciform motif; cross; intersecting arcs; wishbone motif; dots or pecking

Sheehan 1996: 1). This upland landscape provides the setting for the largest known concentration of rock-art in Ireland.

All of the carvings on the peninsula are abstract and geometric in form; no figurative carvings have been located to date. The cup, ring and line form the basis of the motifs within the assemblage. While this may suggest a very limited range of motifs and simple compositions, they are surprisingly elaborate and incorporated together to produce quite an extensive range of motifs and frequently complex compositions. A total of twenty-four separate motifs were identified during fieldwork (Figure 4.2). Of these a small number occur quite infrequently and often exclusively to particular locations.

Approximately 120 rock-art sites occur on Iveragh (O'Sullivan and Sheehan 1996: 1). Of these approximately seventy examples were included in the study. Carvings that were not *in situ* were excluded. On Iveragh a significant portion of the carvings are located quite close together at the heads of river valleys. Within these valleys the carved stones are frequently clustered together; these concentrations were the areas studied. Within four river valleys on the peninsula, five concentrations of rock-carvings were located in which the majority of carvings were *in situ*. These five concentrations of carvings formed the primary study area and included:

- the art in the Kealduff Valley spreading across the townlands* of Derrynablaha and Derreeny;
- the art in the Ferta Valley in the townlands of Teermoyle, Caherlehillan, Gortnagulla and Ballinahowbeg;
- the art in the Sneem Valley in the townlands of Derryleague, Tullakeel, Dromtine and Maulagallane;

Two separate concentrations of art in the Behy Valley are at:

- Coomasaharn; and
- Kealduff.

Each of these carvings has a separate Sites and Monuments Record (SMR) number.†

The situation to date

Relatively little work has been undertaken on rock-art of Ireland, despite the growing number of sites being discovered as intensive survey is undertaken at a national level (e.g. Buckley and Sweetman 1991; Cuppage 1986; Lacy 1983; Power 1992; O'Sullivan and Sheehan 1996). Small-scale local studies have highlighted the rock-art of specific localities, for example Clarke's (1982) examination of the area around Dundalk, County Louth, and academic interest in rock-art is well represented (e.g. Shee 1968, 1972; Shee and O'Kelly 1971). The rock-art of the Iveragh Peninsula has been comprehensively

---

* Townland: a division of land used within Ireland; several townlands make up a parish.
† Sites and Monuments Record: a county-level record of all known historical and archaeological sites and monuments.

surveyed recently by O'Sullivan and Sheehan (1996). Prior to this, little work had been undertaken since the early seventies (e.g. Finlay 1973) or before (e.g. Anati 1963). The study undertaken by Johnston (1989) had not included the carvings of the south-west of Ireland.

The study of rock-carvings from outside of Ireland provided a guide to the approach taken in this study; in particular work in Britain on carvings that are similarly abstract and geometric. Studies by Bradley (1991, 1992, 1993, 1994), Burgess (1990), Jackson (1988), Beckensall (1974, 1991, 1992a, 1992b) and Morris (1977, 1979, 1989) proved most useful, presenting different approaches to the study of abstract carvings. In addition the approaches and methodologies employed in the study of figurative art were incorporated (e.g. Tilley 1991; Malmer 1989) which were based on the Scandinavian experience. The former proved particularly valuable in determining a methodology by which to examine the compositions on the stones. The approach in this study incorporated and adapted a variety of ones used elsewhere in the study of rock-art to study abstract geometric carvings from south-west Ireland.

The dating of Irish and British rock-art is uncertain, although a Late Neolithic date has been suggested by Bradley for Atlantic rock-art including that located in Ireland (1997). He (1997: 65) proposes an origin possibly as early as 3300 BC and suggests a very long period of importance attached to carving rocks in open areas. For a more detailed discussion on the chronology of Irish rock-art prior to this hypothesis see MacWhite (1946), Simpson and Thawley (1972), Johnston (1989) and O'Sullivan and Sheehan (1996). This issue of chronology is not critical to the present study but it is thought likely that Irish rock-art is broadly of a Late Neolithic date. All of the carvings in the study are perceived as being broadly similar in terms of chronology and social context, although local variations are apparent throughout.

The methodology employed

Irish rock-art is located in the open air, either on boulders or outcrops, which are for the most part carved on the dominant rock type in the area, sandstone in the case of Iveragh. The landscape of Iveragh is one in which huge amounts of stone are located strewn across much of the landscape. Thus there was a wide choice of surfaces available to those who carved these stones. The selection of surfaces to be carved over those which were not provides an insight into the operational rules which governed the production of rock-art in the study area. The factors that influenced this selection may be very broad based, including the landscape and topography of a particular area, land use and the cultural perception of an area by those who carved.

In this study two aspects of location are particularly noticed. One is prospect: how large an area and what kind of land are visible from the rock-art location (and, conversely, that area from which the rock-art is visible). The other is accessibility, in terms of topographic location in a rugged landscape, where some hill slopes lead to passes, and others are steeper or sheer and lead only to the heights. The local road network, both as metalled roads today and as the stone tracks of recent centuries, is a helpful guide to those topographical indications, for these ways are lightly engineered and very much prefer to follow the easier ways through the landscape.

Through an examination of the prospect from the carvings, in comparison to that from nearby uncarved stones, the significance of the landscape that the carvings overlook became apparent. From most of the nearby uncarved stones a wide, open, extensive view over the surrounding landscape was apparent in contrast to the more focused, enclosed view of the landscape from many of the carvings.

Through a very detailed examination of the landscapes of the carvings in terms of microtopography, proximity to water and the sea and so on, in combination with use of cartographic sources, it was possible to determine the accessibility of the carvings. A dichotomy in the location of carvings in the landscape became apparent. Carvings could be found in open accessible areas, frequently along obvious route-ways through the landscape, for example close to rivers, which in the study area seem to have provided a most useful means of accessing areas. Alternatively, carvings were located in very inaccessible areas which may be difficult and possibly dangerous to access and frequently overlook route-ways through the landscape, for example high, steep mountain slopes.

The examination of the compositions and the motifs carved focused on trying to determine the overriding rules or 'design grammar' that governed the development of the compositions and the use of particular motifs in particular locations. We do not know what guided the carvers of these abstract motifs here to carve simple cups, there a set of concentric circles, here a small motif, there one a metre or more in diameter. But it is possible to recognize whether motifs on different rocks are much the same or very different, we can distinguish the simple from the complex, and we can certainly observe the comparative size of the figures.

Accordingly, we can explore the placing of the carved rocks in the landscape and the character of the motifs carved in these terms, and thereby hope to observe and to recover some aspects of the controlling logic which drew the prehistoric carvers to decide where to carve and what to carve. That is the purpose of the present study.

The findings revealed are consistent with the logical location of rock-art of the same tradition in northern England and Scotland (Beckensall, Chapter 3, this volume; Bradley 1997). Another region, far from Ireland, where a comparable research approach has been effective is in the Colorado Plateau region of western North America. This is a landscape of deep canyons, in which visibility varies greatly according to whether one is in the canyon or on the plateau above, and varies much within the canyons. Access is even more constrained, for access down or up the canyon is often possible at only a few locations and even there may involve a hard scramble. Accordingly, a compelling study has been made of 'spatial behaviour', the logic of human action in a landscape – in that instance one more constraining and strongly directing than Iveragh – where again the siting of rock-art makes sense in terms of human topography, and one can see patterns also in just what kind of rock-art occurs at just what type of topographical locale (Hartley and Vawser 1998).

The Kealduff Valley – Derrynablaha/Derreeny

The Kealduff Valley is situated to the south of the centre of the peninsula. At the head of this valley an extensive concentration of rock-carvings is located, spreading across the two townlands of Derrynablaha and Derreeny. The carvings are situated on the lower slopes of Mullaghanattin Mountain and Knockaunattin Mountain. A large lake, Lough Brin, is situated at the east of the valley head. The Kealduff River rises in the steep surrounding mountains, flowing south into the Blackwater Valley, and finally enters the sea some eleven kilometres away via the Kenmare River.

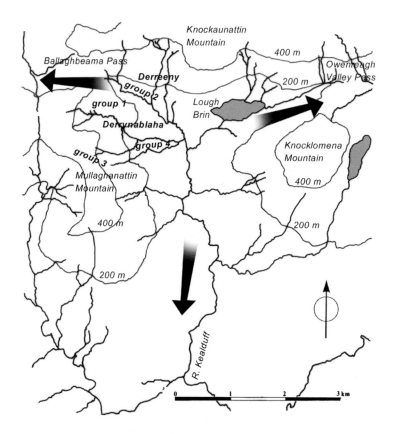

Figure 4.3 The Kealduff River Valley where the carvings in Derrynablaha and Derreeny are located. The three route-ways through the valley are demonstrated with arrows

Within the Kealduff Valley are several important links in a chain of route-ways that provide access to much of the largely inaccessible centre of the peninsula (Figure 4.3). Two mountain passes are located at the head of the valley, the Ballaghbeama Pass and the Owenreagh Valley Pass. The Ballaghbeama Pass is one of the few north–south-running mountain passes cutting through the predominately east–west-running Macguillycuddy's Reeks mountains. Through the Ballaghbeama Pass much of the centre and north-west of the peninsula opens up; the Owenreagh Valley Pass gives access to much of the east of the peninsula. Both of these passes are within the valley head, the Ballaghbeama Pass to the north-west and the Owenreagh Valley Pass to the north-east; they are separated by just two kilometres. Movement between them is relatively easy due to a pathway running along the foot of the mountain that is elevated above the wet valley floor. This path is best described as a natural route-way which is the easiest route between these mountain passes; in general, the modern roads and tracks follow these inviting route-ways whose easy location the topography rather directs.

A total of twenty-nine *in situ* carvings were examined within the valley. These divide into four distinct groups based on the geographical situation of the carving and the view focused on from each one:

- Group 1; SMR numbers 82: 23–1, 82: 23–2, 82: 23–3, 82: 23–4, 82: 23–5, 82: 23–6, 82: 24–1, 82: 24–2, 82: 25–1 82: 25–2 and 82: 27.
- Group 2; SMR numbers 82: 30, 82: 32, 82: 67, 82: 72, 82: 73, 82: 74, 82: 74–1, 82: 74–2, 82: 78, 82: 79 and 82: 80.
- Group 3; SMR numbers 82: 36–1, 82: 36–2, 82: 37, 82: 38 and 82: 39.
- Group 4; SMR numbers 82: 34–1 and 82: 34–2.

Group 1

The group 1 carvings are situated on a south-eastern spur of Mullaghanattin Mountain. The carvings are located at various altitudes on the spur, some on the lower slopes and some extending higher. From the carvings located on the lower mountain slopes there is a wide, open view, particularly in a southerly direction overlooking the course of the Kealduff River down the valley (Figure 4.4). Similarly, towards the east there is also quite a wide view overlooking Lough Brin and the Owenreagh Valley Pass. As one ascends the mountain, the carvings are situated in an increasingly enclosed landscape. They are located within a dip between the spur, extending from the mountain to the east, and the

Figure 4.4 A carving in Derrynablaha group 1, SMR number 82: 24–1, looking south over the Kealduff River Valley. The composition of two pairs of parallel lines and a cup and ring is clearly visible; several additional lines and cup marks are not visible. The mountains of the Beara Peninsula are perceptible in the background

body of the mountain; a small watercourse flows through this dip. The view from these carvings is channelled in a southerly direction along the river valley, the view to the east over the Owenreagh Pass and Lough Brin being completely cut off by the height of the spur, which extends from the mountain and on which the carvings are located.

The motif compositions decorating these stones vary considerably in this group of carvings. Some are quite unelaborated, for example 82: 23–3, with just simple cup and ring motifs and some isolated cup marks, while others, for example, 82: 24–2, are more elaborately decorated with cup and rings and cups with two or more rings. The majority of the compositions are quite elaborate in form. Some of the carved stones in this group stand out by their location on prominent boulders while others are very unobtrusively located, at present ground level or just above. Few are highly visible within the landscape even from very short distances.

The view from the carvings located at a higher elevation is more confined, and oriented in a southerly direction, than from those on the lower mountain slopes. The surrounding mountain slopes cut off the view in all other directions. From some of the latter carvings two route-ways through the valley are apparent, southwards down the valley following the river course and to the east through the Owenreagh Valley Pass. The Ballaghbeama Pass, which runs directly below the rising slopes of the spur on which the carvings are located, is not visible from these carvings.

Group 2

The majority of the group 2 carvings are located within the townland of Derreeny; only two are in Derrynablaha. The carvings are located on the low, rising slopes of Knockaunattin Mountain. Small glacial hillocks (referred to as drumlins) run along the lower slopes just above the valley floor. The carvings are situated within a channel formed between the lower mountain slopes and these hillocks which elevates them above the extremely wet, boggy valley floor, along the course of the pathway, previously mentioned, connecting the Ballaghbeama Pass to the Owenreagh Valley Pass. Both the track-way and the carvings follow the most accessible route between these mountain passes, above the wet valley floor but below the steep mountain slopes.

The view from most of the group 2 carvings, located along the stone track, is confined by the lower mountain slopes and the glacial hillocks, which channel it in a westerly direction. From most of the panels this is the dominant vista towards the Ballaghbeama Pass. However, several of the group 2 carvings are located on the southern side of the glacial hillocks and slightly south of the track. From these carvings there are extensive views down the valley to the south. From here the view towards the west and the Ballaghbeama Pass is cut off by the rising of these hillocks. From several of the carvings on these hillocks there is a view both down valley and towards the Ballaghbeama Pass to the west. From one very unusual carving in this group, SMR 82: 78, there is a view to the east over Lough Brin and the Owenreagh Valley Pass. This carving is unconventional with just pock-marks on it, and may not be rock-art.

From particular carvings within this group the three route-ways through the valley are visible. The location of these carvings in an area from which the view is so obviously focused on the three route-ways through the landscape is most significant. Slight alterations to the location of these carvings could have considerably widened the views from them.

The carvings are located within a relatively confined area and thus it is surprising that there is very little inter-visibility between most of the panels. Most of them are apparent only when viewed from a very close distance (low evening sunshine enhances their visibility significantly).

The carvings in this group are quite different in terms of compositions; some have just isolated cup marks on them, for example 82: 79, but the majority are more elaborate with cup and rings, two or more cup and rings, and meandering lines. These carvings are for the most part quite easily found due to their location along what is best described as a natural route-way.

Group 3

The group 3 carvings are located on the eastern slopes of Mullaghanattin Mountain. Situated between two slightly protruding ridges of the mountain, they are in a slight hollow which is more enclosed than most of the surrounding landscape. Three of the carvings are located on the lower slopes of the mountain and the other two on the high, steep slopes. The view from all of these carvings extends over the eastern part of the valley head, in particular over Lough Brin and the pass to the Owenreagh Valley. The view from the two highest carvings is extremely focused on this area and restricted to it. As one descends the mountain to the carvings on the lower mountain slopes the view, still eastward-looking, is slightly wider, with limited views to the north and the south.

The carvings in this area are elaborate in form. Four of the five have unusual or very elaborate compositions. These carvings are extremely difficult to locate, particularly those at the highest elevation on the mountainside. Two of the panels have the rosette pattern carved on them, a motif found only in the Derrynablaha area. The web motif carved on one of the surfaces is also unusual. Within this group is probably the most elaborate carving on the peninsula: SMR 82: 36–1 has an abundance of cup and rings, and two or more cup and rings, with meandering lines. The carving at the lowest elevation of the five is the most simple of them, cup marks, cup and lines, and cup and rings are carved on this surface.

Group 4

This consists of just two carvings located on the valley floor. The area is extremely wet and boggy, a dense covering of peat concealing much of the earlier landscape. Within this landscape, two extremely large stones stand out above the surrounding valley floor. The view from these carvings is very focused down the valley to the south where a distant view of the Beara Peninsula is to be seen. Neither the Ballaghbeama Pass nor the pass to the Owenreagh Valley is visible.

These carvings are located on extremely large boulders of which only a very small proportion is decorated. The compositions are for the most part quite simple, consisting of cup marks, isolated lines, and cup and rings; part of a cup with two rings is present on one of the stones. The boulders, within two metres of each other, are extremely prominent in the landscape.

Ferta Valley carvings

A small assemblage of eight rock-carvings are located in the Ferta Valley, which is situated several kilometres east of Cahersiveen town. The carvings are located in four townlands within the valley. Seven of the carvings are on the slopes of Been Hill, Mullaghnarakill Mountain and Teermoyle Mountain which surround the Ferta Valley to the east; the other carving is located on the valley floor (Figure 4.5). The valley is enclosed to the north, south and east by high mountains; it is open to the west, where the Ferta flows into an estuary at the Valencia River and on into the sea.

Two mountain passes provide access to and from the valley head. To the south-east of the valley head one of these passes cuts between the low mountains of Caunoge and Keelnagore. The mountain pass, not particularly perceptible in the landscape given its location between these low mountains, connects the Ferta Valley to the Inny Valley. From the Inny Valley large tracts of the central area of the peninsula are accessible. This mountain pass is visible from several of the carvings in the valley. The other pass in the valley head is more obvious and dramatically located. Situated at the northern side of the valley head, it cuts through the impressive Knocknadobar Mountain and Been

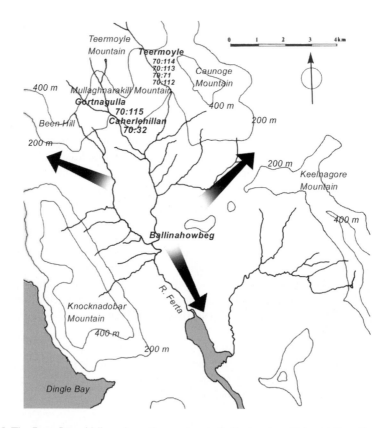

Figure 4.5 The Ferta River Valley where the carvings in Ballinahowbeg, Caherlehillan, Gortnagulla and Teermoyle are located. The three route-ways through the valley are demonstrated with arrows

Hill to access the coast, giving a spectacular view over Dingle Bay and the Dingle Peninsula to the north. However, none of the carvings in this study area has any visibility over this area. The Ferta River runs east–west through the valley; one panel is located within several hundred metres of this.

The carved stone in the townland of Ballinahowbeg is located on the valley floor approximately halfway between the estuary and the lower mountain slopes. The carving is several hundred metres from the Ferta River, which at this point is wide, meandering and quite shallow, therefore providing one of the best crossing points for several kilometres. The proximity of the carving to the river and a possible ford suggests it is located on an important route-way up- and down-river, as well as a crossing point. The carving on this stone is quite interesting; with the grid motif on the surface as well as several cups with two rings and lines, cup marks and cup and rings, it is elaborate. This composition is brilliantly illuminated by the low evening sunshine (Figure 4.6).

Two carvings are located in the townland of Caherlehillan. Approximately 300 metres apart, they are on the southern side of a spur of Mullaghnarakill Mountain. Above these carvings on the high slopes of Been Hill/Mullaghnarakill Mountain is located another single carving in the townland of Gortnagulla. These three carvings overlook the valley floor along the course of the Ferta River as far west as Valencia Island. The carving in Gortnagulla townland, located higher up the mountain slopes, has a wider view encompassing almost the entire valley.

The compositions on the three surfaces vary considerably. Caherlehillan SMR 70: 32 is an elaborate carving, with cup marks, cup and rings, and cups with multiple rings as well as meandering lines. The other carving in Caherlehillan townland, SMR 70: 115,

Figure 4.6 The carving in Ballinahowbeg in the Ferta River Valley. The composition is highlighted in the low evening sunshine

has far fewer motifs carved on its surface. Several cup marks, an isolated ring, and a cup with two rings decorate its surface. Both carvings are on relatively large prominent boulders; their visibility is greatly reduced by peat growth. A Late Neolithic wedge tomb is located on a promontory above the Caherlehillan carvings, although it is not visible from them.

The Gortnagulla carving located up-slope from the Caherlehillan carvings is elaborate: a web motif decorates a large part of the stone's surface. Isolated rings, cup and rings, and a cup with a line and multiple rings also decorate the stone. This composition is on a large stone located at a very high altitude. It is an extremely difficult carving to find, despite its size, as it is concealed within a landscape dominated by outcrop, scree and boulders.

The four remaining carvings are in the townland of Teermoyle on the southern slopes of Teermoyle Mountain. The views from these carvings are more limited. The southern part of the valley floor is visible from the carvings but the upward slope of Teermoyle Mountain cuts off the view of the northern portion of the valley. The pass at the south-east of the valley cutting through Caunoge and Keelnagore mountains is visible from all four panels. Parts of the valley floor are also visible, but that view is more restricted than the one from the Caherlehillan and Gortnagulla carvings. The view of the mountain pass appears to be what is focused on from these four panels. They are located within a small area and are largely inter-visible, however, due to the large amount of scree and boulder dominating this landscape, it is difficult to isolate them from their background.

The compositions on these four stones are simple in form with only a small proportion of the surfaces of the stones carved. Two of the four carvings are composed of cup and rings, some of which have lines attached, as well as cup marks. Of the other two carvings one is composed of two basins, which are unusual motifs, and the other of the web motif, which is again unusual, as well as cup marks.

The Sneem Valley group

The Sneem Valley is at the south-west of the peninsula, where three small rivers converge to form the River Sneem, which flows into an estuary at Sneem town and into the sea at the Kenmare River further south. Six *in situ* carvings in this valley were included within the study area (Figure 4.7). Four are located at the north-east of the valley on the south-eastern slopes of River Hill in the townlands of Tullakeel and Derryleague. A carving in the townland of Maulagallane, located on the valley floor, is about three kilometres south-west of the River Hill carvings, towards the centre of the valley. The final carving is in the townland of Dromtine, approximately two kilometres north-west of Maulagallane in a landscape of small hillocks scattered across the valley floor and lower mountain slopes. The carving is on the western side of one such small hillock overlooking a small lake, Dromtine Lough.

High, impressive mountains encircling the valley floor to the east, north and west dominate the landscape. To the south the valley opens up along the course of the Sneem River. The main route through the valley follows the course of the river and its tributaries from the sea to its mountain sources. A pass on the eastern side of the valley, north of a low ridge called Brackloon, is the only other route-way. From the valley into which this pass opens one has access to much of the central area of the peninsula.

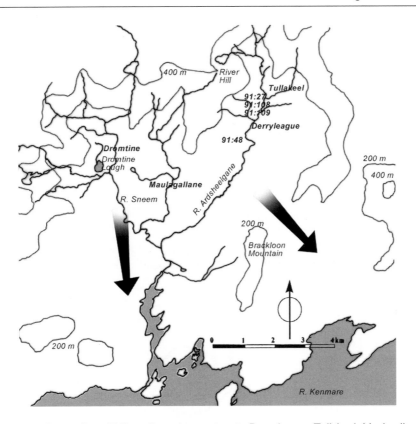

Figure 4.7 The Sneem River Valley where the carvings in Derryleague, Tullakeel, Maulagallane and Dromtine are located. The two route-ways through the valley are demonstrated with arrows

From the three carvings in the townland of Derryleague and the one in the townland of Tullakeel the view is largely in a southerly direction, along the course of the river to the estuary. There is also a view to the south-east of the valley towards the pass north of Brackloon Mountain. The four carvings are all on similarly sized stones, small flat-topped boulders that are unobtrusive in the landscape. Each of these four carvings is difficult to find.

Three of the four compositions on these stones are very similar, carved simply with isolated cups, lines, and rings, as well as cup and rings. The fourth carving, 91: 109, on a stone 1.3 metres long by 0.85 metres wide, is composed of a cup with five rings, and a cup with six rings, one of which has satellite cups within the rings (Figure 4.8). Cup marks, cup and rings, and lines also decorate the surface. This elaborate carving covers a large proportion of the rock's surface, a feature which occurs quite infrequently. In proximity to the Tullakeel carving there is an elaborate carving, which unfortunately has been removed from its original location and is now situated within a field boundary. The stone is decorated with the web motif, cup marks, cup ring and lines, and cup with multiple rings and lines.

From the carving in the townland of Maulagallane there are views both up and down the valley, to the south along the course of the river, and to the north towards the river's

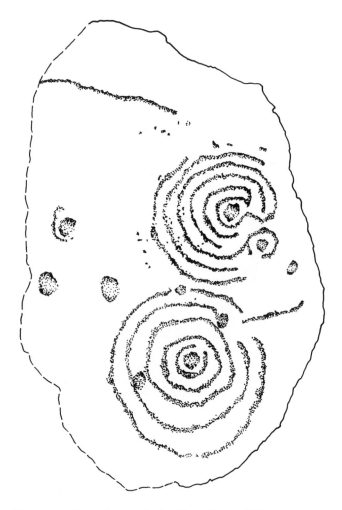

Figure 4.8 The elaborate carving in the townland of Derryleague, SMR number 91: 109

mountain source. There is also a view west towards the pass north of Brackloon, which accesses much of the central area of the peninsula. The panel is composed of cup marks, most of which are surrounded by multiple rings, although many of these rings appear rectangular rather than circular. An unusual feature of this panel is the wide spacing between the rings which enclose the cups, allowing the motifs to have very large overall diameters. The largest of these motifs, approximately one and half metres in diameter, is the largest motif known to this author on the peninsula, and certainly within the study area (Figure 4.9).

Single or double lines develop from most of these carvings. Several of the carvings continue under the surrounding peat, and several cups with partial rings are present also. The surface on which the carvings are located is unfortunately very worn and it is possible that some of the motifs have been weathered away. The carved surface is a large stretch of flat outcrop approximately twenty metres long and 6 metres wide, partially peat

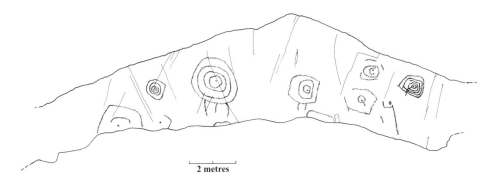

2 metres

Figure 4.9 The carving in the townland of Maulagallane, SMR number 90: 41. The motifs on this carving are the largest recorded on the peninsula

covered, and prominent in the landscape when approached from the south but otherwise, despite its large size, not perceptible. This extensive outcrop makes a natural stage; it would have provided a spectacular location for the carving of the stone, or other ritually based activities, to be viewed by an audience.

From the carving in Dromtine townland there is a wide view down the valley; it is curiously located, perched on a small hillock overlooking Dromtine Lough, suggesting the importance of this natural feature to those who carved the panel. The composition of this carving is quite unusual: two basin motifs are connected by lines to a cup and multiple rings and lines, as well as multiple rings with lines. The multiple-ring motif with lines found twice on this panel is not seen in any other known panel within the study area. This is a large stone that is prominent within the immediately surrounding landscape.

Behy River Valley – Coomasaharn

Towards the north-east of the peninsula near Glenbeigh village, two large rock-art concentrations are spread over two townlands within the Behy River Valley (Figure 4.10).

The Behy River Valley is almost completely encircled by mountains. The valley floor is extensive, and several large lakes are found close to the foothills of the mountains to the south-west. There are several places through which access can be gained to the valley. Following the course of the Behy River from the sea to its mountain source is the most obvious route. The river develops from several tributaries, which emerge from the surrounding steep mountain slopes and the lakes in the valley. Following the many tributaries of the river takes one to almost all sections of the valley. Several kilometres south of where the river meets the sea, the valley narrows considerably, to approximately half a kilometre. The river is funnelled between high and sometimes steep mountains.

On the north-western side of the valley is a mountain pass. Through this access is gained to the coast and the north-western part of the peninsula. Several roads skirt around this low hill and continue through the pass, these modern lightly engineered routes again showing the natural ways through this landscape.

The carvings located in the townland of Coomasaharn are at the south-west of the valley head close to Coomasaharn Lough, and situated on the lower slopes of a spur of

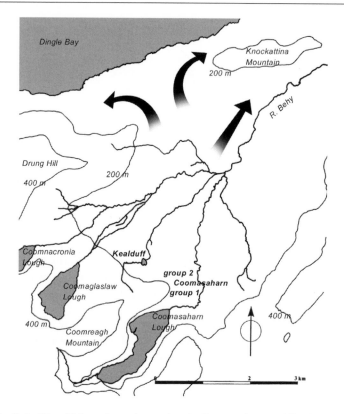

Figure 4.10 The Behy River Valley where the carvings in Coomasaharn and Kealduff are located. The three route-ways through the valley are demonstrated with arrows

Coomreagh Mountain. This mountain spur, lake and the River Behy provide natural boundaries.

From here, the complex of panels at Coomasaharn can be divided into two groups based on their location and the view on which the carvings focus:

- Group 1; 71: 18, 71: 20, 71: 21, 71: 57 and 71: 61.
- Group 2; 71: 10, 71: 11, 71: 12, 71: 13, 71: 16, 71: 58, 71: 59 and 71: 60.

Group 1

The group 1 carvings are located on the south-eastern slopes of Coomreagh Mountain overlooking Coomasaharn Lough as well as the exit of the Behy River from the lake. The area is enclosed by the high, steep slopes of the surrounding mountains, particularly those to the south, east and west of the lake which are virtually impassable due to their very steep gradient. The view is extremely restricted by this landscape; the expanse of valley floor to the north, largely cut off, is only partially visible from one carving in the group.

The compositions on these carvings are simple in form, though several unusual motifs are located among them. A keyhole motif and a web motif are found on panels in this area. Cup marks, cups, rings and lines are also numerous. Only one of the panels has more elaborate cups with multiple rings motif. Most of the carvings in this area are located on or above ground level and are unobtrusive in the landscape. Two are more prominent, one of which is sited overlooking Coomasaharn Lough.

Group 2

The group 2 carvings, several hundred metres north of group 1, are located on the northern slopes of Coomreagh Mountain. From these carvings there is an extensive view of the valley floor towards the sea. There is no view of Coomasaharn Lough. The landscape here is much more open than from the group 1 carvings, the vista extending along much of the course of the river, including the steeply sided pass at Glenbeigh town through which it passes. The pass between Drung Hill and Knockatinna Mountain at the west of the valley is also visible.

The carvings are placed where the mountain slopes converge with the valley floor in an area that was probably regularly traversed when moving through this landscape. It is similarly located to the pathway between the mountain passes in Derrynablaha–Derreeny.

The composition of these carvings varies considerably. Several comprise just cup and lines; others have cup marks with multiple rings with and without lines.

Much of the valley floor in the Coomasaharn area is covered by dense peat and several of the carvings are partially concealed by this. Now very unobtrusive in the landscape, they may originally have been quite prominent.

Behy River Valley – Kealduff

To the north of the Coomasaharn carvings and across a tributary of the Behy River is another extensive rock-art area, located in Kealduff townland. Although the Kealduff carvings are only located approximately one kilometre from the Coomasaharn carvings they are none the less distinct and very cohesive so they form a separate group.

The Kealduff carvings are on the lower, northern slopes of Coomreagh Mountain. To the north and south tributaries of the Behy River limit the location of the carvings. To the west the rising slopes of Coomreagh Mountain and to the east the approach of the valley floor limit the extent of the carvings' location. As the Kealduff carvings are located in the same valley as the Coomasaharn carvings the surrounding landscape setting is as was described earlier.

Thirteen panels were studied from the townland of Kealduff. All are located within very close proximity to each other, just above the valley floor, in both sloping and flat areas. From all of the carvings the course of the River Behy through the valley to the sea is visible, as is the narrowing of the valley, where the town of Glenbeigh is located. The pass to the north-west of the valley between Drung Hill and Knockatinna Mountain is also visible. These panels are located in a landscape similar to the location of the Coomasaharn group 2 carvings, where the valley floor and the mountain slopes converge.

The compositions on the stones in Kealduff are quite unusual; several of the motifs are found exclusively in this area, including the coiled or broken spiral motif, the cruciform motif, the cross, intersecting arcs, and the wishbone motif. There are some carvings with very simple compositions, including cup, rings and lines, and one carving with just lines on it; the majority of the carvings in this area are elaborate in form.

The location of these carvings so close together within a small area is an interesting feature of the art in this location. The carvings are located at the meeting of valley floor and mountain slopes, which was probably an area regularly traversed, and thus along a possible route-way. However, the density of panels within this confined area may reflect an additional importance attached to the place. This may also account for the presence of so many motifs exclusive to the area. Despite the location of these panels within a small area, there is only limited inter-visibility between them. This landscape is strewn with outcrop and boulders and the volume of rock present makes the carvings more difficult to isolate from anywhere more than a short distance away.

The placing in the landscape

Within the five areas examined from the peninsula there exists a dichotomy between those located at viewing-points and those located along route-ways. This is similar to observations produced by Bradley (1991) where the importance of route-ways and viewing-points was noted in relation to the location of rock-art in Britain. Those situated at viewing-points are usually in areas from which the views are restricted and overlook specific features of the landscape, frequently route-ways. Generally the views from uncarved stones very close to the carvings are much wider than those from the carvings themselves; this suggests the precise landscapes to be carved were chosen prior to the selection of stones, largely in the light of landscapes which they overlooked. Within the Derrynablaha–Derreeny clustering, groups 1 and 3 are both in areas of viewing-points; from both groups the views are channelled, by their location, to overlook very specific parts of the surrounding landscape, in this case route-ways. In the carvings in the townlands of Caherlehillan, Gortnagulla, Teermoyle in the Ferta River Valley, those in Coomasaharn group 1, and the carvings in the townlands of Derryleague and Tullakeel in the Sneem Valley this same pattern emerges. Carvings overlook specific parts of the surrounding landscape, and usually marking an important route-way through that landscape.

Many of these carvings located at viewing-points are very difficult to find; stones that were almost concealed within the landscape were chosen for carving, although this does not necessarily imply that they are small in size. Frequently the landscapes in which they are located are dangerous to move through: steeply sloping mountains, small cliffs, an abundance of water and the ease with which one can get lost, particularly when fog suddenly descends. These viewing-point carvings are for the most part not placed along any obvious route-ways and are frequently located at a considerable distance from them. The carvings would probably not be encountered without prior knowledge of their exact whereabouts or a concerted effort to locate them. They are not easily or readily accessible and the audience to which they were addressed was probably restricted.

The carvings located along route-ways through the landscape are in areas that are open and accessible to wide audiences. These include carvings in groups 2 and 4 in the Derrynablaha–Derreeny group, carvings in the townlands of Dromtine and Maulagallane in the Sneem Valley, the carving in the townland of Ballinahowbeg in the Ferta Valley, the Kealduff carvings and the Coomasaharn group 2 carvings, both in the Behy Valley. The Derrynablaha–Derreeny group 2 carvings are located along an important route-way that connects the two mountain passes of Ballaghbeama and the Owenreagh Valley. As the carvings are on a path through the area that would be most easily traversed between these mountain passes they would be encountered by those traversing the route. They may not have been apparent to all, but those who were aware of their presence would eventually find them; it appears that these were open to viewing by a wide and varied audience. The Kealduff and Coomasaharn group 2 carvings are similarly located. The route-way on which they are sited runs along the edge of the valley floor where the lower mountain slopes and valley floor converge. That zone was probably an important route for those who moved through this area. The Kealduff carvings stand out as a particularly important group in two ways: first, by the density of carvings located in such a limited area; second, by the number of motifs within the compositions that are exclusive to this area and the elaborate compositions on many of the surfaces. Kealduff appears an area of considerable ritual significance for those who carved in it.

Locations in proximity to rivers are quite common for many of the other route-way carvings, including Derrynablaha–Derreeny group 4, Ballinahowbeg in the Ferta Valley, and Dromtine and Maulagallane in the Sneem Valley. Those moving through the landscape would have located these carvings with relative ease; many form large panels and are prominent in the landscape, in particular Derrynablaha–Derreeny group 4 and Maulagallane, when approached from the south. The panel at the latter is notable not just for the size of the rock surface but for the large scale of the motifs carved on it. This may be due to the landscape in which the carving is located. In comparison with other panels within the study area, this carving is in an area from which the view is limited: its location on the valley floor reduces visibility of the surroundings. The large scale of the surface and the motifs carved on them may be an attempt to compensate for its being placed in this landscape of ill-defined features.

Given the close location of many of the carvings within each of the five clusterings, it is surprising that inter-visibility between the panels was relatively uncommon. This was particularly apparent in Kealduff, where the panels were placed very close together. It was necessary to be within several metres of the panels before they became visually accessible. Prevailing weather conditions influenced the visibility of many of the carvings, and low sunshine either in the early morning or late afternoon had the potential to enhance the visibility of the compositions, particularly if they were wet.

An obvious dichotomy exists between the location of carvings at viewing-points and carvings near route-ways; but this is not reflected among the compositions carved on the stones. At viewing-points the compositions are varied, with both simple and elaborate compositions represented. All of these groups of carvings have a mix of both simple and elaborate compositions, although sometimes a group is dominated by one type. Only Derrynablaha–Derreeny group 3 has four elaborate compositions out of five. In several cases some of the more unusually occurring motifs are within these compositions.

The compositions of carvings located at route-ways are similarly varied, from the elaborate carvings of Kealduff in the Behy Valley, Ballinahowbeg in the Ferta Valley and Dromtine and Maulagallane in the Sneem Valley to the relatively simple compositions of Derrynablaha–Derreeny group 4 and some of the group 2 carvings. Where an isolated carving is located several kilometres from the next, the composition tends to be elaborate. These differences may be extremely subtle, of a kind not apparent using the structuralist methodology applied in the original study. We cannot be sure that the distinctions drawn between the simple and the complex motifs represent any equivalent variable in the understanding the carvers had of their own art. The landscapes which are carved and, in particular, the views from these areas must heavily influence the interpretation of the compositions presented to the audience. It appears from this study that it is easier to control the placing of carvings within the landscape – those at viewing-points away from route-ways would not be easily encountered – than to use obviously different, and perhaps more enigmatic, compositions to limit interpretation by the viewing audience.

While this central dichotomy between carvings at viewing-points and carvings near route-ways is consistent in all of the five clusters of carvings within the study area, the importance of local variations must not be overlooked. There are many subtle variations in the siting of the rock-art at the local level and in the incorporation of motifs, particularly the unique types within the compositions. What is apparent is the very detailed knowledge of the landscape required by those who carved the art.

Several of the carvings in the study area in both the route-way and the viewing-point locations appear to have an association with lakes; O'Sullivan and Sheehan (1993) suggest a water-cult association with the location of rock-art. The Derrynablaha group 3 carvings and the Coomasaharn group 1 carvings both overlook large, impressive lakes situated prominently within the landscapes in which they are located. In the case of Coomasaharn the view from the group 1 carvings is dominated by this lake. The Dromtine carving in the Sneem Valley is located on the side of a small glacial hillock, below which is a lake, which again dominates the view from the carving. The location of the Kealduff and Coomasaharn group 2 carvings could be perceived as being on a pathway towards three large impressive lakes, although the lakes themselves are not visible from any of these carvings. This association with overlooking lakes or being located on paths to them suggests an importance attached to these impressive natural features probably at both a ritual and an economic level by those who carved these landscapes. Certainly it demonstrates the excellent local knowledge of the landscape held by communities which readily translated into highlighting the important natural features and using them to establish a probable socio-symbolic mechanism whereby landscape setting and the possible use of route-ways assisted the location of rock-art.

Conclusion

This has been a study of a small and limited landscape that is rich in prehistoric rock-carvings. It was conducted at a small scale and results from it should not be viewed as generally applicable to other areas. Although trends emerged which have been recorded elsewhere (Bradley 1991), local knowledge of that environment and that landscape appears to be of overriding importance in the selection of landscapes to be carved.

Several general themes emerged: similar operational rules were apparent which governed the placing of carvings within the landscape. Two factors which influenced this placing of carvings were explored: first, the prospect from the carvings; and, second, the accessibility of them. The importance of other components in the placing of carvings, such as the cultural perceptions of the carvers, was noted but was not examined in this study.

A dichotomy between the location of carvings at viewing-points and along route-ways or pathways became apparent. Viewing-point locations such as Derrynablaha–Derreeny group 3 are difficult to access; the audience to which these panels were addressed appears to be limited and restricted. Carvings along route-ways or pathways such as Derrynablaha–Derreeny group 2 are more accessible and probably open to much wider audiences. Accessibility to carved rocks reflects social divisions among the society that carved them.

It is surprising that this dichotomy is not as pronounced in relation to the motif compositions on the surfaces. Instead simple and elaborate compositions are found together in all of the carving groups at both viewing-point and route-way locations.

Thus it is the location of the carving in the landscape that seemed to determine its accessibility to the audience rather than the composition of that carving. The carvings, abstract and geometric, are polysemic. Those located at route-ways are accessible and open to individual interpretation by all who view them, while those who are excluded from the knowledge of the whereabouts of the viewing-point carvings are excluded from any opportunity to view them. Interpretation and communication are thus controlled. Rock-carvings were produced as a form of communication within a given society at a particular time. It is this communicative element of rock-carvings that when further examined will eventually reveal more of the society that produced it.

Acknowledgements

This work was initially undertaken as a Masters of Arts thesis. It was submitted to the Department of Archaeology at University College, Cork, in November 1994. The original study incorporated a detailed examination of the landscapes and motif use of rock-art on the Iveragh Peninsula in south-west Ireland. Thanks are due to Dr Elizabeth Shee Twohig who supervised the thesis and to my family for help with fieldwork, as well as numerous others who helped along the way. Thanks to Fergus Somers who commented on a draft of the paper.

References

Anati, E. 1963. New petroglyphs at Derrynablaha, Co. Kerry, Ireland, *Journal of the Cork Historical and Archaeological Society* 68: 1–15.

Beckensall, S. 1974. *The prehistoric carved rocks of Northumberland*. Newcastle-upon-Tyne: Graham.

Beckensall, S. 1991. *The prehistoric rock motifs of Northumberland*, 1: *Ford to Old Bewick*. Hexham (privately printed).

Beckensall, S. 1992a. *Prehistoric rock motifs of Northumberland*, 2: *Beanley to the Tyne*. Hexham (privately printed).

Beckensall, S. 1992b. *Cumbrian prehistoric rock-art: symbols, monuments and landscape*. Hexham (privately printed).

Bradley, R. 1991. Rock art and the perception of landscape, *Cambridge Archaeological Journal* 1 (1): 77–101.

Bradley, R. 1992. Turning the world – rock carvings and the archaeology of death, in N. Sharples and A. Sheridan (eds), *Vessels for the ancestors*: 168–176. Edinburgh: Edinburgh University Press.

Bradley, R. 1993. *Altering the earth: the origins of monuments in Britain and continental Europe*. Edinburgh: Society of Antiquaries of Scotland. Monograph Series 8.

Bradley, R. 1994. Symbols and signposts: understanding the prehistoric carvings of the British Isles, in C. Renfrew and E. Zubrow (eds), *The ancient mind*: 95–106. Cambridge: Cambridge University Press.

Bradley, R. 1997. *Signing the land: rock art and the prehistory of Atlantic Europe*. London: Routledge.

Bradley, R., J. Harding and M. Matthews. 1993. The siting of prehistoric rock art in Galloway, south-west Scotland, *Proceedings of the Prehistoric Society* 59: 269–283.

Buckley, V. and D. Sweetman. 1991. *Archaeological survey of County Louth*. Dublin: Stationery Office.

Burgess, C. 1990. The chronology of cup and cup-ring marks in Atlantic Europe, *Revue Archéologique de l'Ouest*, Supplement 2: 157–171.

Clarke, J.P. 1982. Prehistoric rock inscriptions near Dundalk, Co. Louth, *Journal of the County Louth Archaeological and Historical Society* 20(2): 107–116.

Cuppage, J. 1986. *Archaeological survey of the Dingle Peninsula*. Ballyferriter: Oidhreacht Chorca Duibhne.

Finlay, F. 1973. The rock art of Cork and Kerry. Unpublished thesis, Department of Archaeology, University College, Cork.

Fraser, D. 1988. The orientation of visibility from the chambered cairns of Eday, Orkney, in C.L. Ruggles (ed.), *Records in stone*: 325–336. Cambridge: Cambridge University Press.

Hartley, R.J. and A.W. Vawser. 1998. Spatial behaviour and learning in the prehistoric environment of the Colorado River drainage (south-eastern Utah), western North America, in C. Chippindale and P.S.C. Taçon (eds), *The archaeology of rock-art*: 185–211. Cambridge: Cambridge University Press.

Jackson, P.J. 1988. An investigation into the prehistoric cup and ring engravings of the British Isles with reference to Galicia. Unpublished Ph.D. thesis, CNNA, Cambridge.

Johnston, P. 1989. Prehistoric Irish petroglyphs: their analysis and interpretation in an anthropological context. Ph.D. thesis, UMI, Ann Arbor.

Lacy, B. 1983. *Archaeological survey of County Donegal*. Lifford: Donegal County Council.

MacWhite, E. 1946. A new view of Irish Bronze Age rock scribings, *Journal of the Royal Society of Antiquaries of Ireland* 71: 59–80.

Malmer, M.P. 1989. Principles of a non-mythological explanation of north-European Bronze Age rock art, *Bronze Age Studies* 6: 91–99.

Morris, R. 1977. *The prehistoric rock art of Argyll*. Poole: Dolphin Press.

Morris, R. 1979. *The prehistoric rock art of Galloway and the Isle of Man*. Poole: Blandford Press.

Morris, R. 1989. The prehistoric rock art of Great Britain: a survey of all sites bearing motifs more complex than simple cup-marks, *Proceedings of the Prehistoric Society* 55: 45–88.

Nevill, W.E. 1963. *Geology and Ireland*. Dublin: Allen and Figgis.

O'Sullivan, A. and J. Sheehan. 1993. Prospection and outlook: aspects of rock art on the Iveragh Peninsula, Co. Kerry, in E. Shee Twohig and M. Ronayne (eds), *Past perceptions*: 75–84. Cork: Cork University Press.

O'Sullivan, A. and J. Sheehan. 1996. *The Iveragh Peninsula: an archaeological survey of south Kerry*. Cork: Cork University Press.

Power, D. 1992. *Archaeological inventory of County Cork*, 1. Dublin: Stationery Office.

Purcell, A. 1994. Carved landscapes; the rock art of the Iveragh Peninsula, County Kerry. Unpublished MA thesis, Department of Archaeology, University College, Ireland.

Shee, E. 1968. Some examples of rock art from County Cork, *Journal of the Cork Historical and Archaeological Society* 73: 144–151.

Shee, E. 1972. Three decorated stones from Loughcrew, County Meath, *Journal of the Royal Society of Antiquaries of Ireland* 102: 224–233.

Shee, E. and M. O'Kelly. 1971. The Derrynablaha Shield again, *Journal of the Cork Historical and Archaeological Society* 76: 72–76.

Simpson, D.D.A. and J.E. Thawley. 1972. Single grave art in Britain, *Scottish Archaeological Forum* 4: 81–104.

Tilley, C. 1991. *Material culture and text: the art of ambiguity*. London: Routledge.

Chapter 5

Landscape representations on boulders and menhirs in the Valcamonica–Valtellina area, Alpine Italy

Angelo Fossati

Valcamonica–Valtellina and its engraved boulders

The rupestrian tradition of Valcamonica and Valtellina (Lombardy, Italy), a patrimony of inestimable value (from 1979 inscribed in the Unesco World Heritage List), presents a large number of topographic representations. These figures – normally engraved on flat rocks – are sometimes found also on vertical surfaces, especially on boulders, stelae and menhirs, monuments characteristic of the Copper Age (third millennium BC) in the area; some of these images may form topographic maps.

This chapter examines particularly these 'maps', trying to define a precise chronology of the phenomenon and a complete typology of these topographic representations, to delineate a possible interpretation.

Points of discussion will be: what is the distinction between the maps engraved on boulders – stones that can be shifted – and those engraved on flat rocks – surfaces that are immovable? Is there any difference in doing figures on vertical or on horizontal surfaces? And, in general, why did this prehistoric people represent maps? Do these maps represent real or imaginary territories? Are they a sort of mythical representation of the known world? Are these representations linked to an agricultural way of living or to a different exploitation of the land, for example mining? Why are these schematic figures the almost exclusive representations available of a rock-art phase, the period between the Neolithic and the Copper Age?

It will be very difficult to answer these questions comprehensively. In the following paragraphs I have tried to summarize some of these points. For those who do not know too much of the rock-art in the area, I have outlined the chronology and themes of the rock-art of Valcamonica and Valtellina. Then I have condensed into a very short history the research on the subject. I hope the interest of the reader will increase when I present and discuss the boulders of the Copper Age with a short summary of the recurrent elements in these particular monuments and a general interpretation.

The petroglyph complex of Valcamonica and Valtellina

The rock-art existing in Valcamonica and Valtellina, two Alpine valleys in the provinces of Bergamo, Brescia and Sondrio in northern Italy, constitutes an archaeological, artistic, ethnographic and historical patrimony of inestimable value, not only for its antiquity but, above all, for its thematic and iconographic wealth (Anati 1982; De Marinis 1988; Arcà *et al.* 1995).

This rupestrian tradition counts today about 300,000 engraved figures.* At the beginning of this century, only the Cemmo boulders (the 'Massi di Cemmo') were known, due to the discoveries of Walther Laeng, an Italian-Swiss geographer (Laeng 1914). In Valcamonica most discoveries were made during the 1930s thanks to the archaeologist Raffaello Battaglia (Battaglia 1934) and the anthropologist Giovanni Marro (Marro 1930). A more scientific comprehension of the different phases appeared during the 1960s and 1970s, with the works of Emmanuel Anati (Anati 1976) and especially Raffaele De Marinis (De Marinis 1988, 1995). With the discovery of rock-art also in Valtellina, a valley adjacent to the northern part of Valcamonica, in 1966 (Pace 1968), this zone of the central-eastern Alps (that is, Valcamonica and Valtellina taken together) can be considered a single petroglyph area.

Geologically, the valleys were excavated and polished by the glaciers during the last hundred thousand years; the art is mainly located in the open air and on the flatter rocks. From the Iseo Lake, south of Valcamonica, to the sites of Sellero-Grevo in the middle valley, the rocks are composed of sandstone; in the upper part of the valley and in the entire Valtellina they consist of schists. Both are very polished and moulded by the ice. The engravers used both hammering and scratching techniques; those made by hammering are the main and important figures. To hammer the rocks the people used quartz tools: it is possible to find these artefacts as they have been abandoned near to the rocks (Fossati 1993a).

In this area at present the rock-art is distributed along four fundamental periods from the Neolithic to the arrival of the Romans in the valleys (Anati 1976; De Marinis 1988; Fossati 1991, 1993b). They are numbered as the 1st to 4th styles, with some sub-divisions. Obviously the rupestrian tradition does not assume in these phases always the same meaning for the populations that have produced it.

The first phase, a period datable between the end of Neolithic and the Copper Age (fourth millennium BC), runs from the '1st/2nd' to the beginning of the '3rd A' styles of the Camunnian rock-art. In it topographical figures are found, the first representations of the territory whose execution on cliffs perhaps is tied to a real division of agricultural lands sanctioned by the ritual practice of rock-art (Fossati 1993a). Other figures attributed to this phase are spirals and necklace designs. According to other scholars (Sansoni and Gavaldo 1995) – followers of Anati's chronology of rock-art in Valcamonica – the human figures in the so-called position of praying (Italian *oranti*; French *orants*) also have to be attributed to this period. I generally prefer to assign these anthropomorphic figures to the Bronze Age (Ferrario 1992; Fossati 1992, 1993a); but here is not the place to discuss this interesting point.

It is more or less accepted that this first phase is preceded by a more ancient moment, perhaps going back to the end of the Palaeolithic (Anati 1974). The figures of this ancient moment, therefore, are very few; all represent animals, including elk and deer. This preliminary phase, called 'Protocamunian', for its great antiquity and for the content, is

---

* This calculation is based on the number of known rocks engraved in Valcamonica and Valtellina (more then 2000). Every year new rocks are discovered with hundreds of engravings never seen before. The problem for Valcamonica and Valtellina rock-art is the absence of an entire published corpus.

in some way related to the style and the chronology of European Ice Age art. Importantly, that Palaeolithic art is today attested also outside the caves, as testified by the recent discoveries of Ice Age art on open-air surfaces in Spain and Portugal (Abreu *et al.* 1995).

The second phase, which corresponds to the full Copper Age (fourth–third millennium BC), is the '3rd A' Camunian style (Figure 5.1). It is characterized by the phenomenon of the stele and menhir, boulders that represent the first anthropomorphic divinities of Alpine people (Casini and Fossati 1994). Even in this period the topographical representations are known among the figures, but the most important depiction is the sun (Figure 5.2), sometimes represented as a man crowned by a solar circle with beams, and often associated with weapons. Two other personages are represented: one is feminine, adorned with numerous jewels; the second is another male divinity, symbolized by a cloak provided with fringes (Figure 5.3). The iconographic repertoire of the boulders is very rich (Figures 5.4 and 5.5).

The third phase of the rock-art of Valtellina and Valcamonica is the '3rd B–C–D' Camunian styles. This is generally datable to the second millennium BC and corresponds to the Bronze Age (De Marinis 1995). The iconographic repertoire is reduced in comparison with the figures of the Copper Age, but is not for this reason less important: numerous weapons (by then no longer associated with divinities), ploughing scenes, ritual

Figure 5.1 The Capitello dei Due Pini (Capital of the Two Pines) at Paspardo (Valcamonica), a beautiful monumental composition of the 3rd A1 style

Figure 5.2 An anthropomorph with a solar crown, a probable representation of the sun god on the Ossimo 8 (Valcamonica) boulder, 3rd A2 style

Figure 5.3 A cloak on the Ossimo 5 (Valcamonica) boulder, 3rd A1 style

Figure 5.4 Cemmo 4 (Valcamonica).
A stele with anthropomorphic gods, necklace,
weapons, deer in the typical 3rd A2 style

Figure 5.5 The three divine personages on the Ossimo 9 (Valcamonica) menhir, 3rd A2 style

scenes formed by praying anthropomorphs, symbols (solar signs and shovels). It is not so clear at present if some topographical figures are to be considered of this phase. There is a lack in the study of superimpositions regarding just these figures. But this is not the opinion of other colleagues (Sansoni and Gavaldo 1995).

In the Final Bronze Age (twelfth–ninth century BC) the first warrior figures appear, a prelude to the immense repertoire of the Iron Age, the first millennium BC (Fossati 1992). This last phase of the prehistoric rock-art of Valcamonica and Valtellina is the '4th style'. From the thematic point of view it is the most interesting and richest (Fossati 1991), a production tied to the initiation rites of the young people of the warrior local aristocracy. Among these figures are recognizable hunting scenes, ritual duels, races and armed dances, buildings, wagons, weapons, musical instruments, agricultural scenes, symbols (foot-prints, cup-marks, swastikas, stars, shovels), divinities and – not least – topographical representations. The best known of these later maps is the 'Bedolina map' (Turconi 1998).

In Valtellina the prehistoric rock-art tradition stopped earlier than in Valcamonica, probably during the sixth century BC. The motives for this cessation are still unknown (Fossati 1995). In Valcamonica the rupestrian tradition continued until the arrival of the Romans, who reached the area in 16 BC: a legion (about 6000 soldiers), under the direc-tion of the consul Publio Silio Nerva, subjected Triumplini, Camunni and Vennonetes (respectively the inhabitants of Valtrompia, Valcamonica and Valtellina) in a single swift military campaign, as is attested by the registration of these three names in the *Tropaeum Alpium*, the monument constructed by the Emperor Augustus in AD 6–7 at La Turbie (France) (Rossi 1987). The interruption of the rupestrian tradition in Valcamonica is perhaps due to the assumption of Roman culture during the second part of the first century AD (the Flavian Age); the diminution of authority of the social classes that held the power until those days; and the economic, cultural and religious attraction caused by the Roman settlements, in particular the new colony Civitas Camunnorum. These reduced and finally destroyed the power of the social aristocratic classes whose traditional themes had constituted, until then, the iconographic patrimony of the rock-engravings (Fossati 1991).

With the arrival of Christianity, artists came back to the rocky areas that were newly engraved with themes taken from the Christian symbols: crosses, keys, shears, Solomon's knots (a cabalistic design of knot without end to the cords), warriors, castles and – obviously – dates and inscriptions. This art has nothing to do with that prehistoric art of the periods previously delineated. At the moment it is not possible to date this phase (called 'Postcamunian') in a better way, since there still do not exist sufficiently deep studies (Sansoni 1993). In the medieval (or more recent) engravings there are virtually no topographical representations, in the sense of the schematic figures that we have considered as maps. There is only one case in which it is possible to mention a topographic representation: at Rock 1 at In Valle, Paspardo, a castle or a tower has been engraved on a small rock just in front of the real castle of Cimbergo (twelfth century AD).

The maps: a short history of research

The existence of topographical representations in the Valcamonica rock-art tradition was first reported in the 1930s by Raffaello Battaglia, an archaeologist of the Italian state organization. During the first International Congress of Prehistoric and Protohistoric Sciences held in 1932 in London, he mentioned the discovery of the Bedolina map (in Italian 'La mappa di Bedolina'). This composite design is described by Battaglia as 'careful representations of fields and fences', and he dates it to the Iron Age (Battaglia 1934). This was in concordance with his general dating of the phenomenon of rock-art. In 1954 the same scholar, with Ornella Acanfora, published the boulder Borno 1 with the oldest topographical representations that are known. The date proposed for these engravings today is the second half of the fourth millennium BC; these pioneer researchers still dated the rock-art to the Iron Age. At this important but still early stage of research the scholars were usually more interested in publishing figures of animals, warriors or instruments than 'less figurative art', like the topographics.

Another scholar active in the 1950s, Giovanni Leonardi, published the topographical figures discovered by him on a rock in a site called 'Saint Rocco bridge', a rocky surface that emerges directly from the River Oglio (Leonardi 1950). Leonardi also insisted that these figures should be dated to the Iron Age.

The first attempt to establish a more complex and acceptable chronology was made by Emmanuel Anati, who during the 1960s and 1970s divided the Valcamonica rock-art into several phases (Anati 1982). The topographical representations were positioned between the Neolithic and the Bronze Age. The Bedolina map was dated to the middle Bronze Age; the composition on the Borno 1 boulder was attributed to the second phase of his chronology, that is, to the Neolithic (Anati 1966).

In recent years these pictures have again received interest due to new discoveries (Sansoni and Gavaldo 1995; Arcà et al. 1996; Priuli 1997). In Valcamonica they are found at: Piancamuno, Darfo Boario Terme, the high plateau of Borno-Ossimo, Nadro, Cimbergo, Paspardo, Capo di Ponte, Sellero and Sonico. In Valtellina the number of discoveries is increasing; at the moment we know such pictures from Grosio, Grosotto and Teglio (Arcà et al. 1995).

The Valcamonica–Valtellina Copper Age monuments are erratic monoliths which have been divided into: stelae or statue-stelae; boulders; menhirs or statue-menhirs; and immovable landslide blocks (monumental compositions). If the monolith has the shape of a slab, sometimes artificially bevelled, the monument is called 'stele' or statue-stele: this is the prehistoric monument close to what we could call today an anthropomorphic statue. But this is a quite rare phenomenon in the Valcamonica–Valtellina group. Most of the monoliths are just simple erratic boulders, without any bevelling or artificial shaping; this is why we usually call them 'boulders'. Sometimes the engravers have chosen ogival or phallic boulders, naturally shaped; for these we can use the term 'menhir'. Then we have a few instances of immovable boulders; the best examples are the Cemmo Boulders ('I Massi di Cemmo'), stones fallen due to a landslide in the past and utilized by the engravers as available surfaces. It is sometimes difficult to distinguish between the shape of stelae, boulders and menhirs, so this is why the term most used in referencing is that of boulder or statue-menhir (see Casini (ed.) 1994: 31, 59).

Topographic representations: typology and chronology

Topographic representations in the rock-art of the Alps have a strikingly standardized graphic form. The main types occurring in Valcamonica and Valtellina, starting with the oldest, are:

- *Spots* (in Italian *macchie* or *maculae*), sub-rectangular pecked areas which appear both on flat rocks and on boulders.

- *Double rectangles* (in Italian *doppi rettangoli*), which sometimes appear as only simple rectangles. These figures have mostly been drawn in outline by a contour line. Sometimes there is a dot in the centre; occasionally the figure can have a simple quadrangular shape (as e.g. in Grosio, Dosso Giroldo), or it may be completely pecked.
- *Groups of dots*, or lengthened dots (in Italian *gruppi di punti o maccheroni*), also called 'macaroni'.
- *Oval shapes* (in Italian *mappe ovali*), sometimes associated with other forms, such as spots and rectangles, often connected with lines.
- '*Mushrooms*' (in Italian *mappe a fungo*), a distinctive composition combining different motifs: double rectangles, oval shapes, rectangles, dots.
- '*Bandolier*' or shoulder-belt figure (in Italian *bandoliera*), a circular map with one or double contour lines. Two or more semicircular lines, sometimes cut in the middle, occur inside or outside the circle. It is the strangest figure in the repertoire of the topographical representations.

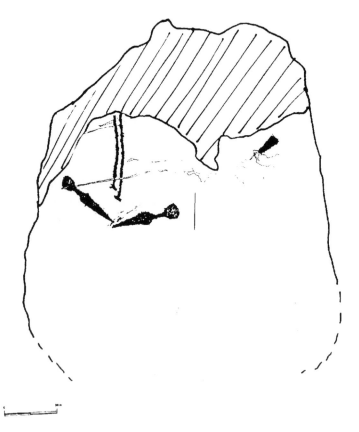

Figure 5.6 The stele Borno 5 (Valcamonica) with two early Bronze Age daggers and two handles of halberds or axes, 3rd A3 style. Scale: width of stone is 0.55m.

All these types appear in the Copper Age monuments – boulders, stelae and menhirs – in Valcamonica. In Valtellina only the 'bandolier' is engraved on the stelae, and the other types occur on flat rocks.

The Bedolina map is more recent, belonging to the Iron Age (Turconi 1998), so it is not discussed here.

The 'spots' are often covered by figures of later periods (Figure 5.6), for instance by the Remedello type of dagger. This is the case on the Borno 1 boulder, where three daggers overlap two spots. This Remedello dagger is very important for dating, as its distinctive form is well dated by its occurrence in tombs of a famous Copper Age cemetery at Remedello, a small town in the province of Brescia, which gives the Remedello Culture its name. The same weapon is frequently engraved on the menhirs and stelae of the Copper Age (Arcà and Fossati 1995; Pedrotti 1993; De Marinis 1996) and also in some rock-shelters, as in the important composition of Les Oullas, Ubaye Valley (France)

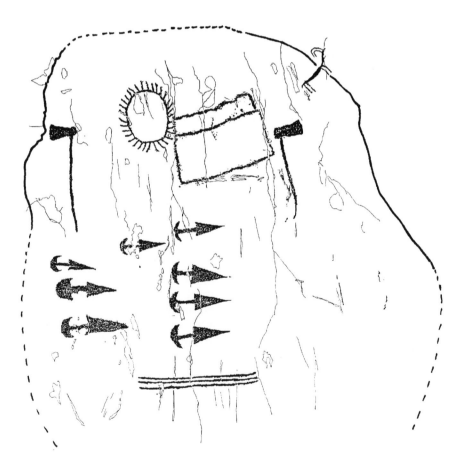

Figure 5.7 The boulder Bagnolo 2 (Valcamonica) with double rectangle superimposed by a solar disc, 3rd A1 style. Scale: daggers are approx. 0.15m–0.18m in length

(Muller *et al.* 1991). It gives a firm 'peg' for the chronology of the megalithic art of Valcamonica and Valtellina (Casini (ed.) 1994). The radiocarbon dates of the Remedello tombs with daggers give it an age of *c.* 2900–2500 BC (the 'Remedello 2' period; De Marinis 1998). The topographical representations superimposed by figures depicting this weapon will be older than this period, which marks the end of the Neolithic and the beginning of the Copper Age in the north Italian archaeological chronology (Fossati 1994). The figures are found on several rocks in Valcamonica, for instance at Vite (Paspardo) (Arcà 1995), and on the Borno 1 boulder (Frontini 1994).

The spots are sometimes superimposed by the double rectangle. The double rectangle on the boulder Bagnolo 2 is superimposed by a solar disk (Figure 5.7) attributed to the Copper Age (3rd A1, Remedello 2 period). So this subject appeared before Remedello 2 (probably around the first half of the fourth millennium BC) in the 'Remedello 1' period' (*c.* 3300–2900 BC; De Marinis 1998). Sometimes this type of figure has the shape of a grill, as on Rock 13 at Vite, Paspardo (Arcà 1992).

The groups of dots, or lengthened dots and oval shapes, are often associated with the double rectangle to form the strange composite figures that we have called 'mushrooms'; these appear on large surfaces and on boulders. By Rock 36 at Vite, Paspardo, where such a figure is present, has been discovered a votive hoard containing a polished stone axe, flint-stones and pottery shards of White Ware type (Fossati 1997). If the hoard is connected with rock-art – as it seems to be – this fact is important for the chronology of the imagery, besides the interpretation of the maps.

The 'bandolier' appears usually on the Copper Age monuments: its association with the figures of the different phases of the Copper Age – the Remedello dagger (Figures 5.8 and 5.9), or the Villafranca halberds dated to the Bell Beaker phase of the Copper Age (*c.* 2500–2200 BC) – puts this type also with the ancient topographical figures belonging to the Copper Age. These figures appear not only on boulders and stelae, but also on flat rocks, as on Vite Rocks 20 or 21, often surrounding the usual double rectangles (Fossati 1994).

Boulders, stelae and menhirs

All these types of topographic representations appear in the Copper Age monuments.

The Valcamonica–Valtellina monuments are stelae in the form of slabs, boulders and menhirs, and of immovable landslide blocks: these are the 'monumental compositions'. Their being anthropomorphic is suggested by the distribution of the engravings, and sometimes by the bevelling of the upper part, to trace the shoulders schematically. The representation of a single personage is rare. In the majority of cases it appears to be a composition of different figures of deep symbolic value. The monuments of this Valcamonica–Valtellina group are distinctive in comparison with monuments of the other Alpine groups of stelae, such as the Lunigiana (De Marinis 1996), the Aosta–Sion (Gallay 1996) and the Trentino–Alto Adige (Pedrotti 1993) monuments. And the Valcamonica–Valtellina group shows a lack of unity in the process of engraving: new figures are added which complete or which efface the previous, a phenomenon that happens through a few centuries or a few decades.

In the Camunian rock-art chronology, this period – as already said – is '3rd A' (De Marinis 1994). It generally corresponds to the Copper Age, within which we can distinguish three different periods of carvings. A first phase, 3rd A1, is characterized by

Figure 5.8 The stele Borno 6 (Valcamonica) with the represention of the bandolier including five Remedello daggers, 3rd A style

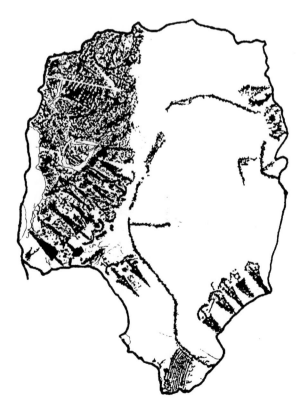

Figure 5.9 Drawing of the stele Borno 6 (Valcamonica). Scale: daggers measure approx. 0.10–0.15m in length

symbolic figures. A second phase, 3rd A2, is marked by anthropomorphic figures. A last phase, 3rd A3, is very short; it has to be attributed, with every probability, to the early Bronze Age (end of third millennium BC).

The iconographic repertoire of the most ancient phase, the 3rd A1 style, is expressed by the Remedello dagger and by all those figures associated with this weapon, which include other weapons (axes and halberds of metal or stone), and a few symbolic figures. The weapons are always associated with the figure of the sun, an aspect that symbolizes the emergence of a social hierarchy; an élite probably saw itself as descendants of the divinities. Even in the statue-stelae of the other Alpine groups, the association between the sun and the weapons refers to male personages who are always indicated by the dagger (Gallay 1996). The double-spiral pendant reproduces a copper jewel symbolically connected with the female figure. A very rich documentation shows the use of this jewel, whose origin is to be found in the Carpathian Basin; there in the Neolithic it is found in the ceramic figurines of the Mother Goddess, as an element of a ceremonial and status dress, a typical motif in representing a goddess (Casini 1994).

The third important symbol is a rectangle filled with vertical lines or a chessboard-like formation; it is adorned, on its vertical sides, with fringes. This motif is often associated with animals: compositions of stags with does (harem) are usually placed below; or a series of wild dogs and chamois are disposed vertically by the sides (Fossati 1993b). The gender association of this symbol is probably masculine; in the anthropomorphic phase (style 3rd A2), it is represented by a phallic anthropomorph associated with the other two gods. The fringes suggest an interpretation of the object as a cloak; on statue-stelae of the Trentino–Alto Adige region a similar motif is represented on the shoulders of the personages (Pedrotti 1993). In this element it is possible to recognize a particularly significant attribute of a god, a characteristic portion that represents him as a *pars pro toto*.

These three main symbols recur singly or together on the same stone, as if this can represent a sort of statue of one single divinity, or of two or three gods (Casini and Fossati 1994).

The iconographic repertoire of the phase 3rd A2 it is not as wide as the previous period. The symbols now become anthropomorphic; but some artefacts – the weapons – remain. These are important for chronology: in particular the Ciempozuelos type of dagger and the Villafranca type of halberd are now engraved, typical weapons of the Bell Beaker period (c. 2500–2200 BC; De Marinis 1994). Animals and human figures are now represented with more realism in a naturalistic way. In general we see a cult to a divine triad (Casini and Fossati 1994).

The 3rd A3 phase shows only anthropomorphic figures, who dance around in circles, and daggers of the Early Bronze Age (De Marinis 1994).

This new interpretation is much changed from previous analysis (Battaglia and Acanfora 1954; Anati 1982). It contradicts Anati's hypothesis of the division into three parts of the stelae and a possible connection to Indo-European ideology and religious ideas (Anati 1977; Gimbutas 1980). The prehistoric people of Valcamonica–Valtellina were surely pre-Indo-European; we know their language from the engraved inscriptions of the following Iron Age, which are in the 'north-Etruscan alphabet', a non-Indo-European language. The monuments of the Valcamonica and Valtellina group must be related to the phenomenon of the other European statue-menhirs, connected to the megalithic tradition of western Europe (Casini and Fossati 1994; De Marinis 1994; Barfield 1996).

Figure 5.10 The stele Vangione 2 (Valtellina) with the representation of the bandolier map, 3rd AI style

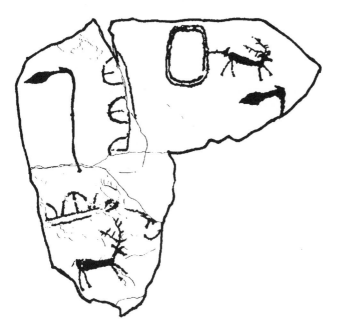

Figure 5.11 Drawing of the stele Vangione 2 (Valcamonica). Scale: red deer measure between 0.20m in length

Drawing: S. Casini and P. Frontini

The maps engraved on the statue-menhirs

On these monuments appear also the topographic representations: the spot type is at the very beginning of the phase (Borno 1), the 3rd A1 (probably during Remedello 1); even the double rectangles start in this first phase, and continue in Remedello 2 (as in Bagnolo 1, and again in 3rd A1). The 'bandolier' type occurs also in the Bell Beaker period (3rd A2), as in the Vangione 1 stele from Valtellina (Poggiani Keller 1989).

At the moment we know topographical representations on four stelae from Valtellina and on five monuments from Valcamonica. In Valtellina the only type represented is the 'bandolier', while in Valcamonica almost all the types are known.

In Valtellina, the bandolier map is engraved on the fragmented stele Valgella 3 and on the stelae Vangione 1, 2 (Figures 5.10 and 5.11) and 3. In Valcamonica this motif is present on the stelae Borno 1 and 6, and on the Ossimo 3 fragment. The composite map (spots, double rectangle, etc.) is present on the Borno 1 and Ossimo 8 menhirs. A single double rectangle is engraved on the Bagnolo 1 boulder (Fossati 1994).

The bandolier is associated with weapons both of the Remedello period and of the Bell Beaker phase. At Valgella 3, Vangione 2 and 3, Borno 1 and 6, and probably Ossimo 3 the bandolier map includes halberds of the laurel-leaf type and/or Remedello daggers. On the Valgella 1 stele the bandolier includes a laurel-leaf-type halberd; it is also associated with a group of three halberds of the Villafranca type (Bell Beaker period). Sometimes animals (deer and ibex) are engraved outside the bandolier, at Borno 1 or on Vangione 1 and 2; in one case the animals are inside, at Ossimo 3.

Maps are also present on the boulders that we can call 'pre-menhirs'. They are big, erratic stones, which have only been studied in recent times; a careful and deeper investigation is deserved by their importance. Patrizia Frontini, in publishing the Borno 1 menhir, had occasion to investigate in a very accurate way the different phases of the engravings (Frontini 1994). While drawing the engravings of the boulder (which we realized together), we noticed that at some special points of the surface (especially on the junctions between the different faces) were evident the marks of ropes utilized to raise the boulder (Figure 5.12). In a few places they overlap the topographic representations, and show that the shifting of the monument was done after the first engraving phase. In her first report (1994) Frontini proposed that the boulder – before it became a real menhir – was lying down. At that time its face B (the one with the maps, made before the Remedello 2 engravings phase) was the only surface engraved; the figures had the form suggested in Figure 5.13. In a following period the boulder was erected to show the other faces, etched with the motifs that we know.

These signs of ropes are not present on boulders recently discovered at Piacamuno (Priuli 1997), Lozio and Ossimo (these last not yet published). So these boulders were not erected in the places where the glacier abandoned them. On their surfaces the first engravers made the topographical representations. Few boulders were reused; at the present stage of research, we know of Ossimo 8 (Figure 5.14) and Bagnolo 1. The type of rock may be important to understanding why these stones were chosen to be engraved. These boulders are always of sandstone. On the Borno–Ossimo *altipiano* (high plateau), where they are found, there is no other sandstone available. There the bedrock is limestone, a type of rock which has usually not been engraved. So the sense in engraving these boulders can have the same meaning as the figures realized on bedrock in the area – around Capo di Ponte, Paspardo and Pià d'Ort – where that bedrock is sandstone. But

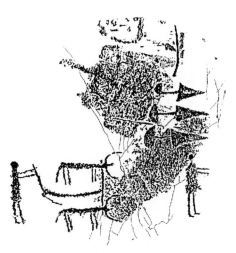

Figure 5.12 Maps superimposed by traces of ropes, Remedello daggers and ploughing scene, Borno I (Valcamonica)

Drawing: A. Fossati and P. Frontini

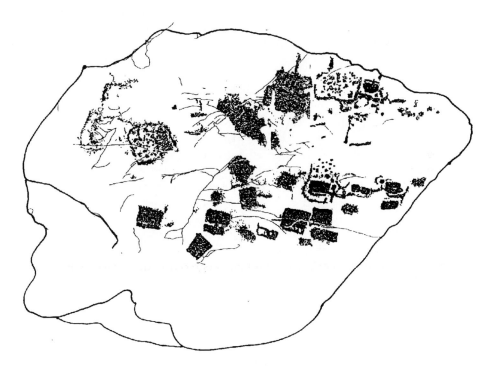

Figure 5.13 How the Borno I boulder could appear before the first shifting of the full Copper Age phases

Figure 5.14 Drawing of the Ossimo 8 boulder (Valcamonica) showing the superimpositions between the figures of the 3rd A2 with the maps

there is maybe little difference in the public visibility of the maps engraved. A boulder is something emerging from a meadow, even if it is not erected as a menhir. A rock usually is positioned in a place where other rocks are available, and sometimes in an area (for instance Vite or Pià d'Ort) which has nothing of the meadow about it. These are steep-sloped and rocky places, sometimes very difficult to reach; they are sites where it is not possible to cultivate anything apart from grapevines or chestnut trees – plants during the Copper Age that were not yet cultivated. The places where the boulders are found, on the contrary, are easy to reach and very good for cultivation or for placing a settlement. So there are some differences.

But why did the artists of the full Copper Age decide to re-engrave these boulders? A first answer can come from the simple remark that in the following periods the engravers usually reused rocks already engraved in previous periods. Probably this was something that could give strength to their ritual acts: this can be called the 'importance of the place'. A second answer can be in the meaning of the maps itself, which was recognized by the Eneolithic artists. If the Copper Age compositions are visions of the world, maybe of a religious world, the maps can represent a cosmological territory, a sort of mythical ancient world, maybe etched on the stone by the ancestors or by the spirits themselves, in the same way as the Australian Aborigines believe for some rock-art figures of their own tradition.* A third idea could link the maps to the economy of the Copper Age that is represented in the compositions: agriculture and farming (the ploughing scenes), breeding (there are representations of goats, pigs and bovids), metallurgy (the weapons representations). Moreover, at the Vite site, a special place for the maps (Arcà 1995), there are copper mines in the open air, on the same rocks as the topographic representations.

Can these maps be a sort of real or mythical land register? It is difficult to say. Battaglia (1934) saw in these prehistoric maps the 'careful representations of fields and fences'. At the present stage of research, we have discovered no Copper Age sites in the area of Valcamonica and Valtellina. How can we recognize on the land traces of these prehistoric descriptions? We have in the land today features that sometimes gives us suggestions of what an ancient engraver could see and represent. The fences for animals, the sheep- or goat-folds (baréch in the contemporary Camunian dialect), are very similar to the oval topographical representations. A suggestion for the double rectangle, if it is not a house, may be that it represents a field where the grass has been cut to produce hay. The grass collected in stacks and left on the field to dry – in a practice still continuing in Valcamonica and Valtellina today – has been associated with the groups of dots. For the 'macaroni', or long dots, there are suggestions in the system of hay-drying still in use in the Austrian Alps. In general, the best comparison is possible where the farmers still use techniques of working the land that may be very similar to the prehistoric ones: hand-cutting the grass, collecting it manually into stacks or sheaves. Other scholars, such as Andrea Arcà, have recently suggested that instead of the grass the topographical representations show the cultivation of corn or rye (Arcà 1999). Both interpretations are linked to farm and agricultural productions, and Arcà suggests many interesting interpretations and similarities in the standardized and distinctive graphic forms used. I will focus on the bandolier that seems to be most represented in the stelae, and was engraved in all the 3rd A phases.

* See, for instance, as a comparison the figures of Bula's cult in Gunn (1992).

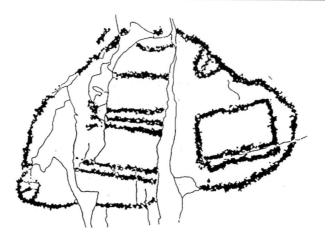

Figure 5.15 Bandolier map on Vite Rock 21, Paspardo (Valcamonica)

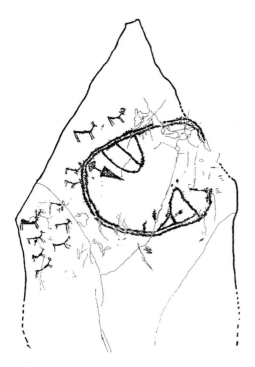

Figure 5.16 The bandolier map on the Borno 1
boulder (Valcamonica)

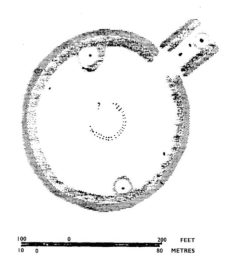

Figure 5.17 The first phases of Stonehenge,
England

From Champion *et al.* (1984)

This bandolier motif (Figures 5.15 and 5.16) has already been compared by Patrizia Frontini (1994) to a plan of a megalithic structure, with ritual or astronomical meaning, as in the first phases of Stonehenge (end of the fourth millennium BC: Cleal *et al*. 1995; Figure 5.17), or with a more practical sense, like Jarlshof in Scotland (a site which began to be used in the first half of the third millennium BC; Ritchie 1988). Andrea Arcà (1999), instead, has underlined a similarity of the bandolier to the fort of Los Millares (Figure 5.18) and other Copper Age sites of the Iberian Peninsula. Ritual or practical, it maybe was a sort of fence, as today we still see in some mountain villages. Probably the semi-circles represent little towers or something else that we do not understand. As I have pointed out (Fossati 1994), this element is not only found in Valcamonica, but also in the megalithic art of Brittany and in the English Channel (Dissignac, Le Dehus, Channel Islands; Joussaume 1985; Figure 5.19), in the rock-engravings of Mont Bego (Lumley *et al*. 1995), and in some rock-paintings in southern Italy, attributed by Paolo Graziosi (1980) to the late Neolithic period.

Even the other types of Valcamonica–Valtellina maps find comparison in the Mont Bego area, showing many and surprising similarities. The Valcamonica 'mushroom' is well known also in Fontanalba, where it is associated with dots, squares, 'macaronies', spots and so on. If the chronology appears the same there, as the typology is, we must answer a few questions. Why have these figures been engraved, and why are they so similar when so far apart? If sometimes the engravers marked on the rock the land that they were seeing, it is quite possible that these figures were only imaginary, maybe a cosmological representation, as are some huts engraved during the Iron Age (Tognoni 1992).

We must underline the importance of the presence of the maps in the engraved menhirs, boulders and stelae. Francesco Fedele (1995; Fedele and Fossati 1996), who recently unearthed two sites in Valcamonica with stelae–menhirs, has put forward the hypothesis that these monuments not only have a sacral value, but that they 'stand to make a new organization of the territory' – an idea already expressed by Colin Renfrew (1976). The topographical representations could be, in this sense, a sign of a new organization of the land, with ritual functions. Their use could also be practical, as a border or a property mark.

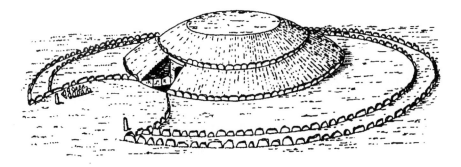

Figure 5.18 The fortress of Los Millares, Spain

From Joussaume (1985)

Figure 5.19 Cross-belt like figure from Porto Badisco, Italy
From Graziosi (1980)

Note

This chapter develops some of the ideas produced in a paper presented at the Vitark – International Rock Art Seminar: 'Rock Art in Landscapes – Landscapes in Rock Art', held in September 1998 at the Vitenskapmuseet of Trondheim, Norway, the proceedings of which are in Sognnes (2000).

Acknowledgements

Andrea Arcà (Cooperativa Archeologica Le Orme dell'Uomo, Cerveno); Stefania Casini (Civico Museo Archeologico, Bergamo); Giacomo Camuri and Giannetta Musitelli (Cooperativa Archeologica Le Orme dell'Uomo, Cerveno); Raffaele De Marinis (Università degli Studi, Milano); Francesco Fedele (Università degli Studi 'Federico II', Napoli); Patrizia Frontini (Civiche Raccolte Archeologiche, Milano); Elena Marchi, Emanuela Tognoni (Cooperativa Archeologica Le Orme dell'Uomo, Cerveno).

Photographs and drawings are by A. Fossati and/or the Cooperativa Archeologica Le Orme dell'Uomo, unless otherwise stated.

References

Abreu, M.S. De, A. Arcà and A. Fossati. 1995. As gravuras nao saben nadar! Le incisioni non sanno nuotare . . ., *Archeologia Viva* 53(anno 14): 28–36.

Anati, E. 1966. *Il Masso di Borno*. Breno: Centro Camuno di Studi Preistorici. Pubblicazione del Centro 2.

Anati, E. 1974. Lo stile sub-naturalistico Camuno e l'origine dell'arte rupestre alpina, *Bollettino del Centro Camuno di Studi Preistorici* 11: 59–84.

Anati, E. 1976. *Evolution and style in Camunian rock art*. Capo di Ponte (BS): Edizioni del Centro. Archivi 6.

Anati, E. 1977. Origine e significato storico-religioso delle statue-stele, *Bollettino del Centro Camuno di Studi Preistorici* 16: 45–56.

Anati, E. 1982. *I Camuni: alle radici della civiltà europea*. Milano: Jaca Book.

Arcà, A. 1992. La roccia 13 di Vite, Paspardo: elementi per un archivio di archeologia rupestre, *Appunti* 19: 25–31.

Arcà, A. 1995. Vite, incisioni topografiche, prima fase dell'arte rupestre camuna, *Notizie Archeologiche Bergomensi* 2: 91–98.

Arcà, A. 1999. Fields and settlements in topographic engravings of the Copper Age in Valcamonica and Mt Bego rock art, in Philippe Della Casa (ed.), *Prehistoric Alpine environment, society and economy: papers of the international colloquium PAESE '97 in Zurich*: 71–79. Bonn. Universitätforschungen zur prähistorischen Archäologie 55.

Arcà, A., C. Ferrario, A. Fossati and G. Ruggiero. 1996. Paspardo (BS), località Val de Plaha: ricerche nell'area Vite-Deria, *Notiziario della Soprintendenza Archeologica della Lombardia (NSAL)* (1994): 46–47. Milano: Soprintendenza Archeologica della Lombardia.

Arcà, A. and A. Fossati. 1995. *Sui sentieri dell'arte rupestre: le rocce incise delle Alpi. Storia, ricerche, escursioni*. Torino: CDA editions.

Arcá, A., A. Fossati, E. Marchi and E. Tononi. 1995. *Rupe Magna, la roccia incisa più grande delle Alpi*. Sondrio: Ministero dei Beni Culturali e Ambientali, Soprintendenza Archeologica della Lombardi, Consorzio per il Parco delle Incisioni Rupestri di Grosio. Quaderni del Parco 1.

Barfield, L.H. 1996. The context of statue-menhirs, *Notizie Archeologiche Bergomensi* 3: 11–20.

Battaglia, R. 1934. Ricerche etnografiche sui petroglifi della cerchia alpina, *Studi etruschi* 8: 11–48.

Battaglia, R. and O. Acanfora. 1954. Il Masso inciso di Borno in Valcamonica, *Bullettino di Paletnologia Italiana* (NS)9 (64): 225–255.

Casini, S. 1994. I pendagli a doppia spirale, in S. Casini (ed.), *Le pietre degli dei: menhir e stele dell'Età del Rame in Valcamonica e Valtellina*: 97–108. Bergamo: Centro Culturale Nicolò Rezzara.

Casini, S. (ed.) 1994. *Le pietre degli dei: menhir e stele dell'Età del Rame in Valcamonica et Valtellina*. Bergamo: Centro Culturale Nicolò Rezzara.

Casini, S. and A. Fossati. 1994. Le stele e i massi incisi della Valcamonica e della Valtellina nell'ambito dell'arco alpino, in S. Casini (ed.), *Le pietre degli dei: menhir e stele dell'Età del Rame in Valcamonica e Valtellina*: 59–68. Bergamo: Centro Culturale Nicolò Rezzara.

Champion, T., C. Gamble, S. Shennan and A. Whittle. 1984. *Prehistoric Europe*. London: Academic Press.

Cleal, R.M.J., K.E. Walker and R. Montague. 1995. *Stonehenge in its landscape: twentieth-century excavations*. London: English Heritage. Archaeological Report 10.

De Marinis, R.C. 1988. Le popolazioni alpine di stirpe retica, in G. Pugliese Carratelli (ed.), *Italia omnium terrarum alumna: la civilta dei Veneti, Reti, Liguri, Celti, Piceni, Umbri, Latini, Campani e Iapigi*: 101–155. Milano: Libri Scheiwiller.

De Marinis, R.C. 1994. La datazione dello stile IIIA, in S. Casini (ed.), *Le pietre degli dei: menhir e stele dell'Età del Rame in Valcamonica e Valtellina*: 69–87. Bergamo: Centro Culturale Nicolò Rezzara.

De Marinis, R.C. 1995. Problèmes de chronologie de l'art rupestre du Valcamonica, *Notizie Archeologiche Bergomensi* 2: 99–120.

De Marinis, R.C. 1996. Le statue-stele della Lunigiana, *Notizie Archeologiche Bergomensi* 3: 195–212.

De Marinis, R.C. 1998. The Eneolithic cemetery of Remedello Sotto (BS) and the relative and absolute chronology of the Copper Age in northern Italy, *Notizie Archeologiche Bergomensi* 5: 33–51.

Fedele, F. 1995. Il contesto rituale delle stele calcolitiche camuno-valtellinesi: gli scavi di Ossimo (Valcamonica), *Notizie Archeologiche Bergomensi* 2: 37–66.

Fedele, F. and A. Fossati. 1996. Centro cultuale calcolitico dell'Anvoia a Ossimo (Valcamonica): scavi 1988–95, *Notizie Archeologiche Bergomensi* 3: 251–257.

Ferrario, C. 1992. Le figure di oranti schematici nell'arte rupestre della Valcamonica, *Appunti* 19: 41–44.

Fossati, A. 1991. L'età del Ferro nelle incisioni rupestri della Valcamonica, in R. La Guardia (ed.), *Immagini di una aristocrazia dell'età del ferro nell'arte rupestre camuna: contributi in occasione della mostra Castello Sforzesco Aprile 1991–Marzo 1992, Milano*: 11–71. Milano: Comune di Milano, Settore Cultura e Spettacolo, Raccolte Archeologiche e Numismatiche.

Fossati, A. 1992. Alcune rappresentazioni di 'oranti' schematici armati del Bronzo Finale nell'arte rupestre della Valcamonica, *Appunti* 19: 45–50.

Fossati, A. 1993a. *Il mondo dei Camuni: l'arte rupestre della Valcamonica*. Cerveno: Edizione della Cooperativa Archaeologica Le Orme dell'Uomo. Valcamonica Preistorica 4.

Fossati, A. 1993b. Deer in European rock art, in G. Camuri, A. Fossati and Y. Mathpal (eds), *Deer in rock art of India and Europe*: 75–117. New Delhi: Indira Gandhi National Centre for the Art. Rock Art series 2.

Fossati, A. 1994. Le rappresentazioni topografiche, in S. Casini (ed.), *Le pietre degli dei: menhir e stele dell'Età del Rame in Valcamonica e Valtellina*: 89–91. Bergamo: Centro Culturale Nicolò Rezzara.

Fossati, A. 1995. Cronologia ed interpretazione, in A. Arcá, A., A. Fossati, E. Marchi and E. Tononi, *Rupe Magna, la roccia incisa più grande delle Alpi*: 99–109. Sondrio: Ministero dei Beni Culturali e Ambientali, Soprintendenza Archeologica della Lombardi, Consorzio per il Parco delle Incisioni Rupestri di Grosio. Quaderni del Parco 1.

Fossati, A. 1997. Un deposito votivo presso la roccia istoriata n°36 di Vite-Deria, loc. Val de Plaha, Paspardo (BS-Valcamonica), *Bulletin d'Études Préhistoriques et Archéologiques Alpines* 5–6: 151–156.

Frontini, P. 1994. Borno 1, in S. Casini (ed.), *Le pietre degli dei: menhir e stele dell'Età del Rame in Valcamonica e Valtellina*: 192–197. Bergamo: Centro Culturale Nicolò Rezzara.

Gallay, A. 1996. Les stèles anthropomorphes du site mégalitique du Petit-Chasseur à Sion (Valais, Suisse), *Notizie Archeologiche Bergomensi* 5: 167–194.

Gimbutas, M. 1980. The Kurgan Wave 2 (c. 3400–3200 BC) into Europe and the following transformation of culture, *Journal of Indo-European Studies* 8: 273–315.

Graziosi, P. 1980. *Le pitture preistoriche della grotta di Porto Badisco*. Firenze: Giunti Martello.

Gunn, R.G. 1992. Bulajang – a reappraisal of the archaeology of an Aboriginal religious cult, in J. McDonald and I.P. Haskovec (eds), *State of the art: regional rock art studies in Australia and Melanesia*: 174–194. Melbourne: Australian Rock Art Research Association. Occasional Publication 6.

Immagini dalla preistoria: incisioni e pitture ripestri: nuovi messaggi dalle rocce delle Alpi Occidentali. Catalogo della mostra in occasione della XXXII Riunione Scientifica dell'Istituto Italiano di Preistoria e Protostoria. Boves: Corall Edizioni.

Joussaume, R. 1985. *Des Dolmens pour les morts*. Paris: Hachette.

Laeng, G. 1914. Cemmo (Capo di Ponte), in *Guida d'Italia del Touring Club Italiano, Piemonte, Lombardia e Canton Ticino*: 595. Milano.

Leonardi P. 1950. Nuove serie di petroglifi della Val Camonica, *Annali dell'Università di Ferrara* 10: 3–20.

Lumley, Henry de, *et al.* 1995. *Le Grandiose et le sacré: gravures rupestres protohistoriques et historiques de la région du Mont Bego*. Aix-en-Provence: Edisud.

Marro, G. 1930. La nuova scoperta di incisioni preistoriche in Valcamonica (nota prima), *Atti della Reale Accademia delle Scienze di Torino* 65: 1–43.

Muller, A., M. Jorda and J.M. Gassend. 1991. Les gravures préhistoriques de la vallée de l'Ubaye (environ du lac du Longet) et les modalités du peuplement de la zone intra-alpine, in *Le Mont Bego, une montagne sacré de l'Age du Bronze, préactes du Colloque*, 1: 155–161. Paris: Laboratoire de Préhistoire du Musée Nationale d'Histoire Naturelle.

Pace, D. 1968. Vestigia di culto arcaico su rupi del territorio grosino, *Bollettino della Società Storica Valtellinese* 21: 14–30.

Pedrotti, A. 1993. *Uomini di pietra: i ritrovamenti di Arco ed il fenomeno delle statue stele nell'arco alpino.* Trento: Provincia Autonoma di Trento.

Poggiani Keller, R. 1989. *Le stele dell'età del Rame*, in R. Poggiani Keller (ed.), *Valtellina e Mondo Alpino nella Preistoria*: 40–46. Modena: Edizioni Panini.

Priuli, A. 1997. Nuovi siti con incisioni rupestri in Valle Camonica, *Tracce* 9: 70–71. www.rupestre.net. Special issue for the 2nd International Congress of Rupestrian Archaeology. Europe Alps, Valcamonica.

Renfrew, A. Colin. 1976. Megaliths, territories and populations, in S. De Laet (ed.), *Acculturation and continuity in Atlantic Europe*: 198–220. Bruges: De Tempel. IV Colloque Atlantique, 1975.

Ritchie, A. 1988. Jarlshof, in *Scotland BC: an introduction to the prehistoric houses, tombs, ceremonial monuments and fortifications in the care of the Secretary of State for Scotland*: 16–23. Edinburgh: Historic Buildings and Monuments, Scottish Development Department.

Rossi, F. 1987. *La Valcamonica Romana, ricerche e studi*. Brescia: Edizioni del Moretto.

Sansoni, U. 1993. Medioevo sulla roccia, *Archeologia Viva* 40: 32–47.

Sansoni, U. and S. Gavaldo. 1995. *L'arte rupestre del Pià d'Ort: la vicenda di un santuario preistorico alpino*. Capo di Ponte: Edizioni del Centro. Archivi 10.

Sognnes, Kalle (ed.). 2000. *Rock art in landscapes – landscapes in rock art*. Trondheim: University of Trondheim. VITARK: Acta Archaeologica Nidrosiensia 3.

Tognoni, E. 1992. La roccia 57 del Parco Nazionale di Naquane e le rappresentazioni di case nell'arte rupestre della Valcamonica. Doctoral thesis, Università degli Studi di Milano.

Turconi, C. 1998. La mappa di Bedolina nel quadro dell'arte rupestre della Valcamonica, *Notizie Archeologiche Bergomensi* 5: 85–113.

Chapter 6

Alpine imagery, Alpine space, Alpine time; and prehistoric human experience

Michael Frachetti and Christopher Chippindale

> The whole of science is nothing more than a refinement of everyday thinking.
>
> Albert Einstein

Space and time

The contributions to the present volume are concerned with landscape, and therefore with many aspects of the spatial order of rock-art as it is distributed at large and small scales across the face of the earth. But it is a small step from that dimension of space to another archaeological fundamental, the dimension of time. In the Alpine region, as in so many places with rock-art, human experience and use of landscape are shaped by seasonality.

The *altopiani* – high but comparatively level mountain plains situated above the lower, steeper slopes of Alpine valleys – provide good summer pastures, to which the flocks and herds climb in the warm-season transhumance. Equally, they become barren and empty lands in the winter season, when their altitude loses them for several months to the snow. At Mont Bego, highest of the Alpine rock-engraving regions, the sheep, goats and cattle today do not go up to the pastures in the rock-engraving zones until mid-June; snow lies in the gullies and protected places until August; and the animals come off the high mountain in September.

So the spatial order of the human landscape is affected by seasonality, and so, too, is the spatio-temporal order of the rock-engravings. We know that the Bego rock-engravings were made in high summer or early autumn because in spring, early summer, late autumn and winter the mountain's high valleys are in the snow, and the rock surfaces buried. Even in the lower-altitude Alpine regions of rock-art, such as Valcamonica–Valtellina, the rhythm of mountain life directs human presence, up the slopes in summer, down into the valley's protection for the cold months. So there is a first cycle of time, that of the annual seasonal routine, which lies behind which marks are made on which rocks during particular seasons.

Alongside this cyclical time goes a linear sense of time. The Alpine lands, becoming available once more for human settlement as the high glaciation came to an end, were reclaimed as a human environment. The celebrated freeze-dried mummy of the 'Iceman' (Hopfel *et al.* 1992; Spindler 1994, 1995; Barfield 1994), found in 1991 on the high ridge of the Hauslabjoch in the Tyrolean Alps, has been a salutary reminder of how – as early as the Neolithic – a sophisticated technology was in place for even the highest mountain conditions; and some of the Iceman's toolkit, with its hints of folk medicine, evokes a world of abstruse knowledge far removed from the simple efficiencies of functionalist modelling. This will have been a world of spirits and gods, as well as one of a measurable number of degrees of winter cold and wind-chill. Our best chance of a glimpse into that world, and the structured human landscape which it was, is through the rock-art of the Alps, among which an extraordinary element is the statue-stele, the carved and decorated rock made human, quasi-human or para-human in form: the 'stones of the gods' as they were well named in the great 1994 exhibition of them in Bergamo, Italy (Casini 1994a).

A singular and striking feature of the statue-stelae is their change over time, in which one sees an old design recarved, recut or effaced by a new one. Monumental objects in the landscape, some of them portable rocks, some of them carved into rock-fast surfaces which could not have been shifted, stand for the other aspect of the Alpine landscape, that part which was created by human knowledge and memory, rather than imposed by the external forces of the seasons as expressed through altitude, aspect, exposure, slope.

In this study we explore how concepts of time are embedded in the iconography of Chalcolithic (c. 2800–2200 BC) statue-stelae of Valcamonica – located in the Italian Alps. We investigate the idea that cyclical and linear conceptions of time have complementary aspects such as that these 'two times' of the Valcamonica statue-stelae underscore the discourse of the prehistoric Alpine social landscape. This is supported by the contextual relationships that are suggested by the iconography, placing emphasis on various aspects of human interaction in the world and society.

Finding time

There are few phenomena that are more fundamental to the way we construct our perception of the world around us than time. Yet discussions of the nature of time are often seen as so abstract that it is impossible to relate them to questions of why 'we' act and think in the way 'we' do. Yet people do express their concept of time, both actively and subconsciously, through the spatially and temporally organized interactions that pervade daily life (Lakoff and Johnson 1980). But why is it difficult to investigate how time manifests itself in a society's culture?

A society's concept of time is highly related to the dynamics and context of social interaction. These conditions of human existence guide the communication and trans-mission of spatio-temporal concepts and social knowledge. Often this transmission is 'non-discursive' (Giddens 1984), subconsciously present within social mechanisms and symbolic structures of everyday life.

Societies have innumerable ways of conveying time, and their linguistic codes are culturally bound – thus the indexical elements of communication can be considerably obscure to outsiders (e.g. Bohannan 1953; Oyvind 1995; Evans-Pritchard 1940). The pressing question for an archaeologist is: what is the material evidence of these indexed contexts, or of any conceptual expression of time?

Calendars are simple examples of material evidence that directly reflects a notion of time. Other examples are clocks or sundials, which also prove a quantification of a specific temporal framework. Interpretable ancient calendars are fairly rare in the archaeological record, though examples include Mayan and Egyptian. However, there are less obvious traces from prehistory that are equally loaded with temporal information accessible to the archaeologist.

Evidence of prehistoric time-reckoning can be embedded in elements of cultural 'output', such as in artwork – often linking particular symbols with aspects of a society's *genre de vie*. The particular form addressed in this study is prehistoric rock-engraving. In order to discern the implicit concepts of time embedded in prehistoric representations, archaeologists must attempt to understand the temporal constraints that apply to various motifs. There are difficulties with this approach, as arbitrary meaning is often loaded into seemingly simple 'realistic' representations (Chaloupka 1993). Therefore, it is sometimes difficult to discuss the exact meaning of a particular rock panel or image – in terms of time and other 'signified' phenomena.

There are limits to our ability to interpret rock-art – as well as other archaeological evidence. One can look to burial studies for the same interpretative problem. In Neolithic Europe reburial and reuse of shaft graves suggest that groups were reusing ancestral cemeteries (Whittle 1996). However, it is possible that the subsequent burials were unrelated to one another; they simply reused the locations for practical reasons. Recent interpretations can never really *prove* this is not the case, yet misinterpretation is avoided if it can be demonstrated that various elements are 'indexed' to a common context. In this study the same technique is used for interpreting the relationship between temporal contexts. Much as similarities in form and arrangement substantiate interpretations of Neolithic reburial practice, similarities between the unique set of motifs etched into the stelae have indexical characteristics that highlight and expose the way in which time was integrated into everyday life and ritual life in Valcamonica.

Alpine rock-art and Chalcolithic statue-stelae

With these concerns in mind, we address the unique forms of communication inherent to the statue-stelae of north Italy, themselves forming a distinctive element within the rock-art tradition of the broad Alpine region (Arcà and Fossati 1995), dated to the 'Remedellian' Chalcolithic (Anati 1993; De Marinis 1994c; Fossati 1995; Table 6.1; and see Barfield (1971) for a broader archaeological survey of the region).

The major zones of Alpine rock-engraving are Mont Bego in the French Maritime Alps and the adjacent valleys of Valcamonica and Valtellina in Italian Lombardy (Figure 6.1). Valcamonica is a long valley situated north of the city of Brescia, between Lake Iseo and the Austrian border (Anati 1961). It is a model of a high Alpine glaciated valley – straight and steep-sided, with a flat bottom, U-shaped profile, and higher flatter areas (*altopiani*) on the valley shoulders. Prehistoric rock-engravings are distributed sporadically on the slopes of the valley; the greatest concentration occurs approximately seventy-five km north of Brescia near the villages of Capo di Ponte, Cemmo, Nadro, Paspardo and Cimbergo, which are within a few kilometres of one another. There are many thousands of these figures, *incisioni rupestri*, pecked and scratched into the metamorphic surfaces of the open hillside that have been exposed and smoothed by glacial action. To the west the second high valley, Valtellina, is also full of rock-engravings.

Closely related to the Alpine rock-engravings are the statue-stelae (Table 6.2; Figure 6.2). Their main Alpine concentrations are in Valcamonica and Valtellina, in the Trentino region of the Alpine Alto Adige, in the Aosta Valley of Alpine Piedmont, and around Sion in the Swiss Vallais (there are no statue-stelae on Mont Bego, the other large Alpine zone of rock-engraving). Also close by is a distinct group in the Lunigiana, on the Italian coast of Liguria (see Figure 6.1 above); and there are related statue-stelae in southern France and as far away as the Caucasus.

Table 6.1 Elements of chronology in Valcomonica–Valtellina

Period	Chronology of Valcamonica stelae	Other groups of stelae	Northern Italian cultural context	Trans-Alpine cultural context
Late Neolithic (c. 3900 BC)			Square-Mouth Vase culture (3) (Bocca Quadrata) Lagozza	Cortaillod/Pfyn/Altheim Mondsee/Balaton – Lasinja Bodrogkeresztur
		Rougergat		
Early Chalcolithic (c. 3400 BC)		Languedoc	Remedello (1)	SOM/Ferrière/Horgen/Baden Mondsee
	III A 1	Lunigiana Aosta-Sion	Remedello (2)	Fontbouisse/Auvernier
Middle Chalcolithic (c. 2800 BC)		Arco Langundo Sion		Schnurkeramik/Vucedol
	III A2	Velturno	Vaso/Campaniform	Vaso/Campaniform/Vucedol
Late Chalcolithic (c. 2400 BC)				
Early Bronze Age (c. 2200 BC)	Borno I		Polada	Bronze (A I)

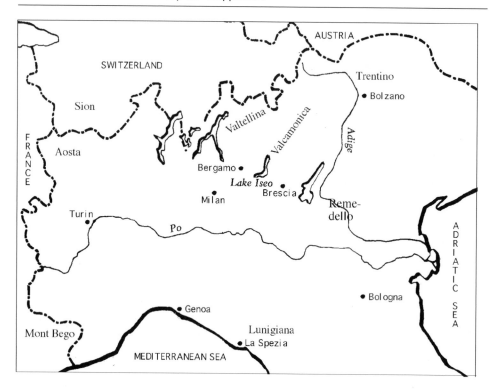

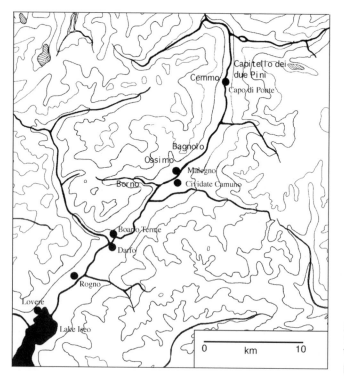

Figure 6.1 Statue-stelae in north Italy and in Valcamonica: regions and places mentioned in the text

Table 6.2 Statue-stelae of Valcamonica and their attributes

Stele name	Sun motif	Animals	Motifs			Weapons
			Agricultural scenes	Human figures		
Masso di Cemmo 4	solar disc-crown type and 'solar-ring'	red deer (male with harem), dogs	–	1 with solar crown		dagger, axe
Relievo di Ossimo 5	–	red deer (male with harem)	2 ploughed fields	–		–
Relievo di Ossimo 7	solar disc small rays: solar crown	red deer (male with harem), pigs, ibex	ploughing scene, ploughed field	3 figures arm to arm, 1 with solar crown		daggers
Relievo di Ossimo 8	solar disc, crown type	red deer (male with harem), pigs, ibex	ploughing scene, planted fields, ploughed field (back panel)	figures arm to arm, 1 with solar crown		–
Capitello dei due Pini	solar disc (fractured) small rays, antler type	1 red deer	–	–		daggers, halberd
Masso di Bagnolo 1	solar disc, small rays, antler type	1 ibex	1 field, unploughed	–		daggers, axes
Masso di Borno 4	solar disc (unique)	ibex	–	–		daggers, axes
Masso di Cemmo 2	solar disc, small rays	ibex, dog, fawns	ploughing scene, cart	6 individuals		daggers, axe, halberd
Masso di Bagnolo 2	solar disc with small rays, antler type	fawns, dogs	ploughing scene	–		daggers, axes
Relievo di Ossimo 9	solar disc, crown type	–	–	3 figures arm to arm		axes
Masso di Cemmo 1	–	red deer (males), ibex, dog, wild pig	ploughing scene	–		daggers, sickle?
Masso di Cemmo 3	solar disc, crown type	red deer (male),	–	44 figures arm to arm		dagger, halberds
Masso Face A	solar disc, long triad rays	ibex	field	2 figures		daggers, axes
di Face B	solar disc, no rays	ibex, dog	ploughing scene, planted fields	–		halberd
Borno Face C	–	red deer (males) fawns,	–	–		–
1 Face D	–	group of red deer	geographic representation	–		dagger

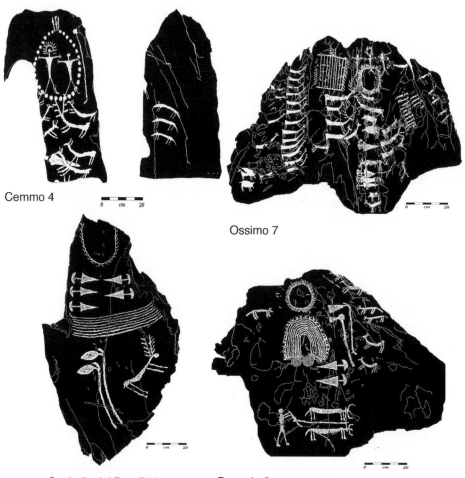

Cemmo 4

Ossimo 7

Capitello dei Due Pini   Bagnolo 2

Figure 6.2 Four of the compositions addressed in the study: Cemmo 4; Ossimo 7; Capitello dei due
Pini; Bagnolo 2. In contrast to the common pattern in rock-art, of individual motifs set
down without apparent regard for each other, the statue-stelae present compositions of
figures. Often a set of similar motifs is placed together in a line

Drawings: Casini (1994a), adapted

The statue-stelae represent a distinct class of standing stones, decorated with incised
and low-relief motifs. In those features they complement and are distinguished from the
simple menhirs, the plainer standing stones ubiquitous among the megaliths of western
and southern Europe. The statue-stelae are reliably dated to the Copper Age by their
iconography, with distinctive forms of halberds and daggers in forms known as physical
objects (Fossati 1995; De Marinis 1994c), and other links to rock-engravings and
monuments of that era. The stelae are set in an *'epoca di grandi transformazione'* (De Marinis
1994a), itself subsequent to the 'creation of new worlds' (Whittle 1996) in the European
Neolithic.

Recent work at Ossimo (below) now gives an archaeological context to a group of statue-stelae, until now generally known as stray individual blocks. Some statue-stelae are anthropomorphic, shaped as a human with distinct heads, bodies and arms – genuine human statues set into the ground at about waist level, as if lacking legs. Most, including those studied here, broadly resemble a human body in proportions but do not have such overtly anthropomorphic features. Some figured surfaces, such as the 'Corni Freschi' and 'Capitello dei due Pini' (Valcamonica), present a distinctive composition on a rock-outcrop surface of statue-stelae type without being standing stones; they further link these detached stones to the more numerous surfaces of engraving on bedrock. *Le pietre degli dei* . . . (Casini 1994a), a catalogue of an exhibition in Bergamo, collates present knowledge of the Valcamonica and Valtellina menhirs and statue-stelae of the Copper Age with a *catalogue raisonnée* and good essays: Casini (1994b); Casini and Fossati (1994); De Marinis (1994a, 1994b, 1994c); Fedele (1994); Fossati (1994b, 1994c, 1994d, 1994e).

General interpretation of statue-stelae can be summarized in three points:

- Statue-stelae/menhirs are anthropomorphic, and they are linked with burial ritual, balanced gender and ancestor worship.
- Statue-stelae/menhirs exhibit a unified phenomenon of megalithic expression, exhibiting uniform distribution, uniform chronology and uniform cultural significance.
- Statue-stelae/menhirs are frequently refigured (Figure 6.3), reshaped, reused and rearranged over time. This is an indication that their symbolic nature may have changed over time.

There are discussions of these points in Barfield (1995), De Marinis (1994b) and Fedele (1994); some scholars might, to a greater or lesser extent, add to or recapitulate them. A thread common to these arguments is their reference to aspects of the stelae that prehistoric people were conveying within their own cultural context. That is, the studies to date have tried to understand the overall discursive significance of these monuments as prehistoric people themselves understood them, and thereby to attempt a 'prehistoric understanding' of their context. Barfield and Chippindale (1997), studying the Mont Bego rock-engravings elsewhere in the Alpine group, address the question: 'What was the meaning of their work?' (see, for these issues more broadly, Zubrow 1994).

Yet we can also understand elements of prehistoric activity, and perhaps more generally prehistoric cognition, by investigating aspects of social activity which are embedded in the iconography and revealed in the relationships between the iconographic elements, which may not have been consciously explicit or intended; they were essentially a form of 'non-discursive expression' (Giddens 1984). Specifically, we propose that we can detect prehistoric conceptions of time at a cosmological level, at a social level (both ritual and mundane) and at a personal level through a rigorous interpretation of these stelae. Using evidence from the engraved stelae, we argue that the understanding of these temporal planes is represented through a structure that integrates various conditions of human experience. Before addressing this pattern directly, we briefly situate this evidence within its Chalcolithic context.

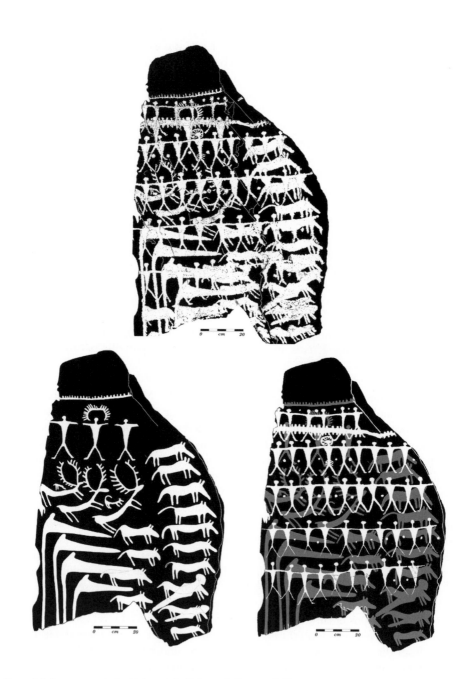

Figure 6.3 Sequence on the main panel of Masso di Cemmo 3. Top: the collected designs on the surface. Lower left: elements of the early phases, A and B. Lower right: elements of the late phases, C and D (in white), cutting through those of the early phases (in grey)

Drawings: Casini (1994a), adapted

The 'Remedello' Copper Age (3400–2200 BC): context for the statue-stelae

The chronology and artefact base for the north Italian Chalcolithic at first depended on the type-site of Remedello di Sotto, on the northern edge of the Po Plain (Barfield 1971; and see Barfield 1985; Whittle 1996). Numerous burial and settlement sites on the Po plain have produced a considerable typology and chronology for the region (see Table 6.1 above), secured by radiocarbon dating and detailed stratigraphy (Casini *et al.* 1995). The primary artefacts that define the period include copper weapons and ornaments – daggers, halberds, axes and pins. Remedello groups are seen as semi-mobile, employing mixed subsistence economies, while dotting the landscape with stelae and other monuments (perhaps also of wood: Whittle 1996: 324); the rock-engraving repertoire corresponds with numerous wild animal motifs as well as images of oxen and ploughs. These Copper Age groups in northern Italy share features with contemporary Corded Ware/Bell Beaker groups in central Europe and the Swiss Alps (Whittle 1996), in terms of both settlement and burial practice (Barfield 1985). Following contemporary interpretation of such communities, we can situate the stelae within a culture that is decentralized, with fragmentary lineage groups replacing the large-scale communities of earlier periods. Like many societies of Europe in the Neolithic and early metal ages, these communities formally maintain a 'Neolithic' subsistence strategy, having domestic plants and animals. Yet at the same time wild animals and plants are conspicuous both in the archaeological record and in the iconography; deer are a common rock-art subject, and deer-and-pig economies are prevalent in the north Italian Neolithic (Jarman 1972).

The images of daggers and halberds date the stelae of Valcamonica to the Remedello period as their forms closely match copper artefacts from archaeological contexts (De Marinis 1994c). The importance of these artefacts, evident in burial contexts, is their relation to prestige and social definition (Whittle 1996: 341), in which a specifically masculine aspect to their import has been demonstrated (Barfield and Chippindale 1997). The engravings on the stelae accentuate this contextual symbolism. The 'Camunian' stelae of this period are ordered by a chronology, established by Anati (1972) and refined by De Marinis (1994c) and Fossati (1995); it places these stelae into a Valcamonica period III A subdivided into III A1 and III A2 (see Table 6.1 above). Valcamonica, off the Po Plain and just outside the geographic zone typically considered 'Remedellian' *per se*, appears broadly to conform to its chronology.

Iconography and structure of the statue-stelae

The engraved statue-stelae from Valcamonica discussed here* are: Cemmo† 1, 2, 3 and 4; Bagnolo 1 and 2; Ossimo 5, 7, 8 and 9; Borno 1 and 4; plus the panel in a bedrock surface of Capitello dei due Pini. In total this represents twelve boulders (plus Capitello) with twenty-three carved surfaces (Table 6.2; Figures 6.2 and 6.4). As is apparent from

---

* The four other stelae in the region (Ossimo 1, 4, 10 and 14) are not considered within this study. Their iconography is decidedly different, and a different interpretation follows.

† The established inventory system for the statue-stelae numbers them in groups by, first, locality and then by numbered sequence within a locality.

Figure 6.4 Detail of Masso di Cemmo 1. The figures on Cemmo 1, a block of schist/slate, are unusually deep cut and unusually clear compared with the more usual material of metamorphic sandstone, on which carvings and their sequences are less distinct. The cutting of newer figures – vertically grouped animals – over older figures – vertically grouped daggers – is plain. The vertical surface in this photograph is dry, with streaks of rainwater running across the face

Photograph: Christopher Chippindale

Table 6.2, these stelae have common iconography, common structure and common arrangement of motifs. This group of stelae has a unique set of motifs, distinct from those of the overtly anthropomorphic stelae in other Italian Alpine regions and across Europe (Casini *et al.* 1995); they make a distinctive group of a partly or wholly different tradition.

The iconography of this group of stelae reflects various combinations of the following motifs:

- sun discs;
- animals;
- agricultural motifs;
- human figures; and
- weapons.

Other motifs that occur less often include spiral rings and lined 'U-collars' (*linee a 'U'-collare*), motifs that seem to relate to the later iconography.

There is little argument concerning the importance of the annual cycle in traditional agrarian society (Thompson 1974; Gell 1992; Bailey 1993). Part of this cycle is revealed through the motifs on each stele depending upon different arrangements of imagery; thus the images demonstrate a relationship to one another based on their temporal nature. If these relationships are reconsidered in ritual terms, a similar temporal structure is revealed. The image of the deer 'harem' represents a natural event of the autumn season, while other images such as the sun are not, on the face of it, specific to any time of the year. Yet when the solar disc is seen in context as part of the greater pattern – which includes ploughs, fields and human figures – it also reveals embedded temporal significance of autumn. In this way the stelae can be situated within a seasonal context. In light of this context the iconography offers information about rituals within society. In each group of engravings is a seamless reference to cyclical temporality and clearly

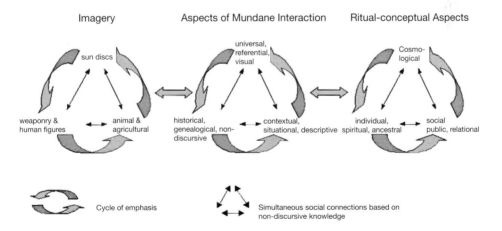

Figure 6.5 Time's cycle. This model illustrates the relationship between the imagery and signified conditions of human interaction. Various aspects are emphasized at different times in the annual cycle. However, each condition plays a role at all times, as they are all part of everyday and ritual/social life

demarcated periods of time that, collectively, represent cosmological, social and personal levels of community interaction.

We will first show how these motifs fit into thematic groups that refer to mundane activity and cyclical time. Second, these thematic groups are related to the ritual nature of the stelae, using both iconographic associations and ritual context. After establishing a model of cyclical time that pervades both everyday and ritual experience (Figure 6.5), the evidence for reuse and alteration of the stelae is addressed. Finally, this reuse is shown to 'incorporate' elements of a historical chronotype into an iconographic framework that reflects cyclical time.

'Two times' of Valcamonica: everyday associations and cyclical time

Let us look at how these elements may show themselves in the material evidence. How do the motifs (on the stelae) relate to mundane life? How are these images of cyclical, seasonal time?

Certain images repeatedly appear within the 'set' of motifs on the stelae. The combinations of figures fit into three general thematic categories. Furthermore, the social interplay between the images and the real world can be realized at various levels. The iconographic themes and corresponding mundane conditions are:

- sun imagery: universal, referential;
- human/weapon imagery: historical, genealogical;
- animal/agriculture imagery: contextual, associative.

The correlation is derived from the prosaic characteristics of these forms. This relationship is not exclusive, as the themes have both substantive and temporal connections. On the one hand, the iconographic subjects depict natural, cyclical tempos in the 'day to day' of the real world. Chalcolithic subsistence strategies in Valcamonica included both domestication and hunting (Anati 1993); temporally, both activities are constrained by seasonal cycles.

Without resorting to environmental determinism, it is not difficult to see how human adaptive strategies responded to these cycles in prehistory. Weaponry, or more generally material culture, is part of a reflexive interaction between society or the individual (Treherne 1995) and aspects of mundane or economic management of environmental cycles (Gilman 1976, 1981; Harding 1984). Also, non-discursive knowledge (Giddens 1984; Gosden 1994) can be transferred through human interaction based on the social history ascribed to material culture. The sun acts as a referential link to the cycles of natural life and the temporality of human activity. Thus this taxonomy is useful in defining common temporal attributes of everyday human interaction as related to the motifs. However, the inherent everyday cycles of these phenomena must be explicitly defined so they can be associated with ritual aspects of social and individual life.

Temporality of the sun

The cyclical nature of the sun is apparent with its short and fast rhythms of day and year. Significant aspects of the annual cycle include the summer and winter solstices, and the spring and autumn equinoxes. On a daily scale, the sun moves across the sky from east to west, its position changing over the course of the year. The rising and setting of the sun against a mountainous skyline and its variable height in the sky serve as seasonal reference points. The attributes of the sun which relate it to everyday activity include:

- universal constancy;
- referential properties;
- visibility.

Although sun symbolism does not convey a 'universal' concept across time and context, Goodison (1989) notes that its use as a 'numinous' or awe-inspiring link between nature and society is marked in prehistory. One can relate the natural appearance of the sun and its consistent cycles to regular human behaviour, both substantially and socially. Regardless of the precision of explicit 'sun-monitoring' on the part of Copper Age societies, we must assume they were able to recognize the daily and annual cycle of the sun. Evidence from the position of other megalithic monuments and studies of variation in seasonal consumption are analogous contexts which support this observation; in the British Isles (Ruggles 1999), for example Newgrange, Ireland, is oriented to the mid-winter solstice sunrise, and Stonehenge's axis is towards the midsummer solstice sunrise/midwinter solstice sunset.

The annual cycle of the sun can affect nearly every aspect of human interaction in that it plays a major role in temperature and available daylight. We use the term 'universal' to indicate the scale at which the sun is integrated into natural cycles, and by default into human consideration. The sun serves as an object of reference, both temporally and spatially. One can situate oneself in relation to the sun's position, in simple result of the visibility of the sun. We see these conditions of everyday human observation and interaction with the world as detailed through sun imagery on the statue-stelae of Valcamonica.

Human/weapon

Human imagery and weapon motifs are less explicit in respect of cyclical time. The temporal nature of human behaviour must be considered within the context represented by the engravings. In order to understand the temporal aspects of the weapon imagery, it must be discussed in terms of its role as active material culture. The temporal information which material culture can provide at an everyday level can be described as:

- historical;
- genealogical;
- non-discursive.

'Natural' evidence for the cyclical nature of genealogical structures is difficult to substantiate. Lineage systems are contextually unique. We suggest that a cyclical genealogical model applies to the Camunian context. The recognition of ancestors allows the event of death to take on diachronic repetition; revisiting and 'reliving' the event are suggestive of this. Burial evidence from Remedello contexts suggests periodical, potentially annual, revisiting and rearrangement of graves. Specifically at Remedello di Sotto, many graves contain disarticulated remains, most likely representing secondary deposition (Whittle 1996: 340). Barfield (1985: 161) also discusses this practice:

> In this rite a period of exposure or burial of the corpse elapses between death and the consignment of the dry bones to an ossuary or ancestral bone house. This period of delay may serve the function of defining the period of mourning, [or] symbolizing the transition of an individual member of the community to becoming a deified ancestor.

The periodic veneration of ancestors is supported by the placement and location of the stelae. Whittle (1996: 340) suggests: 'The context of the individual stelae and menhirs was often remote; they provided the memory of an idea, perhaps of particular individuals, but as plausibly, through part or whole, of wider ideas of community and descent.'

During the Chalcolithic the symbolism and importance of weaponry serves as an example of non-discursive, genealogical information concerning day-to-day individual and group social activity. Many weapons were recycled, reused or passed down from generation to generation, suggested by their absence from the contemporary burial contexts at Ossimo (Fedele 1995). Social history can affect how space is divided, marriages arranged, or resources allocated. Material culture is active in everyday contexts as well as ritual contexts (Treherne 1995; Sørensen 1984). The importance of ritual cycles and regeneration of copper weapons can therefore be extended to everyday interaction. The temporal cyclicity of both human and weapon imagery is expressed through their ancestral histories. A reasonable and long-standing element in interpretation of prehistoric metal-working in Europe is to see the mysteries of copper – its green and coloured ores, its extraction from within the rock, its transformation in smelting into a bright and shining material – as a far from mundane procedure, both prestigious and restricted. Taylor (1999) pertinently addresses the 'envaluation' of copper in the early metal age of Europe, as materially visible in its conspicuous absence from the record.

Animal/agriculture

Seasonal attention is crucial to both agriculture and animal ecology. Seasonality is pronounced in animal cycles that affect hunting patterns as well as herd management.

The cycles of red deer are marked in the iconography of the stelae, such that this motif acts as an excellent seasonal indicator. In the fall (mid-September to late October) the male deer form harems of females for mating. During the winter months the dominant males are solitary. In the spring the fawns are born. During the summer the males' antlers are fully grown, and the bucks form groups, competing for dominance (Camuri *et al.* 1994). Hunting is best during the summer and winter periods, when the males are isolated from the females.

The agricultural imagery is less 'time-specific'; the depicted activities and conditions (ploughing scenes and field layouts) can be related to various seasonal practices in an Alpine agricultural context, at a sufficient altitude to make for a harsh winter. In Valcamonica ploughing and planting would generally take place in the spring; harvesting, ploughing (and possibly planting) during the autumn; planted crops are tended during the summer; unplanted fields prevail during the winter, when the ground is frozen and snow-covered. In Chalcolithic Valcamonica spring-sown wheat and barley were the probable cultivars (Sherratt 1980).* The seasonal pattern suggested here accommodates both environmental and plant constraints. When both animal and agricultural seasonality are considered in light of day-to-day human activity, the corresponding motifs serve to convey the following conditions:

- contextuality;
- descriptiveness;
- situationality.

The phenomenological 'locales' that guide social activity (Tilley 1994) are regulated by seasonally stressed changes and social discourse. The iconography accentuates certain activities which are temporally linked. The time of specific social activities such as ploughing or hunting are determined by their situation within the cycles of these phenomena. Seasonal activities are often use to situate society in the world (Gosden 1994), and serve to describe 'how to go on' on a daily basis (Giddens 1984).

Ritual associations

How does the iconography relate to ritual behaviour? How do the ritual images reflect cyclical, seasonal time?

Particular motifs associate natural phenomena with everyday activity and interaction. They also form a context which denotes a cyclical time concept. This becomes particularly relevant when we consider that these motifs were ascribed to a ritual context – that of the stelae – thereby redirecting their inherent cyclical traits towards ritual activity and expression.

New excavations at Ossimo have reiterated the ritual significance of the statue-stelae (Fedele 1994, 1995; Fedele and Fossati 1995), showing that the stelae are central to ritual activity at various levels. Fedele (1994) has remarked that the stelae have linear align-ment, and generally face towards the east. At Ossimo the adjacent sites OS4 and OS5 are aligned on an east–west axis; the sun iconography at these sites is specifically turned west – looking back towards the other stelae. The arrangements of stelae are located on *altopiani*, with few artefacts or votive offerings.

Fedele (1994) suggests that the stelae were focal locations of funeral rites, which emphasized interaction with the landscape as opposed to material offerings. He has also remarked that in the limited natural space created through the arrangement of the stelae, the rituals must have been small scale and served few people at a time. Finally the stelae symbolized important reference points in the landscape, which served as gathering points and markers for the small communities of the region.

The stelae are also related to burial ritual; there are analogous stelae arrangements in Sion (France) and Val d'Aosta (Italy). Evidence from these regions as well as Lake Garda suggests that the stelae of Valcamonica–Valtellina fall within a larger ritual

---

* The recent dominant crops have been rye (rare in this prehistoric period), maize and potatoes (New World introductions), so the 'traditional' subsistence agriculture of the past millennium is not pertinent for prehistory.

burial tradition accentuating individual, deified ancestors. Taken together, the ritual characteristics of the stelae emphasize cosmological, communal and individual levels of society.

The iconography mirrors the greater ritual employment (as outlined above) of the stelae in the following set of relations:

- sun imagery: cosmological;
- human/weapon imagery: individual, ancestral, spiritual;
- animal/agriculture imagery: social, public, relational.

Ritual sun imagery

As a ritual symbol, the sun motif is primarily associated with cosmological ritual concepts. Sun imagery occurs on nearly every engraved surface on the stelae. The motif is normally located at the top of the statue, which suggests its significance as a cosmological icon (Casini *et al.* 1995; Goodison 1989). The sun is interpreted as having cosmological significance for fairly straightforward reasons. Ritual attention to the sun (and, rarely, also the moon) is characteristic of stone monuments across Europe. In Valcamonica this is supported by the cardinal alignment and orientation of the statue-stelae. In respect to the stelae's imagery, the sun serves as a superstructural icon that 'regulates' the other motifs (providing a link between human/weapon and animal/ agriculture) as an iconographic set. In this way the sun iconography parallels the role of the sun (actual) at the cosmological scale, whereby it mirrors and 'regulates' the cycles of other cosmological bodies like the moon and stars.

Ritual human/weapon

Human/weapon ritual symbolism is correlated with the following concepts:

- individuality;
- ancestor personification;
- spirituality.

These relations are shown by their ritual relation to burial contexts, in which the human/weapon iconography functions as a surrogate for individual inhumation and grave goods. This is shown by three observations concerning the context of statue-stelae across the Alpine region. First, the majority of the statue-stelae across the Alps are explicitly anthropomorphic and individualized – meaning they have engravings of a unique face and/or obvious anatomical parts. The stelae of Valcamonica, not overtly anthropomorphic, are unusual in this respect. Second, the stelae are part of burial contexts which contain relatively few grave goods,* as documented at chronologically later sites such as Sion and

---

* The 'dolmen' type of graves at these sites contain primarily flint daggers and points; they are considered to be earlier (*c.* 3400–2800 BC) than those of 'Corded Ware' type (Whittle 1996: 341; Barfield 1985) found on the Po Plain, which contain more metal objects and pottery.

Aosta, where the stelae are considered to represent specific individuals (De Marinis 1994b), presumably an ancestor of those interred in the grave. Accordingly, earlier (2800–2400 BC) 'burial/ritual' contexts in Valcamonica, such as Ossimo (OS4 and OS5) and Bagnolo, contain neither bodies nor votive offerings. Third, contemporary burials on the Po Plain and around Lake Garda *do* contain individuals and grave goods, which are explained as part of the 'Corded Ware/Bell Beaker' phenomenon which affected much of Europe during this time (Barfield 1985; Whittle 1996). Therefore, since the stelae are directly related to burial contexts, we propose that the imagery on the stelae represents the concepts of individuality and prestige (De Marinis 1994b) which are normally related to single inhumation graves of this period, of which physical evidence is missing from specific ritual burial contexts in Valcamonica. The stelae signify the ritual significance of ancestors; these 'iconographic offerings' replace material offerings of prestige goods, which define their social status (De Marinis 1994b). The idea of ancestor personification, noted above, may indicate a cyclical genealogical structure.

Ritual animal/agriculture

The ritual concepts conveyed through the animal/agriculture iconography are:

* social;
* public;
* relational.

The animal/agriculture iconography, like the other motifs, is integrated into the ritual expression inherent to the stelae. The majority of the animal images are represented in groups – either all males, or male and harem. The animal imagery serves to relate a natural model to human social interaction. It is useful here to think in terms of analogous totemic symbols that are used to explain certain social interactions in ethnographic examples (Lévi-Strauss 1966). A similar communal relation manifests itself through the agricultural imagery. The labour-intensive agricultural activity of the Chalcolithic would have demanded social co-operation (Sherratt 1980).

Rituals often serve society by instituting 'rules' (Giddens 1984) which accentuate group concepts and relate them to elements that are important and understandable even outside a ritual context. By placing ritual importance on agricultural activity, the division of labour and structuring of public relations is bolstered. Moreover, defining rituals in light of animal and agricultural cycles serves to guide the community through stages of development, as individual social roles and task differentiation change over time. The season serves to mark ritual and mundane responsibilities.

Most of the stele iconography emphasizes one season or the other. The stelae Ossimo 8 (Figure 6.6) and Borno 1 (Figure 6.7) have multiple emphases, partly through superimposition of various motifs with different significance. Borno 1 has four panels or faces, each with a different iconographic and seasonal emphasis. Frontini (1994: 77), in her analysis of Borno 1, suggests that the four faces relate to the 'cycle of life'. Her discussion of the motifs is primarily concerned with phases of human reproduction:

> The figures preserve a recognizable symbolic significance [that] seems to recall the sacred world and ritual rhythm of the cycle of life: fertility, reproduction, continual

Figure 6.6 Ossimo 8. Both the grouping of similar motifs and the recutting of figures through and over previous figures are plain. These characteristics permit the reliable recovery of the phases of imagery on a statue-stele

Drawing: Casini (1994a), adapted

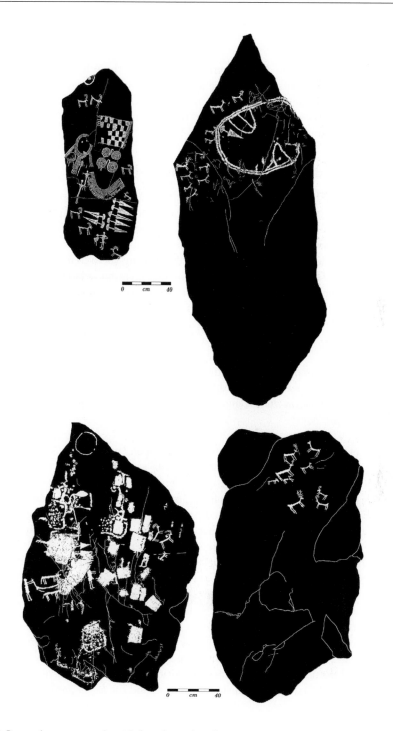

Figure 6.7 Borno 1, a statue-stele with four figured surfaces

Drawing: Casini (1994a), adapted

regeneration and perhaps death – if we recognize the sun and deer [motifs] as signifiers of the afterlife.*

Our interpretation of Borno 1 complements Frontini's, though it relates seasonal *and* natural aspects of the motifs to a broader social significance: the temporal link between mundane and sacred time. Each face of Borno 1 is attributed to a different season; Borno 1 can be interpreted as a standing 'calendar' of ritual and day-to-day human activity in Chalcolithic Valcamonica.

Re-use and re-decoration: linear time

We have argued that a seamless conception of various aspects of human interaction is possible and is evident in the rock-engravings of Valcamonica. Simply stated, humans can understand and integrate various parts of their life without oscillating between different concepts of time. If this is true, we must also be able to integrate various scales of temporal understanding, again without differentiating them in terms of our reference of understanding. This refers specifically to the demarcation between short-, medium- and long-term time-scales – a paradigm made famous by the French Annales school.

Braudel (1949, 1972) outlined a structure for explaining history according to the scale of visible development of human societies (Bintliff 1991). Time and change are classified at various levels:

- Short term – *événement* – events; individual histories; narratives.
- Medium term – *conjontures* – social histories; economic, agrarian cycles; ideologies.
- Long term – the *longue durée* – geo-history; stable technologies; unchanging ideologies/concepts.

Application of these concepts in archaeology has been limited (but see Bintliff 1991; Knapp 1992; Barker 1995), because the Annaliste approach was developed to address historical questions for which the primary evidence is documentary. A simplification of an Annaliste explanation of history sees long-, middle- and short-term changes occurring simultaneously, though not linked to a common reference point; events operating at the short term are separate from changes that are recognizable from the viewpoint of the *longue durée*. The Annaliste approach is inadequate for prehistorians in its original form because, archaeologically, long-term developments are primarily explained from discrete residues of events in the short term (Binford 1981). Yet, distilled and adapted, Annaliste concepts are useful in explaining human experience and time concepts at various integrated scales (Barker 1995).

The Valcamonica statue-stelae comprise a unique *prehistoric* example that illustrates time at various scales, without divorcing the event from long-term change. As noted above, the stelae are not, in and of themselves, synchronic. Stelae such as Ossimo 7 and 8, Cemmo 3 and Borno 1 show clear superimposition of imagery. Decisive work at Ossimo by Fedele (1994; 1995) illustrates the medium term and the *longue durée* of these religious

---

* Authors' translation.

symbols; stelae were reshaped, broken, turned over or otherwise reconfigured at *événements* over a span of hundreds of years. The mutation of the stelae – both iconographically and structurally – is a striking feature of long-term change in Valcamonica, and alludes to concepts of time at a large scale. In opening this chapter, we referred to the commonplace of archaeological sites being returned to and reused. The recutting of the images on the stelae shows a continuing value for these specific stones – there are many other boulders of comparable size and shape to be had were one simply to seek a fresh surface to mark. Recovered at Ossimo have been the fragments of a statue-stele from which the engraved outer surface was entirely hacked over, leaving the rough core exposed. When the meaning of the statue-stelae becomes obsolete or false, they may not go quietly into simple oblivion but are transformed or suppressed.

We have seen that human interaction in Copper Age Valcamonica is depicted through a cyclical viewpoint of time. This has been explained in light of the annual cycle, which affects both ritual and mundane life. In addition to the short-term cycle, each carving or set of carvings can be seen as an event that relates conditions of human experience to larger-scale time and social history. It is significant to see how cyclical time concepts can be applied to a range of scales.

Cyclical time is also useful in explaining how concepts are regenerated and modified over longer periods of time. It is plausible to think that the stelae remained visible — socially as well as optically – throughout time, much like other megalithic monuments of the period, such as Stonehenge (Bradley 1991). The conditions of human interaction that are related to the stelae must also have changed throughout the Chalcolithic. Over the long term the stelae act as markers of past events. The reconfiguration of the iconography and reshaping of the stones may indicate that over long periods of time subsequent generations involved themselves as part of a cycle of ritual and social history. Changes in everyday technology and social organization would be reflected in the iconography, yet the activity would still be in reference to the same focal point(s) as those which came before. A cycle which references numerous planes of social experience (such as those of referential/cosmological, historical/ancestral, situational/communal) could also serve to relate a living group to one which lived 600 years earlier. This type of cyclical concept weds the significance of short-term conditions with the overarching importance of long-term history. A society which has a circular view of time need not be a 'cold', 'history-less' culture (Lévi-Strauss 1966), but can perceive of its history in terms of contemporary symbols and activities. In this framework societies respond to events (*événements*), social rhythms (*conjontures*) and long-term histories (the *longue durée*) in the process of change.

The development of social complexity in the late Neolithic and Copper Age has been discussed as a result of changes in ideology, related to changes in subsistence strategies and group interaction (Shennan 1982; Sherratt 1984). Specifically, it has long been suggested that 'megalithic' burial rituals reflect – to a greater or lesser extent – aspects of social hierarchy. In Atlantic Europe, Shennan (1982) remarks that while society was becoming more stratified in economic terms, the ritual behaviour – in the form of megalithic tombs – focused primarily on group identity and common ancestry. This is suggestive of a separation between the ethos of ritual and production, which we have argued is an oversimplification of social conceptual capabilities.

Sherratt (1984) suggests that the evidence for established social hierarchy has been overstated; though ritual contexts may indeed reflect aspects of prestige, this need not translate into social stratification. The evidence provided here concerning ritual reflection of society supports Sherratt's position. Within the model presented here (see Figure 6.5 above) both individual/genealogical prestige or status and group communality are celebrated, though emphasized at different times of the year. Thus it may be, as Shennan argues, that subsistence strategies did change, but we suggest that ritual practices were structured to accommodate the changes in social organization and the assertion of power that occurred in later Copper Age Europe. Unfortunately, the study of Chalcolithic Valcamonica is hampered by the scarce settlement, human and material remains, so situating 'Camunian society' within broader contemporary changes in ideology and material culture is tentative. The archaeological reconstruction of the society is almost solely based on the rock-engravings, and these must serve as analogues for the grave goods and forms that are discussed elsewhere. If we do transpose the model of cyclical time into the general archaeological context of the region, there is evidence which 'fleshes out' the social conditions which we have suggested are highlighted in Valcamonica by stele iconography both in mundane and ritual terms.

Prehistoric time in modern knowledge

At the genesis of this study is a general and overarching question, yet one which is intricate and complicated to answer directly: when did various societies begin to conceive of time in a historical sense? Numerous ethnographic studies have claimed that linear time is an inappropriate model for many societies, suggesting time-concepts described as: 'static' (Bloch 1977); 'event oriented' (Oyvind 1995); 'hot and cold' (Lévi-Strauss 1966); 'oscillating' (Leach 1961); and 'referential' (Bohannan 1953; Gosden 1994); to name a few. The entirety of time-ethnography cannot be addressed here – though the variety of such ethnographic expositions prompts the anthropologist to look towards prehistoric expressions of time for insights into how time-concepts change in order to understand the relationship between social experience, knowledge and temporal referencing.

This study has examined how time is entwined with human experience in Chalcolithic Alpine Italy and how a cyclical time-concept is embedded in the engraved iconography on Copper Age statue-stelae, with reuse and redecoration of the stelae, generation after generation, aiding the development of a cumulative concept of time. A phenomenon of 'incorporative chronotypes' suggests that changing social experiences and the reflexive nature of the stelae iconography expose a time-concept which is both cyclical and historical (directional).

A consideration of the spatial relationship between social actors and their surrounding landscape hinges upon an understanding of the spatio-temporal concepts which guide a society's definition of the world around them. Any conception of space entails perceptions that are both tangible and ephemeral, and is often considered as inseparable from time (Giddens 1984). Time and space structure the way people behave in their social world. In a colloquial sense humans are able to differentiate between spatial scales; it is clear that material culture, 'artefacts' of social interaction, designate particular spatial relationships in reference to contextual settings – 'locales'. These locales impose spatio-temporal constraints on human praxis. In contemporary Western cultures this translates into concentric categories, such as personal space, living space, village space, regional space, global space and any number of demarcations in between. This essentially is a comparison of indexical scale. For example, spatial contexts that are defined as 'local' refer in the same sense to 'all those things which are not local'. To know where on the scalar continuum of space a specific part of human practice is situated, we need to understand the contextual constraints that might have imposed boundedness upon any single scalar demarcation. Likewise, when understanding temporal phenomenon, in order to understand aspects of historical linearity, it might be useful to understand certain aspects of cyclical time, itself rotating around a set of references which delineates forms of communication in both an everyday and ritual manner.

Image, space, time: world-view

Rock-art offers a unique window into the spatio-temporal framework of human agents, as there is a relationship between the processing of scale in a cognitive mapping sense and the demonstration of spatio-temporal categories in an expressive sense; this is a space–time continuum. What we propose is a way of relating space–time (Giddens 1984) to the study of rock-art and landscape – primarily the translation of a socially defined understanding of spatial scale to a comprehensible spatial analogue on a rock-art panel. In terms of spatial concepts, we situate our experiences according to notions of *short space*, *medium space* and *long space*. In rock-art these are reflected through indexical icons, whose scalar analogue is formulated by incorporating telescopic increments of space and composition – namely millimetre, centimetre, metre and kilometre.

The interpretative challenge lies in differentiating between an agent's mental conception of 'space' constructed in terms of social experience and the translation of this concept that is signified as 'space' in rock-engravings. Like linguistic constructs of space, iconic representations reflect a formulation of a spatial framework that situates the actor *in reference to* other contextually defined parameters (Levinson 1996). If we can better understand the way space and time are defined in reference to specific social contexts we are then able to discuss, in a contextually applicable way, the reciprocal relationship between various spatio-temporal frameworks and human experience.

The model proposed here is simple – various scales and cognitive maps of time and space can be seamlessly relevant and incorporated into a society's world-view. This model becomes more complex when we try to link these ways of understanding the world to the symbolic output of past societies. Yet it is this link which will help us to understand how time and space were structured through social communication and experience.

Acknowledgements

We thank members of the Cooperativa Archaeologica Le Orme dell'Uomo for varied assistance in and out of the field, and other colleagues and friends. The fieldwork for this article was supported by St John's College, Cambridge. The drawings of the rock-art are from those in the splendid book *Le pietre degli dei: menhir e stele dell'Età del Rame in Valcamonica e Valtellina* (Casini 1994a).

References

Abelanet, J. 1986. *Signes sans paroles: cent siècles d'art rupestre en Europe occidentale*. Paris: Hachette.
Anati, Emmanuel. 1961. *Camonica Valley*. New York: Knopf.

Anati, Emmanuel. 1972. *I Pugnali nell'arte rupestre e nelle statue-stele dell'Italia settentrionale*. Capo di Ponte: Edizioni del Centro.

Anati, Emmanuel. 1993. *World rock art: the primordial language*. Capo di Ponte: Edizioni del Centro.

Arcà, Andrea and Angelo Fossati (eds). 1995. *Sui sentieri dell'arte rupestre: le rocce incise delle Alpi: storia, ricerche, escursioni*. Torino: Edizioni CDA.

Bailey, Douglass W. 1993. Chronotypic tension in Bulgarian prehistory; 6500–3500 BC, *World Archaeology* 25(2): 204–222.

Bailey, Geoffrey N. 1983. Concepts of time in Quaternary prehistory, *Annual Review of Anthropology* 12: 165–192.

Barfield, Lawrence H. 1971. *Northern Italy before Rome*. London: Thames and Hudson.

Barfield, Lawrence H. 1985. Burials and boundaries in Chalcolithic Italy, in Caroline Malone and Simon Stoddart (eds), *Papers in Italian archaeology IV: the Cambridge Conference*, II: *Prehistory*: 152–156. Oxford: British Archaeological Reports. International Series 244.

Barfield, Lawrence H. 1994. The Iceman reviewed, *Antiquity* 68: 10–26.

Barfield, Lawrence H. 1995. The context of statue-menhirs, *Notizie Archaeologiche Bergomensi* 3: 11–36.

Barfield, Lawrence and Christopher Chippindale. 1997. Meaning in the later prehistoric rock-engravings of Mont Bego, Alpes-Maritimes, France, *Proceedings of the Prehistoric Society* 63: 103–128.

Barker, Graeme. 1995. *A Mediterranean valley: landscape archaeology and Annales history in the Biferno Valley*. London: Leicester University Press.

Binford, Lewis R. 1981. Behavioural archaeology and the Pompeii premise, *Journal of Anthropological Research* 37: 195–208.

Bintliff, J. 1991. (ed.) *The* Annales *School and archaeology*. Leicester: Leicester University Press.

Bloch, Marc. 1977. The past and the present in the present, *Man* 12: 278–292.

Bohannan, Paul. 1953. Concepts of time among the Tiv of Nigeria, *Southwestern Journal of Anthropology* 9(3): 251–262.

Bradley, Richard. 1991. Ritual, time and history, *World Archaeology* 23: 209–219.

Brandl, Eric J. 1973. *Australian Aboriginal paintings in western and central Arnhem Land: temporal sequences and elements of style in Cadell River and Deaf Adder Creek art*. Canberra: Australian Institute of Aboriginal Studies. Australian Aboriginal Studies 52, Prehistory and Material Culture Series 9.

Braudel, Fernand. 1949. *La Méditerrenée et le monde méditerranéen à l'époque de Phillippe II*. Paris: Librairie A. Colin.

Braudel, Fernand. 1972. *The Mediterranean and the Mediterranean world in the age of Phillip II*. Revised edition, translated by S. Reynolds. London: Collins.

Camuri, G., Angelo Fossati, G. Gatti and G. Musitelli. 1994. *Il cervo: natura, arte, tradizione*. Chuisi della Verna: Commune di Chuisi della Verna.

Casini, Stefania (ed.). 1994a. *Le pietre degli dei: menhir e stele dell'Età del Rame in Valcamonica e Valtellina*. Bergamo: Centro Culturale Nicolò Rezzara.

Casini, Stefania (ed.). 1994b. Il motivo del 'rettangolo frangiato', in Stefania Casini (ed.), *Le pietre degli dei: menhir e stele dell'Età del Rame in Valcamonica e Valtellina*: 93–96. Bergamo: Centro Culturale Nicolò Rezzara.

Casini, Stefania, Raffaele C. De Marinis and Angelo Fossati. 1995. Stele e massi incisi della Valcamonica e della Valtellina, *Notizie Archaeologiche Bergomensi* 3: 221–250.

Chaloupka, George. 1993. *Journey in time: the world's longest continuing art tradition*. Chatswood: Reed.

Chippindale, Christopher and Paul S.C. Taçon. 1998. The many ways of dating Arnhem Land rock-art, north Australia, in Christopher Chippindale and Paul S.C. Taçon (eds), *The archaeology of rock-art*: 90–111. Cambridge: Cambridge University Press.

Cleal, Rosamund M.J. and Michael J. Allen. 1995. Stonehenge in its landscape, in R.M.J. Cleal, K.E. Walker and R. Montague (eds), *Stonehenge in its landscape: twentieth-century excavations*: 464–494. London: English Heritage. Archaeological Report 10.

Clottes, Jean. 1994. Dates directes pour les peintures paléolithiques, *Bulletin de la Société Préhistorique Ariège-Pyrénées* 49: 51–70.

Clottes, Jean. 1998. The 'Three C's': fresh avenues towards European Palaeolithic art, in Christopher Chippindale and Paul S.C. Taçon (eds), *The archaeology of rock art*: 112–129. Cambridge: Cambridge University Press.

De Marinis, Raffaele C. 1994a. L'Età del Rame in Europa: un'epoca di grandi transformazione, in Stefania Casini (ed.), *Le pietre degli dei: menhir e stele dell'Età del Rame in Valcamonica e Valtellina*: 21–30. Bergamo: Centro Culturale Nicolò Rezzara.

De Marinis, Raffaele C. 1994b. Il fenomeno delle statue-stele e stele antropomorfe dell'Età del Rame in Europa, in Stefania Casini (ed.), *Le pietre degli dei: menhir e stele dell'Età del Rame in Valcamonica e Valtellina*: 31–58. Bergamo: Centro Culturale Nicolò Rezzara.

De Marinis, Raffaele C. 1994c. La datazione dello stile IIIA, in Stefania Casini (ed.), *Le pietre degli dei: menhir e stele dell'Età del Rame in Valcamonica e Valtellina*: 69–87. Bergamo: Centro Culturale Nicolò Rezzara.

Evans-Pritchard, E.E. 1940. *The Nuer*. Oxford: Clarendon.

Fedele, Francesco. 1994. Ossimo (Valcamonica): scavi in siti cultuali calcolitici con massi incisi, in Stefania Casini (ed.), *Le pietre degli dei: menhir e stele dell'Età del Rame in Valcamonica e Valtellina*: 135–150. Bergamo: Centro Culturale Nicolò Rezzara.

Fedele, Francesco. 1995. *Ossimo 1: il contesto rituale delle stele calcolitiche e notizie sugli scavi 1988–95*. Gianico (BS): La Cittadina. Quaderni Alpi Centrali 1.

Fedele, Francesco and Angelo Fossati. 1995. Centro cultuale calcolitico dell'Anvoia a Ossimo (Valcamonica): scavi 1988–95, *Notizie Archaeologiche Bergomensi* 3: 251–258.

Flood, Josephine and Bruno David. 1994. Traditional systems of encoding meaning in Wardaman rock art, Northern Territory, Australia, *Artefact* 17: 6–22.

Flood, Josephine, Bruno David and Robin Frost. 1992a. Dreaming into art: Aboriginal interpretations of rock engravings: Yingalarri, Northern Territory (Australia), in Mike J. Morwood and D.R. Hobbs (eds), *Rock art and ethnography*: 33–38. Melbourne: Australian Rock Art Research Association. Occasional Publication 5.

Flood, Josephine, Bruno David and Robin Frost. 1992b. Pictures in transition: discussing the interaction of visual forms and symbolic contents in Wardaman rock pictures, in Mike J. Morwood and D.R. Hobbs (eds), *Rock art and ethnography*: 27–32. Melbourne: Australian Rock Art Research Association. Occasional Publication 5.

Fossati, Angelo. 1994a. Acqua, armi, e ucelli nell'arte rupestre camuno, *Notizie Archaeologiche Bergamensi* 2: 203–216.

Fossati, Angelo. 1994b. Gli animali nei massi incisi, in Stefania Casini (ed.), *Le pietre degli dei: menhir e stele dell'Età del Rame in Valcamonica e Valtellina*: 115–126. Bergamo: Centro Culturale Nicolò Rezzara.

Fossati, Angelo. 1994c. Le figure antropomorfe, in Stefania Casini (ed.), *Le pietre degli dei: menhir e stele dell'età del Rame in Valcamonica e Valtellina*: 127–130. Bergamo: Centro Culturale Nicolò Rezzara.

Fossati, Angelo. 1994d. Le rappresentazioni topografiche, in Stefania Casini (ed.), *Le pietre degli dei: menhir e stele dell'età del Rame in Valcamonica e Valtellina*: 89–92. Bergamo: Centro Culturale Nicolò Rezzara.

Fossati, Angelo. 1994e. Le scene di aratura, in Stefania Casini (ed.), *Le pietre degli dei: menhir e stele dell'Età del Rame in Valcamonica e Valtellina*: 131–134. Bergamo: Centro Culturale Nicolò Rezzara.

Fossati, Angelo. 1995. L'arte rupestre delle Alpi occidentale: confronti con la tradizione rupestre camuna, in *Immagini dalla preistoria; incisione e pitture rupestri: nuove messaggi dalle rocce delle alpi occidentali*: 33–42. Milano.

Frontini, P. 1994. Il masso Borno 1, *Notizie Archaeologiche Bergamensi* 2: 67–78.

Gell, Alfred. 1992. *The anthropology of time: cultural constructions of temporal maps and images*. Oxford: Berg.

Giddens, Anthony. 1984. *The constitution of society*. Cambridge: Polity Press.

Gilman, Antonio. 1976. Bronze Age dynamic in south-east Spain, *Dialectical Anthropology* 1: 307–319.

Gilman, Antonio. 1981. The development of social stratification in Bronze Age Europe, *Current Anthropology* 22: 1–23.

Giusto-Magnardi, Nathalie. 1990. *Les Gravures des bergers dans la Vallée des Merveilles*. Nice: Université de Nice. Mémoire de DEA Anthropologie Générale et Appliquée.

Goodison, Lucy. 1989. *Death, women and the sun: symbolism of regeneration in early Aegean religion*. London: Institute of Classical Studies. Bulletin Supplement 53.

Gosden, Chris. 1994. *Social being and time*. Oxford: Blackwell.

Gould, Steven J. 1987. *Time's arrow, time's cycle: myth and metaphor in the discovery of geological time*. Cambridge, MA: Harvard University Press.

Harding, Anthony F. 1984. Aspects of social evolution in the Bronze Age, in John Bintliff (ed.), *European social evolution*: 135–145. Bradford: University of Bradford.

Helskog, Knut. 1999. The shore connection: cognitive landscape and communication with rock carvings in northernmost Europe, *Norwegian Archaeological Review* 32(2): 73–94.

Hopfel, Frank, Werner Platzer and Konrad Spindler (eds). 1992. *Der Mann im Eis: Bericht über das Internationale Symposium 1992 in Innsbruck*. Innsbruck: Universität Innsbruck. Veroffentlichungen der Universität Innsbruck 187. Der Mann im Eis 1.

Humphrey, Caroline and Urgunge Onon. 1996. *Shamans and elders: experience, knowledge, and power among the Daur Mongols*. Oxford: Clarendon Press.

Jarman, Michael R. 1972. European deer economies and the advent of the Neolithic, in Eric S. Higgs (ed.), *Papers in economic prehistory: studies by members and associates of the British Academy Major Research Project in the Early History of Agriculture*: 125–147. Cambridge: Cambridge University Press.

Knapp, A. Bernard (ed.). 1992. *Archaeology, Annales, and ethnohistory*. Cambridge: Cambridge University Press.

Lakoff, George and Mark Johnson. 1990. *Metaphors we live by*. Chicago: University of Chicago Press.

Lawson, Andrew J. 1997. The structural history of Stonehenge, in Barry Cunliffe and Colin Renfrew (eds), *Science and Stonehenge*: 15–37. Oxford: Oxford University Press for the British Academy. Proceedings of the British Academy 92.

Layton, Robert. 1992. *Australian rock art: a new synthesis*. Cambridge: Cambridge University Press.

Leach, Edmund. 1961. *Rethinking anthropology*. London: University of London, Athlone Press. London School of Economics and Political Science Monographs on Social Anthropology 22.

Leroi-Gourhan, André. 1965. *Préhistoire de l'art occidental*. Paris: Mazenod.

Lévi-Strauss, Claude. 1966. *The savage mind*. Chicago: University of Chicago Press.

Levinson, S.C. 1996. Language and space, *Annual Review of Anthropology* 25: 352–382.

Marshack, Alexander. 1991. *The roots of civilization: the cognitive beginnings of man's first art, symbol, and notation*. Mount Kisco: Moyer Bell.

Oyvind, D. 1995. When the futures comes from behind: Malagasy and other time concepts and some consequences for communication, *International Journal of Intercultural Relations* 19(2): 197–209.

Piggott, Stuart. 1959. *Approach to archaeology*. London: Adam and Charles Black.

Ruggles, C.L.N. 1999. *Astronomy in prehistoric Britain and Ireland*. New Haven, CT: Yale University Press.

Shennan, Stephen. 1982. Ideology, change and the European early Bronze Age, in Ian Hodder (ed.), *Symbolic and structural archaeology*: 155–161. Cambridge: Cambridge University Press.

Sherratt, Andrew. 1980. Water, soil, and seasonality in early cereal cultivation, *World Archaeology* 11(3): 313–330.

Sherratt, Andrew. 1984. Social evolution: Europe in the later Neolithic and Copper ages, in John Bintliff (ed.), *European social evolution*: 123–134. Bradford: University of Bradford Press.

Sørensen, Marie-Louise Stig. 1984. Material order and cultural classification: the role of bronze objects in the transition from Bronze Age to Iron Age in Scandinavia, in Ian Hodder (ed.), *The archaeology of contextual meanings*: 90–101. Cambridge: Cambridge University Press.

Spindler, Konrad. 1994. *The man in the ice: the preserved body of a Neolithic man reveals the secrets of the Stone Age*. London: Weidenfeld and Nicolson.

Spindler, K. *et al.* (eds). 1995. *Der Mann im Eis: neue Funde und Ergebnisse*. Wien: Springer-Verlag.

Stahl, Ann B. 1993. Concepts of time and approaches to analogical reasoning in historical perspective, *American Antiquity* 58(2): 235–260.

Taylor, Timothy F. 1999. Envaluing metal: theorizing the Eneolithic 'hiatus', in S.M.M. Young, A.M. Pollard, P. Budd and R.A. Ixer (eds), *Metals in antiquity*: 22–32. Oxford: Archaeopress. British Archaeological Reports International Series S792.

Thomas, Julian. 1996. *Time, culture and identity: an interpretative archaeology*. London: Routledge.

Thompson, Edward P. 1974. Time, work-discipline, and industrial capitalism, in M.W. Flinn and T.C. Smout (eds), *Essays in social history*. Oxford: Clarendon Press.

Tilley, Christopher. 1994. *A phenomenology of landscape*. London: Berg.

Treherne, Paul. 1995. The warrior's beauty, *Journal of European Archaeology* 3: 105–144.

West, Margie. 1995. *Rainbow sugarbag and moon: two artists of the stone country: Bardayal Nadjamerrek and Mick Kubarkku*. Darwin: Museum and Art Gallery of the Northern Territory.

Whittle, Alasdair. 1996. *Europe in the Neolithic: the creation of new worlds*. Cambridge: Cambridge University Press.

Whittle, Alasdair. 1997. *Sacred mound, holy rings: Silbury Hill and the West Kennet palisade enclosures: a later Neolithic complex in north Wiltshire*. Oxford: Oxbow.

Zubrow, Ezra B.W. 1994. Cognitive archaeology reconsidered, in Colin Renfrew and Ezra B.W. Zubrow (eds), *The ancient mind: elements of cognitive archaeology*: 187–190. Cambridge: Cambridge University Press.

Chapter 7

Rock-art and settlement

Issues of spatial order in the prehistoric rock-art of Fenno-Scandinavia

Per Ramqvist

Rock-art in Fenno-Scandinavia

The western fringe of the Eurasian *taiga* forms the northern part of present-day west Russia, Finland, Sweden and Norway. Even though these areas have similar landscapes and environmental settings they are very different concerning their nature and cultural orientations. North-west Russia and north Norway are directly exposed to or connected with the Arctic Ocean, and in the case of Norway also the Atlantic, while Finland and Sweden are linked to the more closed Gulf of Bothnia. The largest parts of the Eurasian *taiga* in general as well as in Fenno-Scandinavia are, typically, inland areas circling around the large and smaller rivers and lake systems.

In northern Fenno-Scandinavia (Figure 7.1) we mainly find two different traditions of rock-art motifs. The first is the one turning to the vast Arctic Ocean. There we find several examples of carvings with narrative panels, telling us detailed stories about different events connected to the main topics of them all, hunting and fishing. The hunting scenes may very well be more than just a hunting story; it could be these are answers to all the questions about human existence asked by the prehistoric inhabitants. It is highly plausible that the narrative motifs were allegorical. Seen as a whole, the panels by the Arctic Ocean show a broader selection of depicted animals, with large marine as well as the large terrestrial animals; even the large birds like swan and goose have been important hunting game. In the inland areas the elk totally dominates. This, I believe, tells us something of the economic base, of the importance of the depicted features and their reflection in ideology. Since the rock-art is held by almost all scholars to be a religious expression, it is obvious that the main ingredients in the different religions stem from the economy of the religion creators. The religion of the tribes in the *taiga* does not include giraffes!

The question of representativity is of course open to much speculation and diverging ideas, due to the fact that you do not know how much you know. That is true concerning archaeology in general, but especially the distribution of rock-art. This uncertainty has an attraction to some scholars, but is repellent to others. I am not aware if papers about rock-art more often than other archaeological papers are speculative; what is sure is that the papers often are very dynamic and embrace different perspectives. The pictures themselves invite you to a vast range of perspectives in economic, environmental, social and not least religious questions. In that respect the material culture is well suited for modern archaeologists wishing to come close to their prehistoric forefathers. I am not

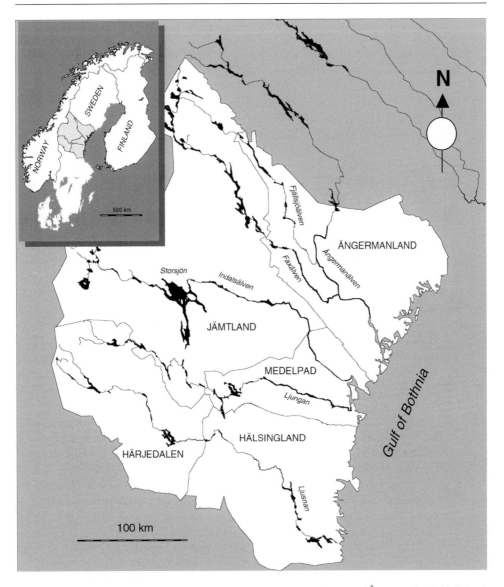

Figure 7.1 Map showing the location of central Norrland: the landscapes of Ångermanland, Medelpad, Jämtland, Härjedalen and Hälsingland

disinterested in human beings of the past, but think it is more fruitful to try to understand what kind of economic, social and religious structures people were part of and dependent on.

So when you try to generalize aspects concerning rock-art you have to be aware that the base of your generalization could be, and probably is, quite brittle.

It is important to try to separate traditions of rock-art styles in order to understand internal and inter-regional communication of the past. It is, however, a hard task to grasp the vast Eurasian *taiga* area with respect to its large size, its fast discoveries of new sites, and the relative slowness of publication. Practically every attempt to publish the whole fails. We have difficulties in the first place to embrace what is already known and in the second to know how much we know. A deeper co-operation between Russian and Scandinavian rock-art researchers is important in looking for regional styles of *taiga*.

On a preliminary level I have found tendencies towards regional differences concerning the depictions of the elk (Ramqvist 1990). We can separate the northern *taiga* from the tundra turned towards the Arctic Ocean as having a 'narrative tradition' with complex compositions of pictures telling stories of hunting sessions, ritual events and so on. These narrative compositions do not seem to be found in the central and western *taiga* area, or at least they are not as clear and easy interpreted. In the inland *taiga* the compositions seem to comprise fewer individual pictures – a human carrying an elk-headed pole standing in a boat, or a row of elk, for instance. Here the compositions seem to be more special-purpose images – unlike some Arctic Ocean compositions which perhaps were part of the larger explanation of cosmos.

The sparseness of the images could mean they represent a way of *pars pro toto*, in which one or a few images may represent a whole complex story, by a kind of summary or reductionism. If this is the case with all the rock-art images – that they are *pars pro toto* representations – it should be even harder to understand what is coded on the rocks. For example, one single elk could represent one story or myth, while an elk-cow with her calf could indicate quite another mythological sphere.

In the central *taiga* area the predominant hunting game was elk. In that respect it is quite different from the Arctic Ocean area where reindeer (and some elk) and the large sea mammals such as whale, walrus and seal were hunted. The Arctic Ocean area had a much broader spectrum of achievable animal resources. In the central *taiga* the hunt was focused on elk, both in real life and as an object for depiction (and therefore religion). This is also evident from the archaeological and osteological record. Bones from elk dominate the faunal remains within dwelling sites (Ekman and Iregren 1984).

We find another interesting difference in the westernmost *taiga*, in Finland, northern Sweden and central Norway. There we can see a quite different distribution of carvings and paintings. In Finland, there have, up to date, not been found carvings on solid bedrock, but instead many sites with rock-paintings (Kivikäs 1995). In Swedish Norrland we have found both types of art, but with a dominance of paintings. In Norway we also find both types, there with a dominance of carvings. Why are the carvings missing in Finland? Is it simply that there are no suitable exposed rocks there? I don't think so, because in Finland we also miss the typical sites at river mouths. These are elsewhere – in Russia, north Sweden and north Norway, the biggest sites – and always provided with carvings, not paintings. The most famous examples of these sites are Zalavruga in the mouth of the River Wyg (Sawwatejew 1984), Nämforsen at the mouth of the River Ångermanälven (Hallström 1960), and Alta in the area of the mouth of the River Alta (Helskog 1988). Why is this kind of site missing in Finland, for example by the mouth of any of the Kemi, Oulu, Kyro or Kumo rivers? Is the successive increase of carvings westwards a sign of two different regions of picture technique? Did the western mode of carving not influence the Finnish, while the Finnish painting mode reached far west? Or are the two techniques in essence the same, each expressing a different function in the society?

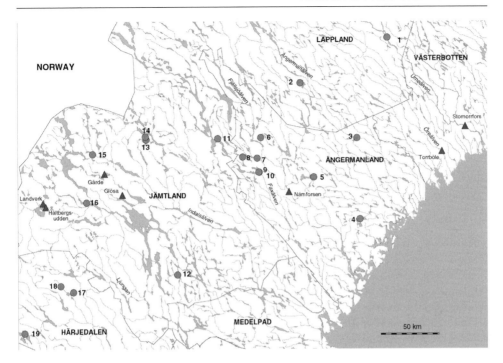

Figure 7.2 All rock-art sites in Norrland known in 1998. The numbers refer to the rock-paintings that are listed in the text. The rock-carvings are named and marked with a triangle

In a third western *taiga* phenomenon, the west Norwegian distribution of rock-art shows a unique sequence (continuation?) of traditions from the supposedly Mesolithic 'Nordland tradition' through the 'ordinary Neolithic and Bronze Age traditions of the hunter-gatherer groups' to the 'South Scandinavian tradition of groups with agriculture'. These three traditions can be found on one and the same spot, as at Hammer in Trøndelag (Hagen 1990: 105ff.). In Norrland we have just vague influences of South Scandinavian motifs at Nämforsen during the Bronze Age (Ramqvist 1992). They are not at all to be compared with the very many sites of agricultural rock-art in the close-lying Norwegian Trøndelag. But in 1998 a small but typical South Scandinavian site with eight or nine partly fragmented carvings was found in Laxforsen (Torrböle in Figure 7.2) by the mouth of the River Öreälven at a height above the sea well corresponding to the Bronze Age (Josephsson Hesse 1999). Also the images are in the 'South Scandinavian' style.

How do we explain these differences in neighbouring districts? As arising through lack of research? Or chronologically? Economically? Organizationally? Cosmologically?

General differences between carvings and paintings in central Norrland

I shall now compare some features in the central Norrland rock-art record, based on what was known in 1998. Even though, on a general level, there are few differences between the two types of pictures, we can make some observations.

Frequencies

There are few sites with carvings, and these contain larger and more complex panels than the painted sites. In this context we are not taking into account the carvings of the 'Nordland tradition', the large-sized and polished carvings probably belonging to the Late Mesolithic period (see Hagen 1976). This tradition is represented in the western part of central Norrland by the carvings at Landverk and Gärde (Figure 7.2). That means that the remaining sites with carvings are Norrfors, Nämforsen and Glösa, and the Bronze Age site at Laxforsen. Also, it is clear that carved sites can be small and contain an individual image or a couple. To conclude: it is obvious that the large carving sites are much bigger than the large sites with paintings.

Verticality

The painted panels only occur on vertical rocks or well-covered sloping rocks; the carvings never or seldom occur on vertical rocks. In the Mesolithic Nordland tradition, however, there are several examples of carvings on vertical surfaces, and there are also examples of Neolithic carvings in north Norway placed on vertical rocks. But the large majority differ totally. Sometimes it is suggested that painted images also were applied to horizontal rocks, but during the millennia these have eroded. This could well be true, but has not yet empirically been shown.

Coastal – inland

The paintings never seem to occur in the direct coastal area, while the carvings occur both by inland lakes and by the coast. No site with paintings has been found in a coastal environment. The closest known site is number 4 at Lake Åbosjön (Figure 7.2) which lies *c*. 200 metres above sea level. If it is of early Mesolithic date it could have been coastal. It is more probable that it belongs to the middle Neolithic period, represented by a shore-displacement curve 60 metres above sea level. The distance to that shoreline is approximately fifteen kilometres. All the rest of the painted sites are placed 'deep' in the forest region. So the paintings seem to be exclusively connected to the forest, while the carvings occur in both environments.

Water connection

All sites known today with carvings are closely connected with water: inland lakes, rivers or the Gulf of Bothnia. The paintings are not dependent on water at all. Of the nineteen painting sites known in central Norrland, eight are not connected with water. For example, one of the most famous and largest sites, at Flatruet (number 18 on Figure 7.2), is placed in a mountain environment (Swedish *lågfjäll*).

The empirical situation in central Norrland

During the 1990s, no fewer than nine of the nineteen rock-painting sites today known in Central Norrland were discovered. Several were found by amateurs in the local communities led by an enthusiastic archaeologist, Bernt Ove Viklund (1997, 1999) in the area of the River Ångermanälven. The discoveries look much like the Finnish example, where thirty-eight of the sixty-one known rock-painting sites were found during the years 1974–1981 (Kivikäs 1995: 324).

In the Norrland rock-art record there are some traits to be noticed. Of the hitherto known 26 sites with rock-art, 19 are painted and 7 are carved. The rock-carvings are published and discussed in several works (among others Hallström 1960; Ramqvist *et al.* 1985; Ramqvist 1990; Forsberg 1993; Lindqvist 1994); for the rock paintings we need up-to-date accounts. Therefore, I here list the painting sites, with a short description and the best reference. Not all are adequately documented. The sites have been numbered according to the numbers on Figure 7.2.

1   Lycksele, Lycksele parish, Lappland: 1 elk, several lines and spots – painted on a vertical rock directly by the River Umeälven. (Fandén 1996.)
2   *Sämsjön*, Åsele parish, Lappland: 4 elk, 1 net image, 1 fragmentary animal, fragmentary spots. On a vertical rock away from the water. (Melander 1980.)
3   *Trolltjärn*, Anundsjö parish, Ångermanland: 3 elk, fragmentary spots. Vertical rock by the small Lake Trolltjärn. (Bertilsson 1992.)
4   *Åbosjön*, Sidensjö parish, Ångermanland: 1 elk, 1 unidentified image. On the vertical side of a large boulder situated in Lake Åbosjön. (Hallström 1960.)
5   *Botilsstenen*, Anundsjö parish, Ångermanland (not adequately documented): 4 fragmentary elk images, some unidentified fragments. The images are painted on a large boulder standing in Lake Storsjön, a setting identical to that of the Åbosjön site (number 4 above). (Viklund 1997.)
6   *Jansjö*, Fjällsjö parish, Ångermanland (not adequately documented): 2 elk images, a vertical line. The images are painted on a large upright stone in the forest. It has no connection to the water, but is otherwise similar to Åbosjön and Botilsstenen (numbers 4 and 5). (Viklund 1997.)
7   *Boforsklacken*, Fjällsjö parish, Ångermanland: at least 7 elk images, 2 possible anthropomorphs, 1 uncertain bear image, also wide lines and spots (probable fragments of images). Situated on a vertical rock and a 45° sloping rock with 'roof overhang'. High up and not close to water. (Viklund 1997.)
8   *Brattfors*, Fjällsjö parish, Ångermanland: 2 elk images – painted on a vertical rock directly by the River Vängelälven. (Jensen 1989; Fandén 1996.)
9   *Högberget I*, Ramsele parish, Ångermanland: 3 certain and 2 fragmented elk images, 2 fragments of anthropomorphs with triangular bodies. Situated a couple of hundred metres from Lake Nässjön, i.e. with no water contact. (Viklund 1997.)
10 *Högberget II*, Ramsele parish, Ångermanland: 3 elk images. Placed high above ground level but easily reachable. No contact with water. (Viklund 1997, 1999.)
11 *Fångsjön*, Ström parish, Jämtland: at least 35 elk images, 1 net image, 1 boat, at least 1 anthropomorphic image, several line fragments. Direct contact with Lake Fångsjön. (Hallström 1960.)
12 *Forsaån*, Bodsjö parish, Jämtland: 4 elk, 1 anthropomorphic image, 1 'snake' zigzag line with terminal ring, fragmentary spots. Vertical rock away from the water. (Rentzog 1993.)
13 *Brattberget*, Föllinge parish, Jämtland: 2 elk, 3 birds (probably), 3 possible anthropomorphs, 2 groups of lines, fragmentary spots. Rock directly by Lake Skärvången. (Hallström 1960.)

14 *Hällberget*, Föllinge parish, Jämtland: 8 elk, 7 anthropomorphs, 1 probable net image, fragments of 10–15 images of which some are elk. Rock directly by Lake Skärvången. (Hallström 1960.)

15 *Hästskotjärn*, Kall parish, Jämtland: 10 elk, 1–2 probable anthropomorphs, 1 'snake' zigzag line with terminal ring (see number 12, Forsaån). Rock directly by Lake Hästskotjärn. (Hallström 1960.)

16 *Hamrebacken*, Duved parish, Jämtland: no information.

17 *Särvsjö*, Hede parish, Härjedalen: 1 elk. Vertical rock in the mountains (*lågfjäll*) away from water. (Hallström 1960.)

18 *Flatruet*, Storsjö parish, Härjedalen: 12 elk, 3 certain and 2 fragments of anthropomorphs, 2 boar-like animals, 1 reindeer, 1 bear, several fragmentary lines and spots. Vertical rock in the mountains (*lågfjäll*) away from water. (Hallström 1960.)

19 *Rogen*, Tännäs parish, Härjedalen: 9 elk, fragments of 2 probable elk. Vertical rock directly by Lake Rogen. (Lööv 1998.)

The distribution of rock-paintings in central Norrland (Figure 7.2) goes from Lycksele in the north-east to Rogen in the south-west, a distance of *c.* 400 kilometres. They are all inland sites.

The number of sites probably represents just a fraction of the original amount. The histories of discovery in Finland and Ångermanland show that a targeted search for rock-paintings gives rich results. The painted sites contain the following numbers of individual images (only the certain images have been counted; see also Figure 7.3):

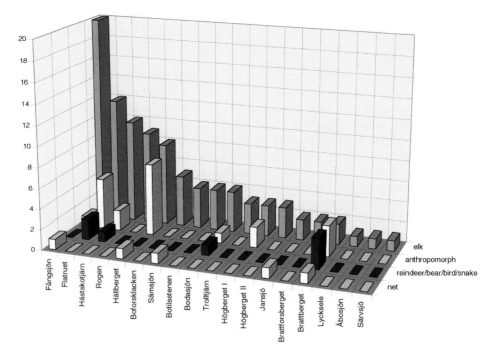

Figure 7.3 The numbers of individual images (certain) on the rock-painting panels in central Norrland. The Hamrebacken site (no. 16) is excluded as no information is available

- 92 elk images
- 18 anthropomorphic images
- 5 net images
- 2 ring-headed zig-zag images
- 3 bird images
- 1 bear image
- 1 reindeer image

Compared to the rock-carvings, the number of individual painted images is small and not really diverging. It is unlikely that all of the rock-art sites belong to the same groups or tribes occupying central Norrland. Instead it is more plausible that several different organizational units populated this part of central Norrland. I see the region on a macro level during the Neolithic as a three-part complex:

- The river tribes, occupying the lower and middle parts of the larger rivers in Norrland. The seasonal use of the river and its tributaries fluctuated from the river mouth up to a certain point; where
- pure inland-oriented tribes had their territories along inland lake systems and the upper parts of the rivers. During the Late Neolithic and Bronze Age these tribes also exploited the high mountain areas (Forsberg 1985).
- To these two main tribal domains we must add the immediate coastal area where coastal tribes had their occupation.

This division of Norrland into three ecologically and culturally different parts could probably be seen from the Late Mesolithic through the Bronze Age to the middle of the first millennium AD. It seems that the biggest settlements of the tribes are represented by the rock-art sites of Nämforsen and Stornorrfors (Figure 7.2), both placed at the mouth of their river valley and in the zone bordering the coastal area. Those positions in the landscape, of course, favour exchange and interaction between tribes and groups living in different environments.

In order to get some structure or contextual grip on the known settlement and rock-art record, I think the River Ångermanälven and its tributaries would be a good case for further study. A good point of departure is the famous site at Nämforsen whose rock-art convincingly has been dated to the Neolithic and Bronze Age by Baudou (1993). The adjacent dwelling site, one of the largest in Norrland, was, however, used until the middle of the first millennium AD.

The tribal territory of the valleys of the River Ångermanälven possibly goes from Nämforsen in the south-east to some point 100 kilometres or so to the north and north-west. It does not go further down into the real coastal zone. Even though Nämforsen during the third millennium BC was at the mouth of the river, it had no real contact with the archipelago since the bay at that time was very deeply cut into the land. In the immediate coastal area, tribes and groups more specialized in seal-hunting and fishing were active probably on a seasonal basis, perhaps just using the close-lying forest areas during parts of the winter. The most famous coastal site dating to the Neolithic is Överveda (Baudou 1977: 42ff.).

I will look now at the sites with painted rock-art within or in a very close contact with the river and lake system of Ångermanälven, and discuss their relation to Nämforsen, their pictorial content, and their role as settlement indicators.

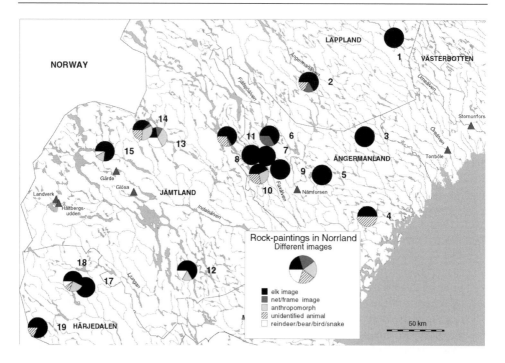

Figure 7.4 Map showing the distribution of the different images on each site with rock-paintings in central Norrland. Relative frequencies. (For absolute numbers see Figure 7.3)

Sites around the Ångermanälven River

Along the valley and side valleys of the Ångermanälven River there are seven sites not very far from Nämforsen (numbers 5–11 on Figure 7.2). They all lie north and north-west of Nämforsen, and could perhaps be made by the same tribe. These sites today represent 37 per cent of the known Norrland painted sites. Their content regarding images is as follows:*

- 37 elk images
- 3 anthropomorphic images
- 1 net image

That means that 40 per cent of the elk, 17 per cent of the human images and 20 per cent of the net images are represented on the seven painted sites close to Nämforsen. Even though the numbers are small, there is a tendency for elk more to dominate each individual site than at the sites in Jämtland and Härjedalen (Figure 7.4).

---

* Only the certain images are counted, as at practically each site there are painted lines, spots and surfaces that are difficult to interpret.

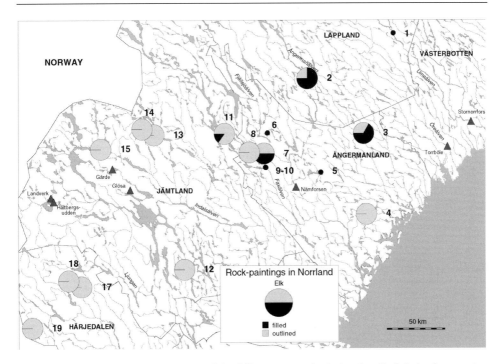

Figure 7.5 Map showing the distribution of the different ways of painting the elk. Relative frequencies. (For absolute numbers see the list in the text)

If we look at the painted elk pictures as a whole in central Norrland, we have 92 clearly identified elk images; 79 occur on sites where some kind of documentation has been done. Of these 79, 69 images are drawn with an outer line only ('outlined'), and 10 are filled in with solid colour ('filled'). An interesting feature is seen in Figure 7.5: at all the sites in the western part of central Norrland the elk are outlined; among the sites in the river system of the Ångermanälven and sites north-east thereof there are several sites where elk are painted in both modes.

The counterparts to these painting conventions in the carvings at Nämforsen are the images made with an engraved defining line ('outlined'), and those in which the whole area has been engraved ('scooped out'). On the whole, these have relatively equal frequencies. These two different ways of depicting elk (and of course other images) occur at Nämforsen in relatively even numbers: there, according to Hallström (1960), 346 (52 per cent) of the 661 certain elk images are scooped out. Studying this relationship in detail (Ramqvist 1992), I found that across the sixteen separable areas within the Nämforsen site the proportion varies considerably. On a 'tribal level' it could be significant that the carvings and the paintings of the elk are made in this same 'mode'. Carvings (at Nämforsen) and paintings (at sites numbers 5–11 in Figure 7.2) were made in both the outlined and the filled/scooped-out form by the tribe living in the Ångermanälven River system. Another example of such a tribal unit could be represented by the sites around the carvings at Glösa. At these sites, like those numbered 13–15, all the elk are outlined (Figure 7.5). Could this kind of habit be a matter of tribal unity, indicating the spatial distribution of different tribal entities?

The differences between the 'outlined' and 'scooped-out' images have been discussed before. Malmer (1981: 100ff.), Forsberg (1993) and Lindqvist (1994: 138) see them as chronological indicators, while others see them as clan indicators (Tilley 1991) or as bearers of other meaning (Ramqvist 1992). Over a larger scale it seems there are regional (local) traditions concerning the technique of in-filling. In the River Wyg localities the scooped-out images dominate totally. We know these carvings were made as late as during the transition from the Late Neolithic to the early Bronze Age (Sawwatejew 1984: 201); but they were probably produced from the beginning of the fourth millennium BC. In Alta in north Norway the engravings were produced between *c*. 4000 and 500 BC (Helskog 1988: 31ff.); there, very few pictures are scooped out. The same is true for the Late Neolithic site at Stornorrfors in Västerbotten (Ramqvist *et al.* 1985). Therefore, I don't think that the chronological issue is of importance regarding the way of depicting elk, despite the fact that Forsberg (1993) mentions (but does not demonstrate) several cases at Nämforsen where outlined images overlap scooped-out images.

Rock-art and settlement

One of the few who has tried to see the Nämforsen site in connection with other close-lying sites is Evert Baudou (1992). He sees the dwelling site at Nämforsen as one of several sites making up a settlement system. That includes sites on the river upstream as well as downstream, and by the archipelago. He suggests that the Rå-inget site a few kilometres upstream from Nämforsen (see Figure 7.6) could be a year-round settlement, a base camp. As seasonal aggregation camps, he suggests Nämforsen during the summer

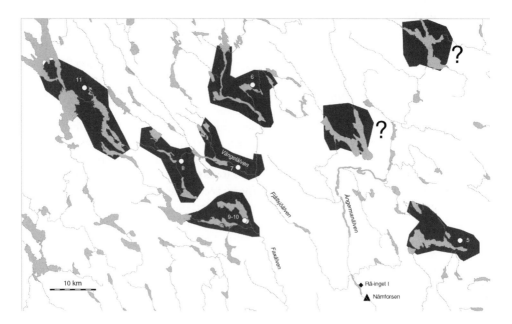

Figure 7.6 Map showing the proposed areas used from the base camps connected to the 'Ångermanälven River tribe'

when masses of salmon migrate upstream and the Överveda site in the archipelago during the autumn when the seals gathered in the bays. There are, in other words, several types of contemporary sites around the Nämforsen site which indicate that we can find some kind of settlement pattern. As mentioned earlier, I don't think that the archipelago, i.e. the site at Överveda, belonged to the same system as the river dwellings like Nämforsen and Rå-inget. The best argument for that is that the coast shows a quite different development through the millennia according to the material culture. The similarities that do however exist are due to intensive interaction between the coastal and river groups.

Whatever functions and terms these different sites should be given, they can be ordered with regard to size and content (a study which has not yet been done). A precedent has been sketched by Ingela Bergman (1995: 8ff.) for the area around Lake Hornavan. Her site categories are (with a slight modification by myself):

- Base camp: the centre of a resource utilization area, occupied by a group for a longer period of time, several seasons.
- Field camp: occupied by part of a group for a shorter time, season or part of season.
- Extraction camp: occupied by a task group for a couple of days in order to exploit a specific resource.
- Aggregation camp: the largest site of all where several groups from different tribes gathered for a shorter period of time. This type of site is located in areas rich in food resources, preferably during the summer and perhaps close to border lines between tribe territories.

It seems increasingly plausible that the settlement organization followed a model of this character during the Neolithic and Bronze Age. A relatively large variation of settlement types is found, from the smaller extraction camps to the bigger base and aggregation camps. The dwelling site at Nämforsen was clearly an aggregation camp, predominantly used during the summer months. During the autumn the groups returned to their base camps in their different tribal territories for autumn, winter and spring activities. If we look at the system north and north-west of Nämforsen the 'Ångermanälven River tribe' could have been distributed according to the areas shown by the rock-painting sites (Figure 7.6). I have also marked an area of approximately 100 square kilometres around these sites. An interesting feature to notice on Figure 7.6 is that the rock-painting sites are connected with larger lake systems occurring within the large river systems. It follows from this observation that in the other comprehensive lake system there should also be found sites with rock-paintings (in the two areas marked with question-marks in Figure 7.6). Could these areas contain the base camps, field and extraction camps used during the cool seasons by an 'Ångermanälven River tribe'?

On practically all of the river and lake shores, dwelling sites of different types have been found. Minor analyses have also addressed the relationship between painting sites and dwellings (Fandén 1996). A typical finding is that there is no direct or point relationship between the two kinds of features; instead, the area directly around the painted sites seems not to have been settled. That unsettled zone probably represents a 'holy area' separating the 'zone of religion' from the 'zones of everyday activities'. The same distancing could be seen in the habit of placing carving sites on islands in the rivers – as at Nämforsen, Stornorrfors, Zalavruga and so on – obviously to achieve a spatial separation.

If the idea of the eight base-camp areas is of any significance, the painting sites are indicators to be taken seriously. These sites should be the 'holy places' at a lower level of organization than the carving site at Nämforsen, the pan-tribal site for religion, social and exchange activities. Interpreted in that way, we could see the images at Nämforsen as a result of the cosmology of the whole community, while the images on painted sites are more oriented towards the religious needs of the different groups. Their needs may primarily be connected to survival during the more difficult seasons of autumn, winter and spring. Therefore, the painted sites most often are smaller and less varied than the carved sites. As a consequence it follows that the painted sites also were made during the cooler seasons, something suggested earlier, but from a different point of departure (Taavitsainen 1978; Ramqvist 1992).

I have tried in this chapter to organize and discuss empirical data of various kinds and of various quality in order to get some new ideas about the life and organization of the hunter-gatherer in the *taïga* region. I hope that the discussion will also be of some interest to other scholars working with the subject of understanding the genetic relationship between such different things as rock-art and dwellings.

References

Baudou, E. 1977. Den förhistoriska fångstkulturen i Västernorrland, *Västernorrlands förhistoria*: 11–152. Härnösand.

Baudou, E. 1992. Boplatsen vid Nämforsen, *Arkeologi i norr* 3: 71–82.

Baudou, E. 1993. Hällristningarna vid Nämforsen – datering och kulturmiljö: ekonomi och näringsformer i nordisk bronsålder, *Studia archaeologica universitatis Umensis* 3: 247–261.

Bergman, I. 1995. *Från Döudden till Varghalsen: en studie av kontinuitet och förändring inom ett fångstsamhälle i Övre Norrlands inland, 5200 f Kr–400 e Kr*. Umeå: Arkeologiska institutionen, Umeå Universiet. Studia Archaeologica Universitatis Umensis.

Bertilsson, U. 1992. En nyupptäckt hällmålning vid Trolltjärn i Anundsjö: Arkeologi nolaskogs: fornlämningar, fynd och forskning i norra Ångermanland, *Skrifter från Örnsköldsviks Museum* 3: 55–58.

Ekman, J. and Iregren, E. 1984. *Archaeo-zoological investigations in northern Sweden*. Stockholm: Kungl Vitterhets Historie och Antikvitets Akademien. Early Norrland 8.

Fandén, A. 1996. Den norrländska hällmålningstraditionen: tolkning av funktion och symbolisk betydelse. Unpublished paper, Department of Archaeology, Stockholm University.

Forsberg, L. 1985. *Site variability and settlement patterns: an analysis of the hunter-gatherer settlement system in the Lule River Valley, 1500 BC–BC/AD*. Umeå: Department of Archaeology, Umeå University. Archaeology and Environment 5.

Forsberg, L. 1993. Ekonomi och näringsformer i nordisk bronsålder: en kronologisk analys av ristningarna vid Nämforsen: ekonomi och näringsformer i nordisk bronsålder, *Studia Archaeologica Universitatis Umensis* 3: 195–246.

Hagen, A. 1976. *Bergkunst: jegerfolkets helleristninger og malinger i norsk steinalder*. Oslo: J.W. Cappelens Forlag.

Hagen, A. 1990. *Hellerisningar i Norge*. Oslo: Det norska Samlaget.

Hallström, G. 1960. *Monumental art of northern Sweden from the Stone Age, 2: Nämforsen and other localities*. Stockholm: Kungl Vitterhets Historie och Antikvitets Akademien.

Helskog, K. 1988. *Helleristningene i Alta: spor etter ritualer og dagligliv i Finnmarks forhistorie*. Alta: Alta Museum.

Jensen, R. 1989. Hällbilder och fångstboplatser: arkeologi i fjäll, skog och bygd, 1: Stenålder – tidig järnålder, *Fornvårdaren* 23: 57–82.

Josephsson Hesse, K. 1999. Laxforsen: hällristningar i brytningstid. Unpublished paper, Department of Archaeology, Umeå University.

Kivikäs, P. 1995. *Kalliomaalaukset, muinainen kuva-arkisto*. Jyväskylä: Atena.

Lindqvist, C. 1994. *Fångstfolkets bilder: en studie av de nordfennoskandiska kustanknutna jägarhäll-ristningarna*. Stockholm: Stockholm University. Theses and Papers in Archaeology NS A5.

Lööv, L.-I. 1998. Nyupptäckt hällmålning, *Jämten*: 109–111.

Malmer, M.P. 1981. *A chorological study of north European rock art*. Stockholm: Kungl Vitterhets Historie och Antikvitets Akademien. Antikvariska Serien 32.

Melander, J. 1980. Dokumentation och undersökning av hällmålning raä nr 151, Sämsjölandet 1: 1, Åsele sn, Västerbotten. Unpublished report, Umeå: Västerbottens Museum.

Ramqvist, P.H. 1990. Fångstristningar och deras användning vid tolkningen av samtida kulturhistoriska sammanhang: kalliotaidetta-tutkimusta ja tulkinta: hällristningar – forskning och tolkning, *Åbo Landskapsmuseum Rapport* 11: 41–51.

Ramqvist, P.H. 1992. Hällbilder som utgångspunkt vid tolkningar av jägarsamhället, *Arkeologi i norr* 3: 31–53.

Ramqvist, P.H., L. Forsberg and M. Backe 1985. . . . And here was an elk too . . . a preliminary report of new petroglyphs at Stornorrfors, Ume River, in *Honorem Evert Baudou: archaeology and environment* 4: 313–337. Umeå: Department of Archaeology, Umeå University.

Rentzog, S. 1993. Älg och 'orm' var målade med rött på lodräta hällen, *Populär Arkeologi* 2: 4–6.

Sawwatejew, J.A. 1984. *Karelische Felsbilder*. Leipzig: Veb. E.A. Seeman Verlag.

Taavitsainen, J.-P. 1978. Hällmålningarna – en ny syn på Finlands förhistoria, *Antropologi i Finland* 4: 179–195.

Tilley, C. 1991. *Material culture and text: the art of ambiguity*. London: Routledge.

Viklund, B.O. 1997. Nyupptäckta hällmålningar i Anundsjö, Fjällsjö och Ramsele i Ångermanland, *Oknytt* 3–4: 20–33.

Viklund, B.O. 1999. Älgar målade i älgens eget rike – nyupptäckta hällmålningar i Ångermanland, *Tidsspår*: 49–57.

Chapter 8

Marking the landscape
Iberian post-Palaeolithic art, identities and the sacred

Margarita Díaz-Andreu

Rock-art and landscapes

In this chapter my aim is to look at the ways in which the ritual aspect of the landscape has been analysed in rock-art studies. I will propose that the use of the concepts of ritual depth of the landscape and of identity of the actors who lived through rock-art landscapes can greatly improve our understanding of the ritual landscape. I will apply both concepts to the examination of a specific case-study, the post-Palaeolithic paintings of Villar del Humo (Spain), and argue that their use gives us a far deeper understanding of how landscapes were ritualized through rock-art.

In the last few years in the archaeological literature there has been a significant growth in the use of the term 'ritual landscape'. 'Ritual landscapes' – also 'ritual seascapes' or 'sacred landscapes' – are an increasing concern in rock-art studies (Bradley 1997b: 124; Hedges 1993; Rault 1997; Sognnes 1994) as well as in other fields of archaeological inquiry (Kinnes 1998; Saunders 1994). Yet discussions on the religious significance of prehistoric art are not new. Some took place right at the outset of rock-art studies (Bégouen 1929; Reinach 1903). The early authors hypothesized about hunting magic, fertility magic and totemism. However, after early interest in this type of approach, archaeologists in the culture-historical tradition tended to abandon these questions and concentrate on more aseptic descriptions (Breuil 1952). Leroi-Gourhan (1967) went a step further with his rejection of all use of ethnographic parallels. Albeit maintaining a basic vocabulary connected to religion (for example, he often alluded to 'sanctuaries', meaning the painted caves), his analysis of art was largely unconcerned with the field of ritual. Parallel to his work, in America and Britain New Archaeology scholars also detached themselves from the field of religion and focused their studies on art as adaptation, taking the environment – or aspects of it, such as its potential in economic terms and the way its changes affected society – as one of the main explanatory factors behind the production of art (Gamble 1982; Jochim 1976). It is only since the 1980s that scholars have rescued the symbolic and religious significance of rock-art (but see Hartley and Vawser 1998). Scholars have turned their eyes from socio-economic approaches to environment to the study of 'ritual landscapes'.

Recent studies of ritual landscapes have focused attention on several issues: ethnicity, shamanism and the topography of the area in which the art has been produced. Some of these questions are new but others represent novel perspectives on known fields of discussion. One example of the latter is the reassessment of one of the main fields of enquiry of New Archaeology, art as information and as such its potential for economic adaptive strategies. Authors such as Taçon have made a connection between the hypothesis of art as information and the religious world of past peoples. Looking at the role of rock-art in the association of certain features in the landscape with ancestors, Taçon argues that a long-term perspective is needed. He maintains that when the first humans arrived in Australia – as in other parts of the globe – 'features of the earth's geology and landscapes made impressions on human consciousness' (Taçon 1994: 118). These first impressions 'created' the landscape for all later human use when the first colonizers became the ancestors of subsequent generations. Rock-art was used as a medium of passing information to later generations about the more functional aspect of the landscape (Taçon 1994: 118). Taçon maintains that one of the main types of data which rock-art may have served to convey regarded ethnicity. He points to ethnographic examples which seem to back up the ethnic meaning of rock-art (Taçon 1994: 120–121) and concludes, perhaps over-optimistically,* that 'rock-art, at least in Holocene times, has been used to signal clan, language and other group identity differences between people' (Taçon 1994: 123). Finally, he asserts that, at least for contemporary people, sites with outstanding natural signifiers are regarded as the most powerful parts of the landscape.

Taçon is not alone in considering topography as important to the relationship between ideology/religion and landscape. In the case of the prehistoric rock-art of Norway, Sognnes (1994: 39) discusses the location of rock-art on the shore (but see Bradley 1997a) as the result of its perception as a liminal locale (at the meeting-place between sea, land and sky), which would confer upon the place a ritual meaning (Sognnes 1994: 43). A different view of the same type of art in its spatial setting has been developed by Hood, who sees rock-art 'as a signification system connecting a set of social relations over space' and points out how the geographic fixation of the discourse narrated in the rock-art 'sets up tensions in regional spatial relations' (Hood 1988: 65). Hood argues that in prehistoric Norway, groups living far from the coast would be disadvantaged regarding their participation in the discourse which was mainly controlled by the coastal groups.

Topography has also been seen as increasingly significant by the expanding group of researchers who give weight to the shamanistic origins of rock-art. †Universal explanations of shamanism point to a belief in the underworld as the dwelling place of the spirits. Because of this, it is argued that artists–shamans painted on rocks either when recalling shamanistic experiences of the supernatural (Lewis-Williams and Dowson 1988), or perhaps as a preparation for such experiences (Kinahan 1999). The importance of the underworld has led other authors to argue for a role of the rock itself. Von Werlhof (1992: 3), for example, argues:

> the relationship the shamans achieved between their art and rock surfaces is seen to us only in spatial form, but one needs to go beyond the perception of matter to see how the art fuses with the rock, blending symbol with substance. This is art of the highest order, a total synthesis, and certainly was the greatest achievement of the shamans.

---

* For my view on ethnicity and the very limited degree to which archaeologists can study this identity in prehistoric periods see Díaz-Andreu (1998a).
† It is not the aim of this article to develop my counter-arguments on the relationship established by some between prehistoric rock-art and shamanism.

The issue of topography has been examined further by some researchers who point to the link between stunning visual and auditory topographical features and rock-art. Bradley (1997a: 123–124), for example, has emphasized that rock-art is located at 'entrances' in the natural terrain that he subsequently defines as ritual. This ritual landscape, furthermore, is characterized in many instances by its impressive setting (Bradley 1997a: 132–135). Ken Hedges (1993) interprets the link between rock-art with prominent features in the landscape – lakes, rocks, a mountain and so on – as a *hierophany*, a manifestation of the sacred. In his study of the rock-art of the American South-west, Hedges indicates how the relationship between Navajo and Hopi belief in the sacredness of certain mountains and rock-art is manifested both in the location of the art and in the orientation of the shelters chosen to be painted.

Hedges's (1993) and Bradley's (1997a: 213) studies go further in their consideration of topography: they not only point to the significance of the location of rock-art itself, but also to the importance of the rocks on which art has been produced. In addition, Hedges suggests the existence of other special features like the sound-effects of rocks (rocks that ring like a chime when struck, for example) for their selection, proposing that senses other than the visual may have been important. He further argues that this may even have been the case with the earliest art, as studies by Dams (1984, 1985) for the Upper Palaeolithic, and by Coles (1991: 133) and Sognnes (1994: 39) for Scandinavian post-Palaeolithic rock-art indicate. In the latter case Sognnes, following Coles, believes that the sonority produced by the sea may have been an important element connected to the location of the art.

The attention paid to the landscape by the authors discussed above has provided a fresh, much needed corrective to the previous, dehumanized analysis of the landscape. Yet, here I propose that the inclusion of two further elements, the ritual depth of the landscape and the question of identities, are fundamental for an adequate understanding of the landscape.

Rock-art and landscapes: ritual depth and identity

The recent interest raised by ritual may have led some authors to overstate the role of rock-art in ritualizing landscapes.* This is the case, I believe, with authors such as Sognnes (1994: 30, 43), who only seems to consider possible the ritualization of the landscape through the making of rock-art. Yet, not all ritual landscapes are decorated with rock-art. Types of material culture other than art that can also be instrumental in this respect. An example of a different type of material culture which can stress the identity of special places is that of prehistoric stone axes. As Cooney (1998: 111–113) argues, in Ireland stone-axe quarries are characteristically located at liminal places, either in mountains (in many societies places are sacred because they seem to touch the sky) or small islands (which Cooney considers as liminal, special places). He suggests (1998: 113) the possibility of quarries having acted as sacred places and landmarks in the past. A further example† is that of the building of megaliths, seen by most authors as another

---

* We could also add that not even all rock-art is primarily religious. Some of it has a marked secular aspect as shown in the examples of some Aboriginal rock-art.
† Although in this case it could be argued that megaliths are a form of art.

means of ritualizing a landscape, to establish, in Tilley's (1993: 80) words, 'a particular form of ordering and domesticating in the landscape bound up with stressing ancestral presence through architectural orders'. The possibility of ritualization of the landscape through other types of material culture is something that rock-art researchers should not ignore. However, the lack of data – a problem which I have encountered in this case-study – makes the integration of this factor impossible.

The novel emphasis on the field of ritual has not led all researchers to forget the secular aspect of the landscape. As Tilley stresses, there is no 'polar divide between a supposed economic rationality and a cultural and symbolic logic, but rather . . . each helps to constitute the other' (1994).* This issue has been dealt with by rock-art specialists such as Bradley (1997b). In his discussion of post-Palaeolithic Atlantic rock-art, he argues that 'to say that . . . [the landscape] was both sacred and secular is merely to perpetuate a division of experience found in contemporary society. This distinction would have been incomprehensible in prehistory' (Bradley 1997a: 152). In this, Bradley follows Tim Ingold, who has argued (Ingold 1986: 140–141) that

> the distinction between religion and economy, upon which western legal and anthropological argument sets such store, has no meaning for native people . . . The very provisioning of society is thought to depend upon the proper conduct of ritual activity, whose object is periodically to revitalize the environment, thereby securing the reproduction of all animal and plant life.

Bradley seeks to integrate the economic/secular with the sacred/ritual aspects of the landscape. He argues (1997a: 88, 91) that rock-art might have been located at vantage-points and also along paths or trails, and usually at or beyond the limits of fertile land: a secular account of its placing. At the same time the author (1997a: 123) considers rock-art as signalling the entrance or at least marking a ritual landscape.

Thus, the recognition of both sacred and secular represents an important step forward in understanding landscape but, in my opinion, this is not enough. A simple equating of the sacred and secular may be as unsatisfactory as considering them as polar opposites. To assimilate the secular to the sacred, or to conflate them, may result in an over-simplification. This is because the relationship between them is problematic and full of tensions which need to be integrated in our enquiry. I therefore propose that we can usefully add to our analysis the idea of the ritual depth in the level of sacredness versus secularity that a place holds in the landscape. The uneven ritual depth of landscape is apparent in that some sites are more ritually charged than others. The degree of secularity and sacredness of a megalith, for example, cannot be equated to that of a house. Daily tasks and practices in the domestic space may be guided by basic religious schemata, but

---

* Yet, despite Tilley's intention, the symbolic logic of the landscape predominates over any economic significance: ideology takes precedence in his reflection on landscape. Both Colin Richards's (1993) and Julian Thomas's (1993) studies on the hermeneutics of megalithic space also show a similar bias towards the ideological aspect of landscape. The authors seem to imply that the secularity of the landscape is secondary to its sacred significance. Despite their step forward in breaking the duality of sacred and secular, the praxis of their analyses still shows a certain reluctance to accept the implication of their own ideas. In practice, the old emphasis on the 'secular landscape' has been transformed into an exclusively focused 'ritual landscape'.

to a great extent they are connected to what we understand nowadays as secular activities. The different depth of secularity/sacredness of each site is something that studies of ritual landscapes seem to have overlooked.

An adequate understanding of the concept of ritual depth of the landscape, however, cannot be complete without paying attention to the question of identities. The balance between the sacredness and secularity of a place cannot be considered as fixed. The magnitude of sacredness of a place is not rigidly fixed by a system of beliefs. The perception of sacredness/secularity of a place depends on who is experiencing a particular space. Individuals are a complex, mutating sum of their identities and each of these identities may affect the way in which the character of the space is perceived. Different audiences may live through a place in diverse ways, and even the same person may experience a place disparately in different moments in his or her life. The religious significance of a place depends, therefore, on a sum of circumstances that can only be partially grasped from a present-day perspective.

In the remainder of this chapter my aim is to illustrate this hypothesis through a case-study, that of the post-Palaeolithic paintings of Villar del Humo (Spain). I will try to explain how the inclusion in the studies of ritual landscapes of the concepts of ritual depth and the consideration of the multiple identities of the actors who produced and/or experienced rock-art in the landscape can enrich our understanding of them.

The landscapes of Iberian post-Palaeolithic art

Spain is a country rich in rock-art. It has a wide variety of periods and styles, from Palaeolithic cave and open-air art to Linear-Geometric, Macroschematic, Levantine and Schematic post-Palaeolithic art. Despite the potential of such diversity, rock-art studies in Spain – especially those on post-Palaeolithic art – are generally limited to bare descriptions of the paintings. Analyses are still largely taken under the culture-historical perspective. Within this paradigm, references to the ritual significance of the paintings, although not common, lurk untheorized in publications: allusions to 'sanctuaries', the 'mother goddess', 'shamans', 'sorcerers' and 'hunting and fertility magic' are made. There are two exceptions to this rule: the articles by Llavori de Micheo (1988–1989) and Criado Boado and Penedo Romero (1993). Llavori explains the restriction of Levantine art to mountain areas as the result of Mesolithic communities being confined to these areas by Neolithic populations. For this author, Levantine art was produced by Mesolithic communities as a means to give a symbolic meaning to their territory in opposition to that of other territories whose reality – that of agropastoral productive economies – was alien to them. A similar proposal has been made from a more classic culture-historical approach by Martí Oliver and Hernández 1988 who not only relate the earlier Levantine paintings to Mesolithic populations but link the Schematic style to contemporary Neolithic societies. For their part, Criado Boado and Penedo (1993: 200) discuss Levantine art as the result of the emergence of a new concept of space and time, by which the interaction between culture and environment was active and positive.

Despite the novelty of Llavori's and Criado Boado and Penedo's suggestions, neither really discusses the framing of the art in the landscape. Yet, this approach can provide an enriching, refreshing and novel perspective to the understanding of post-Palaeolithic art styles. My discussion will only marginally deal with the earlier post-Palaeolithic styles, the Linear-Geometric and the Macroschematic – although the location of the latter in a

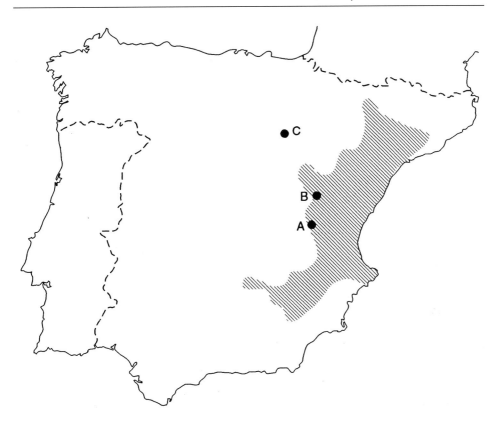

Figure 8.1 Map of the Iberian Peninsula. The shaded area indicates the area where Levantine paintings are found. A: Villar del Humo; B: Albarracín; C: Valonsadero

specific region in the province of Alicante certainly deserves closer analysis. Instead, I will mainly focus on Levantine and Schematic art. The most accepted hypothesis nowadays is that Levantine rock-art originated either in the Mesolithic around the sixth millennium BC (Alonso Tejada and Grimal 1996: 281) or during the early Neolithic, some time in the fifth millennium BC (Alonso Tejada and Grimal 1996; Martí Oliver and Hernández 1988: 36). Levantine paintings are found in an area about 250 km wide along the Mediterranean coast of the Iberian Peninsula (Figure 8.1). Schematic art is also thought to date from the the Neolithic (Marcos Pous 1981; Martí Oliver and Hernández 1988: 45). Its distribution covers practically the whole of the Iberian Peninsula. Schematic art is not only found in painted shelters, but also on carved rocks, on plaques and stelae, as well as in megaliths, where painted and engraved motifs were made on the megalithic stones forming the structure.

A closer look at the distribution of sites with Levantine and Schematic paintings immediately makes it clear that not all areas have rock-art. Painted shelters tend to be grouped together in specific zones. In some regions the absence of sites can be explained by a lack of appropriate rock-shelters to paint, but this is not the case in all instances, for many areas with shelters potentially suitable for decoration were never used. It is usually the case that only mountain areas were selected, but not even all of these display rock-art. The decisions made by prehistoric peoples regarding which areas were eligible to be painted is a subject that requires further thought, and the lack of reference to this issue in specialized publications is surprising indeed (although see Beltrán Martínez 1992: 22).

The concentration of rock-shelters in particular areas denotes that the locales selected for painting post-Palaeolithic art were not arbitrarily chosen. Prehistoric communities, through their paintings, specified the identity of place. The reasons behind the choice of landscape to be decorated, however, need to be elucidated. Yet, geomorphological features and economic potential of the various decorated zones vary widely: it does not seem that there is a sole reason behind all these choices. Different areas might have been selected for different motives. I centre my discussion on the Villar del Humo rock-art area. Yet, similar rock-art areas where there is a high concentration of rock-art sites are to be found both within the Levantine region (shaded in Figure 8.1) and in the territory where only Schematic paintings are found (practically the whole Iberian Peninsula with the exception of the Galician region). Valonsadero in the province of Soria (Gómez Barrera 1982) is an example of the latter. This chapter, however, will not discuss the case of Valonsadero, and will only refer to Albarracín in the Levantine area when undertaking a comparison with Villar del Humo. This is because both Albarracín and Villar del Humo share not only the use of the same rock-art styles but also a very similar topography. They have a number of special characteristics in common. I will suggest that the concentration of sites in both is probably linked with a wish of prehistoric communities to convey the (religious) singularity of the area by marking it. The specific reasons that I propose led prehistoric communities to decorate both Villar del Humo and Albarracín are not necessarily the same as those that lie behind the painting of other areas. I aim to answer why Villar de Humo and Albarracín produced such spectacular rock-art, while neighbouring territories did not, and what led prehistoric communities to select both areas to be decorated.

Villar del Humo: the ritual meaning of landscape

Villar del Humo is nowadays one of the most isolated villages in the province of Cuenca. Access to the village is not easy, as it is surrounded by a rugged landscape comprising mountains. These form part of the mountain chain of the Macizo Ibérico. The decline of the traditional economies – animal husbandry and hunting – and high emigration has deterred the authorities from investing the large sums of money needed to build a road to facilitate access to the village from the north. In recent years the mayor decided that the only way to lift the village out of its decline was to exploit its two potential sources of wealth: its prehistoric paintings and the unique geomorphology of the area. As will be suggested, rather than being two discrete assets, these two are interrelated. The prehistoric paintings were made in Villar del Humo precisely because of the extraordinary geomorphology of the area.

Most of the Villar del Humo district is characterized by a peculiar geology, a spectacular red sandstone known locally as *rodeno*. Outside the *rodeno* area, the geology is replaced by limestone, the bedrock which characterizes most of the mountains in the Macizo Ibérico. In Villar del Humo the relationship between red sandstone and rock-art is manifest when the location of sites is mapped against geomorphology: *all* rock-art is located in the red sandstone area (Figure 8.2). This strong relationship between location and geomorphology seems to point to the importance of the *rodeno* in creating a special meaning for

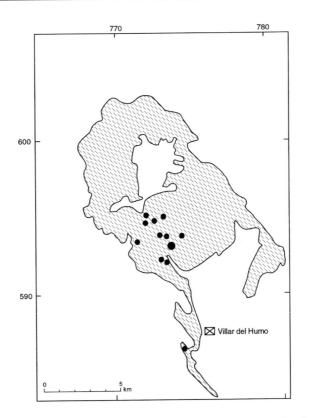

Figure 8.2 Rock-art sites in Villar del Humo. The shaded area indicates the *rodeno* landscape

the area, a meaning (following the studies discussed in the section on rock-art and landscape above) that I consider as ritual. This consideration is backed up by the fact that no other reason seems to exist for the selection of this area; from an ecological point of view, the sandstone is not distinct from the limestone area. It is probable that the sacred significance of the *rodeno* led Villar del Humo to be perceived by prehistoric hunter-gatherers as a spatial node with ritual importance even before it was decorated. The paintings were made by prehistoric communities as a way of stressing the specificity of place, probably actively to manipulate its meaning, to underline its peculiarity, and to ritualize further its landscape.

Villar del Humo is not the only area in Cuenca or indeed in the Macizo Ibérico mountains with red sandstone. As is clear in Figure 8.2, Villar del Humo forms part of a wider zone of the *rodeno*. The lack of sites in the remaining *rodeno* area may seem surprising to someone unaware of the history of research in the area; it is probably due simply to lack of surveys in the province of Cuenca. Moreover, the archaeological study of the Villar del Humo area has been subject to a high degree of negligence. Discovered in 1917, it was first briefly mentioned in 1921 (Hernández Pacheco 1921). Further publications only offered partial accounts of the area (Alonso Tejada 1984, 1985; Alonso Tejada *et al.* 1982; Beltrán Martínez 1968a, 1968b; Hernández Pacheco 1959; Jordá Cerdá 1975; López Payer and Soria Lerma 1991). Only recently has an amateur archaeologist published a comprehensive description of the rock-art of Villar del Humo (Romero Sáiz 1996). The regional government has never financed official surveys in the area, and those undertaken so far have been funded by other means and never directed to the location of rock-art sites (Díaz-Andreu 1994: ch. 3; Díaz-Andreu and Montero 1998: ch. 4). The discovery of a new rock-art site about twelve kilometres to the east of Villar del Humo in the neighbouring municipal district of Henarejos in 1998, the Cueva del Tío Juanico site, is only a hint of what is still to come. This site, now under investigation by the University of Alicante, is not isolated, for further information coming from other districts in the province of Cuenca seems to point to more sites in the *rodeno* (Romero Sáiz, personal communication).

The relationship between the red sandstone and the rock-art becomes clear when a comparison is made between Villar del Humo and Albarracín, about a hundred kilometres to the north in the province of Teruel. As in the case of Villar del Humo, all rock-art sites known in Albarracín are located in the *rodeno* (Figure 8.3). This indicates a careful selection of the areas to be decorated. Some authors have remarked upon this (Almagro Basch 1974: 31; López Payer and Soria Lerma 1991), but there has been no attempt to explain the similarity. A clarification of the processes which led to this pattern is, therefore, much needed.

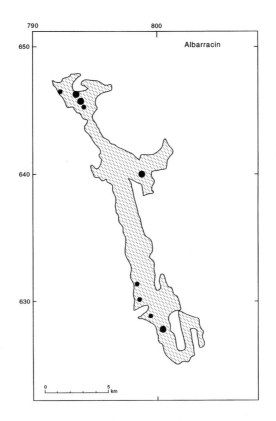

Figure 8.3 Rock-art sites in Albarracín. The shaded area indicates the *rodeno* landscape

A secular use of the landscape was most probably in play. Surveys undertaken in areas with Levantine art usually highlight the occasional association between the paintings and Mesolithic and Neolithic sites (Almagro Basch 1949; Fortea 1974; Galiana Botella 1992; Utrilla Miranda 1986–1987). Rock-art sites with Schematic art have also been related to Chalcolithic sites (González Cordero and Alvarado Gonzalo 1985). In most cases these non-rock-art sites are interpreted as habitation sites and nothing in them – location, material culture or any other feature – indicates that they were distinct from other sites in areas without rock-art. There is no reason, therefore, to conclude that these archaeological sites had a particular ritual character. Regarding Villar del Humo, there is little to say in this respect, for surveys undertaken there have been far from appropriate in order to locate sites of the type frequent in the earlier periods of prehistory. (But some Neolithic material is known from a neighbouring area: Díaz-Andreu 1994: 138; and from the same mountain range in Cuenca: Fernández-Miranda and Moure 1975; Moure Romanillo and Fernández-Miranda 1977.) In Albarracín, though, excavations have unearthed Mesolithic material (Almagro Basch 1949). As in the other cases, the excavator did not point to a difference between these archaeological sites and others elsewhere. In addition, nothing in the specialized literature on the economic geography and economy of the region indicates noteworthy differences between the *rodeno* and neighbouring sandstone areas.

The likeness, at an economic level, of both the red sandstone and the limestone areas does not explain, therefore, why Villar del Humo and Albarracín were selected to be decorated. If this selection was not informed by an economic incentive – despite the areas being used for secular purposes – there must have been a different justification for their being painted. I argue that it was the striking topography and colour of both areas which conferred on the landscape a symbolic–ritual significance. The location of rock-art sites in both was most likely connected with a desire of prehistoric communities to communicate the ritual personality of the area by signing it. The similarity of these archaeological sites connected with rock-art to others supports the considerations expressed above regarding the absence in small-scale societies of a spatial separation between the secular and the sacred. This means that in Villar del Humo and Albarracín economic activities were incorporated into the sacred landscape.

Yet, as it stands this hypothesis is not fully satisfactory. As we have seen, similar theories to the one outlined above have been developed by other authors such as Sognnes (1994), Hedges (1993) and Bradley (1997a). But in my opinion these can be nuanced and perhaps even challenged by the addition of two elements: the concept of ritual depth of the landscape and the consideration in the analysis of the identities of the actors who lived through rock-art in the landscape.

The ritual depth of the Villar del Humo rock-art landscape

So far I have discussed the location of sites in Villar del Humo and Albarracín in relation to the broader landscape and the (ritual) geology of the area. Yet, other factors can be discussed regarding landscape: for example, the selection of specific shelters to be decorated. I again centre my research on the area of Villar del Humo. Here, rock-art sites can tentatively be divided into two broadly defined groups as regards the types of place painted: the shelters of Marmalo, La Peña del Escrito and Castellón de los Machos are situated in places of high visibility; Selva Pascuala and Fuente de Selva Pascuala (to which one could add the disappeared site of Cueva del Bullón) are in more semi-visible locations. I suggest that the topographical scenery selected for each group of sites differs significantly, and that this difference is again meaningful. It is this location which led the sites to be decorated in two divergent ways, conveying distinct messages.

In the first group, consisting of the sites of La Peña del Escrito, Marmalo and Castellón de los Machos, motifs common in Levantine and in Schematic art predominate (Figure 8.4). In the second group, formed by the sites of Cueva del Bullón, Fuente de Selva Pascuala and to a lesser extent Selva Pascuala, more unique scenes occur (Figure 8.5). In the Cueva del Bullón, two sexually ambiguous human figures were depicted. In Fuente de Selva Pascuala the designs found are also extraordinary, as they represent what seems to be a unusual type of sun and a hand (Figure 8.5). The specificity of the motifs is further stressed by the peculiarity of the place in which they are located. As against sites of the

a

b

Figure 8.4 Villar del Humo rock-art. a: Marmalo III; b: Marmalo IV

From: the recording made by the Centro de Estudio de Arte Rupestre de Albarracín

a

b

Figure 8.5 Villar del Humo rock-art. a: Fuente de Selva Pascuala; b: Selva Pascuala

From: recording made by the Centro de Estudio de Arte Rupestre de Albarracín

first group, Fuente de Selva Pascuala has no spectacular views, for it is in a low area. The singularity of the place is further stressed by its location close to a natural tunnel of about 20 metres, which points in the direction of Selva Pascuala, about 150 metres away.

The different features which characterize both groups seem to indicate that the ritual topography of Villar del Humo was not even. Not all places had the same significance, the same degree of sacredness. A site which stands out is Fuente de Selva Pascuala. A natural tunnel leading to this rock-art site, the low location and the motifs depicted suggest that prehistoric peoples conferred on Fuente de Selva Pascuala the highest degree of sacredness – the highest peak in this metaphoric ritual landscape that I am depicting – of all the sites.*

* This ritual topography consisted of elevated imaginary peaks in the Villar del Humo rock-art area. These peaks coincided with places which were conferred a high degree of ritual. The ritual topography of Villar del Humo, however, would flatten out outside the *rodeno* area.

Depth, however, is not the only new factor I want to consider. Until now I have made generalizations about the landscape of Villar del Humo and about the ritual degree of its landscape. This, however, needs more thought, for the implication is that all members of the community perceived the art in the same way. Yet the perception of sacredness or secularity of a place depends on who is experiencing a particular space. I now turn towards the issue of identities and explore how the inclusion not only of the concept of ritual depth but also of identities can seriously affect the considerations first made regarding the ritual landscape of Villar del Humo.

Identities and the distinct perceptions of the sacred

A crucial issue to take into account in studying how people may have perceived places is the role of individuals' identities. I shall analyse four types of identities that may have influenced how people read Villar del Humo's locales; these are age, gender, status and ethnicity. None of the depictions in Villar del Humo seems to depict children. This is not exceptional in post-Palaeolithic art, for the representation of infants is rare. Post-Palaeolithic art was basically, therefore, an adult language which children may have been asked to learn in their training for adulthood.

Does this imply that all adults could provide authorized readings of the art? A consideration of gender is instrumental in order to answer this question. In post-Palaeolithic art most anthropomorphs are either sexually indeterminate or seem to represent men. In Villar del Humo, with the exception of the ambiguous figure of the Cueva del Bullón, no clear female representation is found. In comparison with the proportion of infants, female representations are more frequent; even so, they are rare. Indeterminate human motifs outnumber those of men; and both indeterminate and male human motifs together outnumber those of women. In a previous work on gender in Levantine art I suggested that there are two possible readings of this. Either the representation of gender was irrelevant or, on the contrary, Levantine art was a masculine art in which men represented their own world, appropriating the human body as the male body (Díaz-Andreu 1998b). I try now to answer this dilemma for the case of Villar del Humo.

An examination of the thematic of Levantine art can help in deciding whether indeterminate human depictions were more likely to represent men than women. A high proportion of panels in Levantine art represent hunting scenes. Recent ethnographic studies have stressed the involvement of women in hunting expeditions, something previously ignored or minimized in the ethnographic literature and completely disregarded by archaeologists. However, despite exceptions (Bird 1993: 23), while women may participate in hunts when young (Parks 1998: 274), when adults their hunting is mainly directed at small-sized animals. That is to say that hunting – and in particular the hunting of big game – was still mainly a male activity (but see Wadley 1998). Levantine art scenes are centred on the animal world, with a focus on big animals, and this points to this being mainly a masculine art. Indeterminate human representations in hunting scenes, therefore, most probably were meant to represent men. In the same way as occurs with language nowadays, I propose that men in the prehistoric past appropriated the 'neutral' representation of the human figure in Levantine art to portray themselves. This must surely have affected the way in which men and women perceived landscape. The ritualization of the landscape (or the emphasis on its ritual character) through rock-art was mostly connected to the men's world. Women lived through it, and probably ritualized it through different means. Songs, perishable objects left at the bottom of trees and special festivals are just three alternatives, among many others, women may have used which unfortunately leave no trace in the archaeological record.

But were all (adult) men capable of providing authorized readings of the rock-art? Had status a role to play in the way rock-art was approached? Or perhaps religion? All information on this has been lost long ago. I propose, however, that access to at least some of the sites might indeed have been restricted in part to social agents. The natural tunnel of Fuente de Selva Pascuala (Figure 8.5) might be illuminating in this respect, for it represented a barrier – psychological more than physical – for access. The information contained in it might have been used in controlling a specific (but not necessarily the only) discourse of the landscape by a particular group in society. Those most probably with the power to control the sacred landscape were the ritual specialists (a neutral name for the more charged one – and therefore unacceptable in my opinion – of shamans, medicine men or women). The control of the manifestation of the sacred may well have been managed by the ritual specialist. The Villar del Humo landscape, or at least part of it, might have been partly dominated by an exclusive group in society. Because of its exclusivity, however, it is possible that some women may have been included in this group. The majority of sites, however, probably either remained accessible only to men or were significant only for them. The rock-art's ritual meaning, therefore, remained fundamentally masculine.

A final identity to take into consideration is ethnicity. Fuente de Selva Pascuala seems to have been the most significant locale in the Villar del Humo area. Yet, there are problems with this assertion. Although most theories point to Levantine and Schematic styles originating some time during the fifth millennium BC, it is generally agreed that they were still produced for several millennia. Most of my discussion has been concerned with the period of the fifth to mid-third millennium, and probably even earlier given that the linear-geometric paintings of the rock-art shelter of Cueva del Tío Juanico also in the *rodeno* area can be dated to before the fifth millennium BC. However, in Villar del Humo there are reasons to argue for a late use of the landscape, for one scene at Selva Pascuala represents domestication of a horse, an activity that in the Iberian Peninsula can only be dated from the final Bronze Age onwards (i.e. to the first millennium BC). At that time was Villar del Humo still perceived as a sacred landscape? Many things had changed since the fifth millennium. The invisibility – in archaeological terms – of the Mesolithic and Neolithic non-rock-art sites has meant that for this period there is a lack of data on them. This changed dramatically during the Chalcolithic and especially during the Bronze Age. Then communities moved to the top of defensible hills, creating a landscape of violence (Díaz-Andreu 1994: ch. 3). During the late Bronze Age and Iron Age the violence continued. The population became increasingly centred on some sites, while others were abandoned. The disjuncture between the Neolithic and later period must necessarily have radically transformed the ritual landscape. Iron Age communities may have painted in the same sites but the socio-symbolic reasons for this were different. Given that the meaning of the sacred had radically been transformed (Espacios y lugares 1997), it is highly improbable that the *rodeno* still maintained its ritual meaning at that time. By then a major separation between the sacred and the secular had occurred.

Although this examination of the Villar del Humo rock-art area at first reached similar conclusions to those of other recent rock-art studies of the ritual landscape, the addition of a discussion of the concepts of ritual depth and of identities has served further to enrich the analysis. As regards the ritual depth of the landscape, it has been made clear that the generalizations that are usually made by rock-art scholars may be too simplistic. In the case of Villar del Humo, the examination of the location of sites and of the themes painted in them reveals different degrees of sacredness, highlighting that the ritual depth of the area of Villar del Humo was not even. On the contrary, we could visualize it as characterized by an irregular ritual topography with peaks of different heights each representing a rock-art site, the most prominent of them being that of Fuente de Selva Pascuala. The inclusion of the element of social identities, however, has further nuanced this perspective, for it is highly unlikely that in any society all individuals perceive paintings – and therefore the sacredness of the landscape – in a similar way. First, the study of the identity of age has revealed that the paintings were mostly directed to adults and not to children. A discussion on gender has indicated that the paintings were predominantly a male language. However, the discussion of the issue of status/religion qualified this view, given that probable exclusive access to at least the Fuente de Selva Pascuala site may have made it possible for some women (acting as ritual specialists, for example) to break the gender rule. Finally, the inclusion of ethnicity – in the only way I think this identity can be studied in this example – into the study suggests that my account is only valid for perhaps the Mesolithic and above all the Neolithic (broadly speaking fifth and fourth millennia BC), for the meaning of rock-art shifted after this period. Even if paintings continued to be produced in the Iron Age (first millennium BC), their meaning had changed, for the expression of the sacred had been radically transformed by that time.

The addition of the concepts of ritual depth of the landscape and identities has convincingly enriched the interpretation of the landscape of Villar del Humo. It is therefore apparent that their consideration by rock-art researchers would help not only in this case but in many – if not all – others, to avoid gross generalizations in studies of ritual landscapes.

Acknowledgements

I would like to thank the many people who have helped with this article, in particular Ana Piñón, Ardle MacMahon and Yvonne Beadnell for helping with the elaboration of the figures; to Angel Smith for having patiently edited my English; and to Octavio Collado Villalba for allowing me to use the rock-art recordings made by the CEARA (Centro de Estudio de Arte Rupestre de Albarracín). A first version of this article was presented at the 1998 IRAC Conference in Portugal at a session organized by George Nash and Sven Ouzman.

References

Almagro Basch, M. 1949. Un nuevo grupo de pinturas rupestres en Albarracín: 'La Cueva de Doña Clotilde', *Teruel* 1(2): 91–116.
Almagro Basch, M. 1974. Cuatro nuevos abrigos con pinturas rupestres en Albarracín, *Teruel* 51: 5–33.
Alonso Tejada, A. 1984. Los conjuntos rupestres del vallejo Marmalo y Castellón de los Machos, *Ampurias* 45: 8–29.
Alonso Tejada, A. 1985. Villar del Humo: un núcleo rupestre olvidado, *Revista de Arqueología* 45: 12–23.

Alonso Tejada, A. 1992. Algunes reflexions sobre la cronologia de la pintura rupestre Llevantina, in R. Vilardell and X. Llovera (eds) *Estat de la Investigació sobre et Neolitic a Catalunya*. 9è Col. loqui Internacional d'Arqueología del Puigcerdá, Andorra. Institut d'Estadis Cevetans: 49–51.

Alonso Tejada, A. and Grimal, A. 1992. El Arte Levantino o et 'trasiego' cronológico de un arte prehistórico, *Pyranae* 25: 51–70

Alonso Tejada, A. and A. Grimal. 1996. *El arte rupestre prehistórico de la cuenca del río Taibilla (Albacete y Murcia): nuevos planteamientos para el estudio del arte levantino*. Barcelona: Published by the authors.

Alonso Tejada, A., M. Melgarejo, O. Medina and A. Carrión. 1982. Las pinturas rupestres de la Peña del Castellar, *Zephyrus* 34–35: 133–140.

Bégouen, C.H. 1929. The magic origin of prehistoric art, *Antiquity* 3(9): 5–19.

Beltrán Martínez, A. 1968a. *Arte rupestre levantino*. Zaragoza: Universidad de Zaragoza. Monografías Arqueológicas IV.

Beltrán Martínez, A. 1968b. Sobre la pintura de un caballo cazado a lazo, del abrigo de Selva Pascuala en Villar del Humo, in *Miscelánea José M. Lacarra. Estudios de Arte y Arqueología*: 81–86. Zaragoza: Universidad de Zaragoza.

Beltrán Martínez, A. 1992. Sobre el arte levantino, especialmente de Albarracín, ideas generales para un debate, *Caesaraugusta* 69: 7–31.

Bird, C.F.M. 1993. Woman the toolmaker: evidence for women's use and manufacture of flaked stone tools in Australia and New Guinea, in H. du Cros and L. Smith (eds), *Women in archaeology: a feminist critique*: 22–30. Canberra: Australian National University.

Bradley, R. 1997a. Death by water: boats and footprints in the rock art of western Sweden, *Oxford Journal of Archaeology* 16: 315–324.

Bradley, R. 1997b. *Rock art and the prehistory of Atlantic Europe: signing the land*. London: Routledge.

Breuil, H. 1952. *Four hundred centuries of cave art*. Montignac: Centre d'études et de documentation préhistoriques.

Coles, J.M. 1991. Elk and Ogopogo: belief systems in the hunter-gatherer rock art of northern lands, *Proceedings of the Prehistoric Society* 57: 129–148.

Cooney, G. 1994. Sacred and secular Neolithic landscapes in Ireland, in D.L. Carmichael *et al.* (eds), *Sacred sites, sacred places*: 32–43. London: Routledge.

Cooney, G. 1998. Breaking stones, making places: the social landscape of axe production sites, in A. Gibson and D. Simpson (eds), *Prehistoric ritual and religion*: 108–118. Stroud: Sutton.

Criado Boado, F. and R. Penedo Romero. 1993. Art, time and thought: a formal study comparing Palaeolithic and postglacial art, *World Archaeology* 25(2): 187–203.

Dams, L. 1984. Preliminary findings at the 'organ' sanctuary in the cave of Nerja, Málaga, Spain, *Oxford Journal of Archaeology* 3: 1–14.

Dams, L. 1985. Palaeolithic lithophones: descriptions and comparisons, Oxford *Journal of Archaeology* 4: 31–46.

Díaz-Andreu, M. 1994. *La Edad del Bronce en la Provincia de Cuenca*. Cuenca: Diputación de Cuenca. Arqueología Conquense 13.

Díaz-Andreu, M. 1998a. Ethnicity and Iberians: the archaeological crossroads between perception and material culture, *European Journal of Archaeology* 2(2): 199–218.

Díaz-Andreu, M. 1998b. Iberian post-Palaeolithic art and gender: discussing human representations in levantine art, *Journal of Iberian Archaeology* 0: 33–51.

Díaz-Andreu, M. 1999. Shamanism in Iberian post-Palaeolithic art? Paper given at the Rock Art and Shamanism Conference organized by the Prehistoric Society and the University of Durham, Durham, 20 February.

Díaz-Andreu, M. and I. Montero. 1998. *Arqueometalurgia de la Provincia de Cuenca*. Cuenca: Diputación de Cuenca. Arqueología Conquense 14.

Espacios y lugares cultuales en el mundo ibérico, *Quaderns de Prehistòria i Arqueologia de Castelló* 18 (1997).

Fernández-Miranda, M. and J.A. Moure. 1975. El abrigo de Verdelpino (Cuenca): un nuevo yacimiento neolítico en el interior de la Península Ibérica, *Noticiario Arqueológico Hispánico. Prehistoria* 3: 191–235.

Fortea, F.J. 1974. Algunas aportaciones a los problemas de Arte Levantino, *Zephyrus* 25: 225–257.

Galiana Botella, M.F. 1992. Consideraciones en torno al arte rupestre levantino del Bajo Ebro y del Bajo Aragón, in P. Utrilla Miranda (ed.), *Aragón/Litoral Mediterráneo: Intercambios culturales durante la prehistoria*: 447–454. Zaragoza: Institución Fernando el Católico.

Gamble, C. 1982. Interaction and alliance in Palaeolithic society, *Man* 17: 92–107.

Gómez Barrera, J.A. 1982. *La pintura rupestre esquemática en la altimeseta soriana*. Soria: Diputación de Soria.

González Cordero, A. and M. Alvarado Gonzalo. 1985. Pinturas esquemáticas y grabados rupestres de Los Barruecos (Malpartida de Cáceres), *Actas de las II Jornadas de Metodología y Didáctica de la Historia*: 154–168. Cáceres: Universidad de Extremadura.

Hartley, R., and A.M. Wolley Vawser. 1998. Spatial behaviour and learning in the prehistoric environment of the Colorado River Drainage (south-eastern Utah), western North America, in C. Chippindale and P.S.C. Taçon (eds), *The archaeology of rock-art*: 185–211. Cambridge: Cambridge University Press.

Hedges, K. 1993. Places to see and places to hear: rock art and features of the sacred landscape, in J. Steinbring *et al.* (eds), *Time and space: dating and spatial considerations in rock art research*: 121–127. Melbourne: Australian Rock Art Research Association. Occasional AURA Publication 8.

Hernández Pacheco, E. 1921. Exposición de arte rupestre prehistórico español, *Arte español: revista de la Sociedad de Amigos del Arte* 5(7): 315–339.

Hernández Pacheco, E. 1959. *Prehistoria del Solar Hispano*. Madrid: Real Academia de Ciencias Exactas, Físicas y Naturales de Madrid. Memorias 20.

Hood, B.C. 1988. Sacred pictures, sacred rocks: ideological and social space in the north Norwegian Stone Age, *Norwegian Archaeological Review* 21: 65–84.

Ingold, T. 1986. Territoriality and tenure: the appropriation of space in hunting and gathering societies, in T. Ingold, *The appropriation of nature*: 130–164. Manchester: Manchester University Press.

Jochim, M. 1976. Palaeolithic cave art in ecological perspective, in G. Bailey (ed.), *Hunter-gatherer economy in prehistory*: 212–219. Cambridge: Cambridge University Press.

Jordá Cerdá, F. 1975. La Peña del Escrito y el culto al toro, *Cuadernos de Prehistoria y Arqueología Castellonense* 2.

Kinahan, J. 1999. Towards an archaeology of mimesis and rain-making in Namibian rock art, in R. Layton and P. Ucko (eds), *The archaeology and anthropology of landscape: shaping your landscape*: 336–357. London: Routledge.

Kinnes, I. 1998. From ritual to romance: a new western, in A. Gibson and D. Simpson (eds), *Prehistoric ritual and religion*: 183–189. Stroud: Sutton.

Layton, R.H. 1992. *Australian rock art: a new synthesis*. Cambridge: Cambridge University Press.

Leroi-Gourhan, A. 1967. *Treasures of prehistoric art*. New York: Harry N. Abrams.

Lewis-Williams, J.D. and T.A. Dowson. 1988. The signs of all times: entoptic phenomena in Upper Palaeolithic rock art, *Current Anthropology* 29(2): 201–245.

Llavori de Micheo, R. 1988–1989. El arte postpaleolítico levantino de la Península Ibérica: una aproximación sociocultural al problema de sus orígenes, *Ars Praehistorica* 7–8: 145–156.

López Payer, M. and M. Soria Lerma. 1991. Análisis estilístico de los conjuntos de Canjorro de Peñarrubia, Doña Clotilde, Abrigo del Tío Campano y Selva Pascuala, *Espacio, Tiempo y Forma*, Serie I: *Prehistoria y Arqueología* 4: 219–239.

Marcos Pous, A. 1981. Sobre el origen neolítico del arte esquemático peninsular, *Corduba arqueológica* 9: 63–71.

Martí Oliver, B. and M.S. Hernández. 1988. *El Neolític Valencià: art rupestre i cultura material*. Valencia: Diputació de València.

Mauss, M. 1954. *The gift*. London: Routledge and Kegan Paul.

Moure Romanillo, J.A. and M. Fernández-Miranda. 1977. El abrigo de Verdelpino (Cuenca), *Trabajos de Prehistoria* 34: 31–84.

Parks, R.1998. Size counts: the miniature archaeology of childhood in Inuit societies, *Antiquity* 72: 269–281.

Rault, S. 1997. From Anneville to Zedes: a ritual seascape? Megaliths and long-distance contacts in western Europe, in G. Nash (ed.), *Semiotics of landscape: the archaeology of mind*: 5–16. Oxford: Archaeopress.

Reinach, S. 1903. L'art et la magie: à propos des peintures et des gravures de l'Age du Renne, *L'Anthropologie* 14: 257–266.

Richards, C. 1993. Monumental choreography: architecture and spatial representation in later Neolithic Orkney, in C. Tilley (ed.), *Interpretative archaeology*: 143–181. Oxford: Berg.

Romero Sáiz, M. 1996. *La maravillosa tierra de Pabovi*. Cuenca: Miguel Romero Sáiz.

Saunders, N.J. 1994. At the mouth of the obsidian cave: deity and place in Aztec religion, in D.L. Carmichael *et al.* (eds), *Sacred sites, sacred places*: 172–183. London: Routledge.

Sognnes, K. 1994. Ritual landscapes: toward a reinterpretation of Stone Age rock art at Trøndelag, Norway, *Norwegian Archaeological Review* 27(1): 29–50.

Taçon, P.S.C. 1994. Socialising landscapes: the long-term implications of signs, symbols and marks on the lands, *Archaeology in Oceania* 29: 117–129.

Taçon, P.S.C. and P. Faulstich. 1993. Introduction: expressing relationships to the land by marking special places, in J. Steinbring *et al.* (eds), *Time and space: dating and spatial considerations in rock art research*: 81–90. Melbourne: Australian Rock Art Research Association. Occasional AURA Publication 8.

Thomas, J. 1993. The hermeneutics of megalithic space, in C. Tilley (ed.), *Interpretative archaeology*: 73–97. Oxford: Berg.

Tilley, C. 1993. Art, architecture, landscape [Neolithic Sweden], in B. Bender (ed.), *Landscape: politics and perspectives*: 49–88. Oxford: Berg.

Tilley, C. 1994. *A phenomenology of landscape: places, paths and monuments*. Oxford: Berg.

Utrilla Miranda, P. 1986–1987. Nuevos datos sobre la relación entre el arte rupestre y yacimientos arqueológicos del valle del Ebro, *Bajo Aragón, Prehistoria* 7–8: 323–339.

Wadley, L. 1998. The invisible meat providers: women in the Stone Age of South Africa, in S. Kent (ed.), *Gender in African prehistory*: 69–82. Walnut Creek: AltaMira Press.

Werlhof, J. von. 1992. The rock in rock art, in K. Hedges (ed.), *Rock art papers*, 9: 1–4. San Diego: San Diego Museum. Papers 28.

Chapter 9

The landscape brought within

A re-evaluation of the rock-painting site at Tumlehed, Torslanda, Göteborg, west Sweden

George Nash

Rock-art and narrative

The idea that art represents a (semiotic) language or narrative is not new. Davidson and Noble (1989), Bourdieu (1977), Shanks and Tilley (1987a, 1987b) and, more recently, Tilley (1991) and myself (Nash 1997a) have put forward the notion that symbols – be they rock-art or portable art – create or establish a narrative; a story or language. Therefore, one cannot consider art as merely 'art for art's sake'. Arguably, art possesses power, discourse and, in the case of prehistoric symbols such as rock-painting, rhetoric. Nordbladh (1987) and Tilley (1991) have noted that both rock-painting and carvings are not just single events. Additions to the rock surface may occur, maybe over long periods of time (seasonally or annually). Further, motifs may change status, meaning and importance depending on particular social, political, economic and symbolic mechanisms of influence. One can therefore propose that 'art' is not stagnant but fluid and linear through time and space. Morphological changes can be experienced within the rock-art and, more poignantly, through changes in rock-painting style. This can be clearly seen with the change in style and form from painted art to carved art in northern Scandinavia between the late Mesolithic/Neolithic and the Early Bronze Age. Similarly, during the same transition period, there is a change in subjects: from hunting and fishing scenes to farming, warrior and boat scenes. This change in style probably relates to changes in social, political and economic identity. Interestingly, the Tumlehed panel appears to embrace both styles. With this particular site, the artist or artists have expressed a need to change and integrate certain elements on the panel. Generally, in painting a site, the artist can obliterate, alter, deface, add to and cover over earlier designs. By contrast, rock-carvings can be regarded as a more permanent statement; yet even carvings can be debased, cut through or defaced (Nash 2001). The act of defacement may be applied periodically and may be the signature of new or well-established socio-cultural ideas.

In the past there have been concerns about the authenticity of painted sites in Bohuslän (Nordblabh 1987: 306). The Tumlehed panel is considered authentic due to the positive testing of pigment penetration of the rock surface as well as pigment weathering and lichen growth over some of the images. In this chapter I shall discuss the designs and their spatial organization as a narrative, a series of contextual statements that will create an alternative account for site location. In addition, I will explore the ideology and

Figure 9.1 Landscape in miniature: the Tumlehed rock-painting, Torslanda

Photograph: G.H. Nash

intricacies of performance, focusing on the 'language' of metaphor, rhetoric and contradiction.

Art acting as a language

The rock-painting site of Tumlehed in Torslanda Parish, approximately five kilometres north-west of Göteborg (south-west Sweden) has, over the past twenty years, received much attention (Cullberg *et al*. 1975; Nordbladh 1987; Coles 1991). Discovered in 1974, the panel has been re-evaluated according to what can be seen under certain atmospheric conditions (Figure 9.1). The pigment – varying shades of red-orange-brown – contains a iron derivative, probably haematite; the pigment colour was analysed using a scanning electron method and X-ray fluorescence analysis (Cullberg *et al*. 1975: 78, 86). In places there is streaking from some of the motifs which suggests paint was running down the rock-face possibly during, or just after, application. The site was photographed in 1975 using a number of photographic techniques. It was hoped that the photography might tease out some of the more obscure images, especially within areas of panel where lichen growth and pigment streaking occurred. The photographic techniques included various (daylight) colour filtration, infrared and ultraviolet film. However, each process did not enhance the picture beyond what could already be seen (Cullberg *et al*. 1975: 85).

In 1993 I photographed the same panel using a variety of techniques, including colour filtration, monochrome infrared photography with different film formats (35mm and medium format). The filtration results were generally disappointing in that no new images, aside from a fish and single wavy-line, were discovered – the results of the ideal atmospheric conditions. The moisture along with low temperatures within this part of the valley appeared to tease out the pigments on the panel. Indeed, successive visits to this site revealed less pigmentation and fewer figures than I had experienced earlier. My best results were achieved using a medium-format camera and low-speed colour transparency film (50 ASA).

The initial visit in 1993, along with the comments and a survey plan of the panel in 1975 (to a scale of 1: 15), revealed the following figures: one large red deer (*Cervus elaphus*); five fish, possibly salmon;* four boats; six horizontal wavy-lines (five on the 1975 and 1987 plans); a single stylized 'stick' anthropomorphic figure; and a complex net-like design which is incorporated into the antlers of the red deer (Figure 9.2; and see Table 9.1). Additional figures may be present below the red deer and the lower boat, but pigment streaking across this part of the rock-face has rendered the area indecipherable. Other figures which have not been covered by pigment streaking may be present above the human figure and to the left of a vertical row of four fish and a vertical natural fault line.

The red deer is approximately sixty centimetres in height; it has been painted as a flat side-on figure possessing four legs. The head, legs and torso are in proportion with each other. The antler set is difficult to decipher due to the overlay or incorporation of a net-like design. Compared with other painted cervid designs from this period and within

---

* Only two fish were noticed and recorded on the 1975 plan. This number increases to four, present on a survey plan by Nordbladh (1987).

Table 9.1 Design complexity and spatial dominance I

Site name	Animal	Cervid	Bird	Fish	Human	Male	Female	Geometric design	Colour stain
Allestorp	x	x	–	–	x	–	–	–	–
Brattbergen	x	x	–	–	–	–	–	–	–
Brattberget	x	x	–	–	x	–	–	x	x
Brureberget	x	x	–	x	–	–	–	–	x
Fångsjön	x	–	–	–	–	–	–	x	x
Grannberget	x	x	–	–	–	–	–	x	–
Hällberget	x	x	–	–	x	x	x	x	x
Hästskotjärn	x	x	–	–	x	–	–	x	x
Medbo	x	x	x(?)	x	x	x	–	–	x
Ruändan	x	x	x	–	x	–	–	x	x
Sundsbyn	–	–	–	–	x	x(?)	–	–	–
Skarstad	x	x	–	–	x	–	–	x(?)	x
Tumlehed	x	x	–	x	x	x	–	x	x
Åbosjön	x	x(?)	–	–	–	–	–	–	x

After Cullberg et al. (1985).

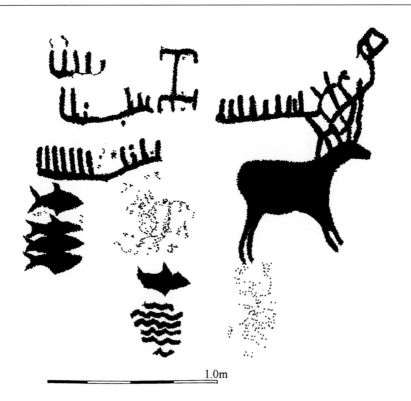

Figure 9.2 Animals on the Tumlehed panel
From Nordbladh (1987)

the region, the Tumlehed red deer is one of the most naturalistic. Other painted cervidae such as the single elk figure at Brattbergen and the reindeer at Medbo are less naturalistic in form and are painted with only two legs – a flat image. However, at the Brureberget site, semi-naturalistic reindeer (possibly male) and stylistic female elk, some with calves, appear as quadrupeds (Figure 9.3). Although these sites have been interpreted as Mesolithic hunting-art sites, different localized styles and traditions are present.

The four boats, including the one incorporated into the red-deer antler set, are all of the same style and appear to resemble the earliest carved-boat phases (boat stage I) of the Bronze Age (Malmer 1981). Each boat is constructed of a single painted line which represents the hull. On three boats, at the bow-end the continuous hull-line curves to form a short vertical line which possibly represents a simple prow. The vertical lines between the prows have been interpreted as a crew (Marstrander 1976). This early boat type, however, is also similar in design to boats of the central Norwegian (Mesolithic) hunting-art traditions as seen at the petroglyph sites of Evenhus (on panels I, III, V, IV, VII), Nord-Trøndelag, Vistnesdalen (I and II), Rødøya (12) and Forselv (19) in Nordland (see Hallström 1938; Sognnes 1987, 1988).

Between the three boats and the red-deer antler set is a stick anthropomorph which has very little stylistic affinity with other painted or carved human figures of this date or later within the region. However, several identical figures are found on Mesolithic portable art

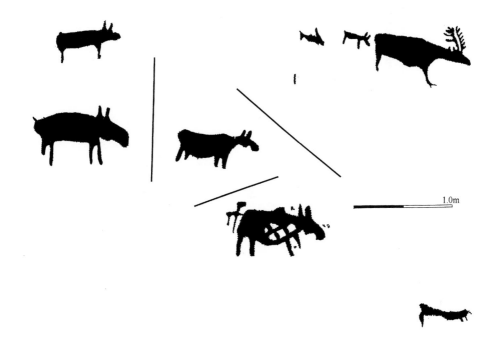

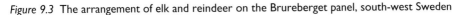

Figure 9.3 The arrangement of elk and reindeer on the Brureberget panel, south-west Sweden

from Denmark (Nash 1998, 2000, 2001). Six pieces, two amber and four bone or antler, are inscribed with up to nine anthropomorphs which, like the Tumlehed figure, have a stick-like torso, extended bent upper limbs and inverted 'U'-shaped lower limbs. Although the figures from the Danish portable art assemblage can be categorically assessed as human figures, the Tumlehed stylistic figure cannot. The figure may, in fact, form the central part of a large boat which extends from the red-deer antler set to the central boat on the left part of the panel. It may be the case that the human figure is incorporated into the boat design. There are many examples of large carved Bronze Age boats with crews and a single identifiable human, usually male with accompanying weapons present in Bohuslän (Coles 1990). However, these figures, along with the boats, are fully recognizable.

Below the boats, on the left section of the panel, is a series of five fish and six wavy-lines. The fish designs are similar to other designs found elsewhere in northern Scandinavia, for example at the nearby Medbo site. The shape of dorsal and tail fins, plus their size in relation to the red-deer and other components on the panel, suggests that they may be salmon (*Salmo salar*). But from their body shapes, ignoring proportion, they could be marine mammals such as whale or porpoise. Finally, the wavy-lines, located below a centralized fish and symbolizing water are unique for any rock-art, painted or otherwise, in Scandinavia.

Dating the individual motifs on the panel is problematic in that there are at least two possible additions over time. Here, the boat, typical of the Early Bronze Age farming-art tradition (for western Sweden), may have been added to the top part of the red-deer antler set, the largest and arguably earliest design on the panel. These additions are not so much a defacement, but more a build-up of the panel design through time. The

Table 9.2 Design complexity and spatial dominance II.

Site name	Wet (W) or dry (D) images	Horizontal (H) or vertical (V) design-plane	Dominant motif	Location of motif on panel	Location of panel
1 Sundsbyn, Holmedal Parish, Värmland	D	H and V	anthro.	periphery	lakeside
2 Brattbergen, Nedre, Blomsjon, Värmland	D	H	elk(1)	–	lakeside
3 Brureberget, Nedre, Blomsjon, Värmland	D	H	reindeer	periphery	lakeside
4 Allestorp, Kville Parish, Tanum, Bohuslän	D	V	reindeer	periphery	cliff–dry valley
5 Medbo, Bohuslän	W and D	H	reindeer and net	central	dry valley
6 Stranderang, Bro Parish, Stangenas, Bohuslän	?	H	abstract	–	fjord
7 Skarstad, Bro Parish, Stangenas, Bohuslän	D	H	reindeer(s)	periphery	dry valley
8 Tumlehed, Torslanda Parish, Goteborg	W and D	H and V	reindeer	periphery	dry fjord

organization of the panel figures appears deliberate. The series of six wavy-lines, five fish and three boats is clustered to the left of the red deer; all the designs, although located on the seaward side, nevertheless face inland (Nordbladh 1987: 305). These figures, along with the red deer, are organized into two generic (design) groups, one terrestrial, the other marine – or what I term *dry* and *wet* designs (see Table 9.2).

These dry and wet figures appear to be deliberately segregated by a natural fissure which divides the two design groups. The fissure, cutting vertically through the centre of the panel, was probably present when the panel was first commissioned. The complete design field possibly represents a cultural 'map' which delineates the dry and wet features of the surrounding landscape: a type of geographical binary opposition. I have chosen the terms dry and wet to contrast designs that are land-based (the red deer and net design) with those that are water-based (boat, waves and fish). The panel itself, sited above the narrowest point of the fjord, possibly marks the shoreline during the Bronze Age (and earlier). The (then) eastern shoreline is possibly represented by the natural fissure on the panel. The figures within the panel design would thus represent a spatial dichotomy, a division between dry and wet figures.

Different landscape, different meanings

Along with the panel, the landscape surrounding the site has also received comment. However, an approach involving site location and the phenomenology of landscape, plus the interplay between figures and landscape, has not. The rock outcrop on which the panel is located is now a valleyside of a dry fjord which forms part of an extended archipelago. The present shoreline is located approximately two kilometres to the west. During the Neolithic/Bronze Age, the fjord would have been flooded, possibly to a point just below where this rock-painting is sited.

In order to place this site into a contextual landscape, one needs to think primarily about prehistoric sea levels for this part of the south-west Swedish coastline. This aspect obviously significantly changes the landscape perception of the site and, more importantly, what the images are trying to say. Shoreline displacement curves document how this fjord has undergone a number of geomorphological changes over the past 8000 years. During the Boreal-Atlantic period (Sand Darna phase), around 8000 BP, shoreline displacement curves place a sea-level rise at about twelve metres along this section of coastline. This greatly increased at around 5000 BP (Funnel Beaker phase) when the sea-level rise was a further nine metres. By the emergence of a Scandinavian Bronze Age (the Swedish–Norwegian Battle Axe Culture), at around 4000 BP the rise was a further eight metres (Nygaard 1989). Therefore, after the retreat of the Fennoscandian ice sheet, the flooding of this and many other fjords along this stretch of the coastline was indeed rapid. However, at roughly 4000 BP, isostatic uplift of the land exceeds sea-level rise, and the fjord shoreline begins to recede slowly to its present position.

It is believed that this panel dates from around 7000 BP; it is similar in artistic form and merit to that of other sites within the Bohuslän region (Nordbladh 1987: 309). Elsewhere, typological and stylistic forms have been correlated with shoreline displacement curves as the basis of chronological arguments concerning the dating of rock-art in both Sweden and Norway (Bakka 1979: 184). Similar sequential structuring, style and formal analysis has been applied to the Alta Fjord, Finnmark, northern Norway (Helskog 1987).

Figures 9.4 and 9.5 Moving through a landscape – approaching the art from the south
Photograph: G.H. Nash

At present the panel is tweny-five metres above sea level and located on a vertical south-facing rock-face. Below the panel a series of natural steps fall away some nineteen metres to the valley floor. During the fourth or fifth millennium BC, it is probable that the painting site would have been only a few metres above the shoreline and may have been less accessible than at present. Within the immediate area of the site, the land rises to expose rock outcropping. The site also marks the narrowest point of the lower and upper sections of the Tumle Valley. Both the rising of the valley landscape and its narrowing may point to where the terminal point of the flooded fjord was. Cullberg *et al.* (1975: 86) claim that the painting is visible at a distance of approximately a hundred metres (directly opposite, from the southern upper slopes of the valley). However, the painting cannot be seen from either the valley floor or the lower slopes, on the opposite side to the panel (Figures 9.4 and 9.5).

Replicating landscape: macroscape to microscape*

By 'mapping' the designs in this way the panel becomes divided according to social and economic topography. A language is therefore encoded through the use and application of zoomorphic and anthropomorphic figures, boats and zigzag lines (waves). The map is further subdivided with motifs that represent above and below the water-line. This visual statement may suggest an economic as well as a symbolic code. Similar structuring of panels exists on other painting sites within the region such as the fish and reindeer present on the nearby Medbo and Skarstad panels (Figure 9.6).

Bradley (1993, 1997, 1998) has suggested that carving panels are located on marginal land, outside the main domesticated areas. The Tumlehed panel, although positioned on a large rock ledge, is close to high-density settlement – Neolithic/Bronze Age in date (Cullberg *et al.* 1975: 85). One can argue that although the main theme of this painting is in the hunter-gatherer domain, its application may originate from nearby farming communities. Two possible arguments to why this and other painted panels were commissioned by pastoralists can be put forward. First, the painting may represent a 'history' and a sense of belonging to the old order – that of the 'Mesolithic' hunter-gatherer-fisher. More probable is that a mixed economy of farming and hunting, fishing and gathering may have existed, and painting was considered merely to be fashionable at that time. The components on the panel do refer to both economies: the style and form of the boats represent a farming tradition, while the red deer and fish acknowledge the hunter/fishing-art tradition. Nordbladh (1987: 305) has suggested that the boats possess crews; this style, indicative of carved boats within the region, would represent an early Bronze Age tradition (see above).

Coles (1991: 130) argues that, in addition to boats, a net also forms part of the antler set of motifs. The hunting of reindeer and elk using nets is depicted on a series of coastal Norwegian (carved) panels at Skogerveien (Buskerud) and Skavberg III (Troms) and on one other Bohuslän painting site, Medbo (Figure 9.6). Here, a rectangular net is placed

---

* The concepts of macroscape and microscape were introduced by the author in 1997 when looking at the spatial relationship of the inner and outer façade areas of the La Hougue Bie passage grave, Jersey, Channel Islands (Nash 1997b: 114).

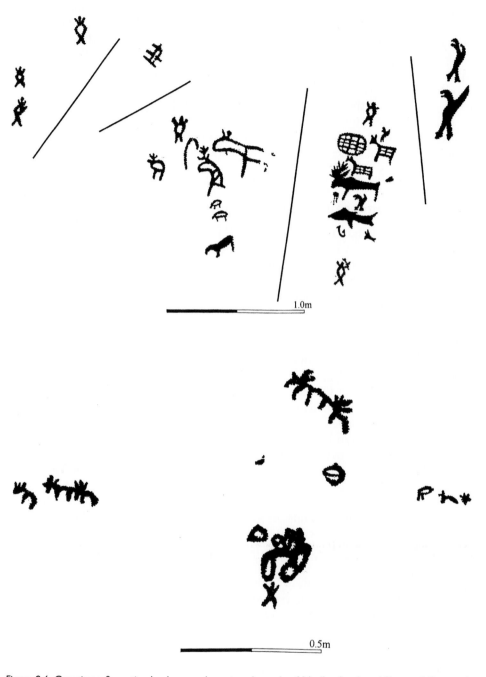

Figure 9.6 Creating a figurative landscape: the painted panels of Medbo (top) and Skarstad (bottom). The Medbo panel extends over a number of metres, and the figure above merely represents the position of individual figures and groups of figures

From Nordbladh (1987)

between two (female) elk. Above both animals is a single human, possibly the owner of the net. Again, a similar distinction of dry and wet figures can be put forward for this, and for the two Norwegian sites. Also present is the 'stick' anthropomorphic figure. These elements, the fish, red deer, human and wavy-lines appear to be embedded within the (earlier) hunting tradition. The arguably later four boats may represent a metaphorical statement that substitutes hunting and fishing of the sea for 'farming' the sea – in other words, a seasonal *control* of landscape is in operation. The boat, which represents the 'domestic' bonds to the wildness of the red deer, creates a link between the two economies which may be sequentially spaced. The art, therefore, could well signify a history, a release outside the domesticate and agriculture to the hunting and fishing economies which may have been considered more symbolic activities. Moreover, the arrangement of these figures on the panel and the social geography of the surrounding landscape appear to express a cultural map whereby figures located on the left of the panel represent the fjord and open sea while figures on the right represent the land. It is my view, therefore, that a socio-cultural rather than a ritual–symbolic language is present: the panel provides the liminal space between a landscape that is socially familiar (the locality) and one that is symbolically unfamiliar (the outer fjord and sea).

Socio-economic concepts of controlling landscape and its resources – farming the landscape – are most prevalent during the Bronze Age. Rock-art, particularly from southern and coastal regions of northern (Atlantic) Europe, depicts an economy obsessed with the control and appropriation of nature. For example, herding animals, such as reindeer, are deliberately placed centrally within petroglyph panel designs. Along the coastal fringes of Norway and Sweden, human figures and geometric designs are usually placed on the panel peripheries – encircling and, arguably, controlling animals (Nash 1998). On the panels at Bardal (Nord Trøndelag) and Tennes B (Troms), male human figures appear to be engaged in herding and/or corralling activity, usually of reindeer (Hallström 1938). On the Rødøya and Forslev panels – both in the county of Nordland – human figures are involved in fishing expeditions as well as terrestrial activities (Gjessing 1932, 1936; Sognnes 1987). In all cases human figures are located on the edges of the panel narrative. Not only does this pattern create a visual image of control, but it also possibly delineates cultural and natural boundaries. In all cases, landscape features are not depicted on any of the panel designs. By placing a physical extent or boundary around the animals using human figures, the artist is creating a metaphor, whereby humans and animals possibly portray the extent of landscape or, at least, part of that landscape that is most beneficial, in this case prime herding routes/migratory paths around the intermediate slopes and upland plateaux. Elsewhere, Bradley *et al.* (1994: 381) have suggested that rock-panels may act as (way)markers, whereby animals are ritually escorted along corralling paths, there to meet their (ritual) deaths. In the case of the Tumlehed panel, the red deer may be a representative figure from a nearby herd which was periodically tracked, stalked and hunted.

Microscape: elements of creating a performance

So far, I have discussed the individual characters on the panel and placed them into a spatial/temporal context. As yet, I have not discussed the relationship between artist, subject and audience. I have argued previously that rock-art constitutes a performance (Nash 1997a). Obviously this concept is not new. One must consider that when initially commissioned and executed this panel must have been a very important and powerful place. This site, along with others in the county, conforms to a distinct landscape pattern; panels are usually sited on the intermediate slopes of dry fjords or inland lakes, on near-vertical cliffs or overhangs. Likewise, similar landscape affinities are present within the coastal Norwegian petroglyph assemblage (Hallström 1938; Sognness 1988; Sognness 1998). During prehistory, many of the painted sites in Bohuslän would have had difficulty of access due to then-flooded fjords and lakes. It could be the case that these sites were only periodically visited during special events in the hunting calendar and that the audience was restricted to certain members of a small hunting groups. The subjectivity of the panel – representing both hunting and fishing – leads us to see it as arguably bound up within a wider ritual performance which is constructed both spatially and temporally. This not only represents the performance of picture-making itself, but involves other components such as gesture, song, place and oral tradition (Bowra 1962). It is well known that both painting and carving on portable and static surfaces used in many contemporary non-Western hunter-gatherer societies are bound up in a wider ritual and symbolic mechanism. Despite the fact that these acts consume large amounts of time and energy, they are essential for the well-being and social organization of the community and form part of a complex socio-symbolic unit. Other forms of visual expression, too, are treated in the same way, such as dress, dance and mime. These forms of visual expression involve social, political and religious organization, and would have invariably formed part of the 'painting experience' during the Mesolithic.

1 Rock surface (the natural)
2 Preparing the surface (the synthetic)

Liminal space

3 Application to the surface (humanizing the surface)
4 Use and reuse of the surface (creating a history)

Figure 9.7 The conversion plane
From Munn (1976)

Within most tribal societies the organization of art activity is controlled by one person and conforms to a strict series of rules, usually gender encoded. Each act within the performance is bound up in ritual. For example, Munn (1976, 1983, 1986) has recognized a symbolic process concerning the preparation, construction and exchange of canoes (*gawa*) on the island of Kiriwana in the Trobriand Islands, Melanesia. Here, Munn refers to each of these construction phases as a conversion plane (Figure 9.7). At each stage the canoe changes its form, shape, identity and symbolic meaning, from the felling of the tree, what I call the natural, through to production, the raw material, to initial exchange of the canoe, what I refer to as maker to user, and eventually on to the main exchange system (*Kula*). Likewise, the preparation, application and adoption involved in applying paint or a carving on to a static surface may be regarded as a series of conversion planes. At each stage the nature of the design, the surface and the artist may change and may have been restricted to particular individuals.

Munn's conversion plane for boats recognizes six stages within the design/build/exchange sequence. Likewise, I have used four stages for the construction and use of rock-art. I would suggest that at all stages a ritual element is applied. Choosing the right panel and preparing the surface may have been just as important as applying the first images to the surface. By preparing rock-art in this way, the act of producing art becomes ordered and controlled. Establishing order may be gender-encoded or manipulated by different social strands such as elders or initiates. Certainly, Munn (1963, 1973) reinforces this notion when researching the importance of secrecy between the genders when producing sand stories by the Walbiri of central Australia. Here, art becomes visually restrictive, secretive and exclusive. As important are the idiosyncrasies such as dress, gesture and choreographic dance used by participating individuals which become part of the complete performance.

Macroscape: enculturation and dissemination

I have suggested earlier that a component group – dry and wet – is structurally opposed. Of course, other groups are also present, such as male:female, culture:nature, human: animal and so on; the list could be endless. Lévi-Strauss first recognized the value of binary oppositions or encoding two elements within his *Structural anthropology* (1963). He regarded binary systems as a series of universal elements that were placed within a cultural vocabulary which included basic functions such as centre:periphery, right:left and, of course, nature:culture. These elements incorporating social structure, myth and symbolism were used to establish contradictions that are basically inherent within society. Arguably, binary systems such as those expressed above underlie universal social structures concerning the meaning of myth and human cognition (Lévi-Strauss 1964: 72). In the case of the dry and wet subjectivity expressed on the Tumlehed panels and on other (Mesolithic) painted sites within Bohuslän there appears to be an iconography that is either terrestrial (dry) or marine (wet). For the sake of this chapter, I do not want to venture beyond the intrinsic arguments that are present between structuralism and post-structuralism, as I believe that the painted art within this region was probably considered universal during this phase of prehistory.

The Tumlehed panel possesses a series of binary oppositions which in some ways promote harmony, but at the same time create a number of contradictions. First, there are dry and wet images. Although harmonious, they contradict each other in that there are terrestrial mammals being associated with marine animals; fish, red deer and boats represent a hunter-gather-fisher economy but they also represent wildness. Second, the presence of a single human figure accompanying a series of boats is in direct opposition to the natural images on the panel. The position of the human figure and the boats – at the top of the panels – subordinates and overlooks the natural elements of the panel (culture over nature). Finally, as stated earlier, the various components on this panel appear to show various harmonious elements of landscape metaphorically – creating a form of cultural map – which establishes a macroscape, symbolized, manipulated and turned into a miroscape. The spatial arrangement of each of the components appears to be deliberately positioned to inform an audience, an onlooker, of what resources are where and how they fit into the wider landscape.

According to Shanks (1992: 184), maps are familiar and transform natural, recognizable features into something abstract. However, maps also create social and political order and make the landscape more familiar and accessible; they inform people where they are and how they fit into a landscape. Those who construct maps promote control and a

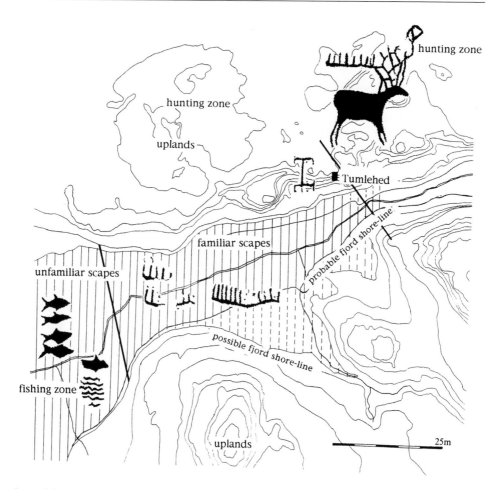

Figure 9.8 Making a map: the rearranged figures and their relationship to landscape

unique language of symbols and signs which can be either universally read or restrictive to certain people. Like a language, signs and symbols need to be fully understood in order to gain maximum information. With symbols, a map can construct a number of things, including delineating social and political territoriality as well as locating prime hunting and fishing resources. In the case of the Tumlehed panel, rock-art provides a link between the maker, the landscape and the audience (Figure 9.8).

Speaking from the rocks

So far, I have argued that the Tumlehed panel may represent a cultural map in which symbols are metaphorically used to construct an abstract image of the surrounding landscape. This exercise is arguably convenient. The old adage, 'The answer's yes, now what's the question?' may spring to most minds when looking at rock-art, especially where different things are portrayed on the same panel. However, there appears to be a conscious decision deliberately to place certain figures in particular places; this is not just confined to the Tumlehed panel. On the panel, boats and the single human figure appear above the 'water-line', while fish and wavy-lines (water) are present below the water-line (as they should be). On the right of the panel the single red deer represents a terrestrial environment (as it should). Likewise, on the Medbo panel a similar arrangement is present, with a single male and two female reindeer above a single fish and fish hook (Figure 9.6). Flanking these figures are several human figures which appear to be corralling or at least controlling the animals. Again, the panel structure is deliberate and is 'speaking' the same language as the figures on the Tumlehed panel. Taking this a stage further, Saussure's *Course in general linguistics* (1960 [1916]) sees a distinct difference between language and, say, speech; language being a collective discourse that is recognizable between individuals. Underlying language is a set of well-defined rules that is universally recognized. Similarly, one can see this with gesture; the nodding of one's head, for example. These signs generally cross the barriers of speech. Barthes (1977, 1984) has used similar arguments on garment, food and furniture systems to express the universal rules of language. Tilley (1991: 16) has argued that material culture (in this case, rock-carvings from Namförsen, north-east Sweden) articulates a language or, more precisely, a speech (based on a generative (grammar) language):

> So far I have made the basic point that material culture, speech and writing all share the same qualities but that communication through speech is more direct. They involve different transformations of the same materialist practice of spacing, differentiation, articulation. In other words all these practices are structured in precisely the same way through breaking up space, creating and establishing difference, articulating and rearticulating units.

I would add that material culture, in this case the rock-art, formulates a general grammar that can be manipulated to suit its audience. Obviously, the artist is in control and would have decided which image goes where. By rearranging certain figures on the Tumlehed panel, a different (and probably very much shorter) story would have emerged from this chapter.

Conclusion: bringing the landscape within

Duality within rock-art itself is common; the Tumlehed painting is no exception to this rule. The basic form of duality which I have identified exists primarily between culture and nature (red deer versus boat or human versus fish/red deer). Similar structural oppositions are present on other Swedish and Norwegian painted panels. Harmonizing relationships are also present, for example in copulation scenes involving both humans and mammals. Subtly, in the case of the Tumlehed panel, landscape is delineated by the position of particular animal species – thus creating (in the eyes of this archaeologist) a (socially constructed) cultural map. The position of the panel – at the termination point of a once-flooded fjord – is also important in determining the social and symbolic space within landscape (i.e. the siting of particular zoomorphs pertaining to landscape). The concept of landscape demarcation would have been an important component within the socio-political division of space, especially when, arguably, the resources for group sustainability became increasingly important during the latter part of the Neolithic and succeeding Bronze Age (Nygaard 1989). More importantly, panel demarcation and landscape form may portray different kinds of space, known and unknown. The distribution of settlement activity (including lithic scatters) suggests that known space was limited to areas around the inner fjord. Unknown spaces were probably confined to the surrounding uplands, the outer fjord and the open sea. All three spaces would have probably provided much anxiety to people venturing to their unknown world. Certainly, the spatial arrangement of figures on the Tumlehed panel and other panels within Bohuslän and neighbouring Värmland appears to portray a cultural map where the surrounding landscape (the macroscape) is brought within.

At the Tumlehed rock-painting site, there appear to be a number of 'acts' that constitute both a history and the socio-ritual division of space. Arguably, this rock-painting site not only tells a story but culturally divides the landscape into a cognitive map whereby the outside (the landscape) may be bought within (to the panel). The 'macroscape' is being reproduced as a 'microscape'. Similar approaches to prehistoric map-making have been recognized by Zubrow and Daly (1999: 162–174), Fossati (this volume, Chapter) who discusses maps as forming a spatial, cultural and symbolic behaviour which is inherent within the human psyche. Maps can thus be placed into a general categorization which include the following points: maps are 'drawn' using limited and restricted scales, thus localizing a world view (what one can see, one draws); (in some cases) prehistoric maps have practical uses (e.g. the Bedolina map, Valcamonica, showing field systems and settlements; as one progresses through prehistoric time, maps become broader and more complex (and subject specific); prehistoric maps emphasize cultural and symbolic activity (for example, hunting, honey collecting, dancing, warfare and so on); prehistoric maps do not use distance–perspective scales; subjectivity is confined to local borders with no cross-cultural or ethnic representation present; finally, prehistoric maps delineate ethnic identity. Of course, many of these generalizations can be considered for rock-art in general.

Acknowledgements

This paper is the result of visits to the Tumlehed site in 1993 and 1995. In ideal atmospheric conditions further motifs were discovered: a fish and single boat-line. Apart from excellent weather conditions and Swedish hospitality, I am indebted to Jarl Nordbladh, Mike Shanks and Tim Yates, for their comments on this paper.

References

Bakka, E. 1979. On shoreline dating of Arctic rock carvings in Vingen, West Norway, *Norwegian Archaeological Review* 12(2): 114–122.

Barthes, R. 1977. *Image–music–text*. London: Fontana.

Barthes, R. 1984. *Writing degree zero and elements of semiology*. London: Cape.

Bourdieu, P. 1977. *Outline of a theory of practice*. Cambridge: Cambridge University Press.

Bowra, C.M. 1962. *Primitive song*. London: Weidenfeld and Nicolson.

Bradley, R. 1993. *Altering the earth*. Edinburgh: Society of Antiquaries of Scotland. Monograph Series 8.

Bradley, R. 1997. *Signing the land: rock art and the prehistory of Atlantic Europe*. London: Routledge.

Bradley, R. 1998. *The significance of monuments: on the shaping of human experience in Neolithic and Bronze Age Europe*. London: Routledge.

Bradley, R., F. Criado Boado and R. Fadregas Valcarce. 1994. Rock art research as landscape archaeology: a pilot study in Galicia, north-west Spain, *World Archaeology* 25(3): 374–390.

Coles, J.M. 1990. *Images of the past: a guide to the rock carvings and other ancient monuments of northern Bohuslän*. Uddevalla: Skrifter av Bohusläns Museum och Bohusläns Hembygdforbund 32.

Coles, J.M. 1991. Elk and Ogopogo: belief systems in the hunter-gatherer rock art of northern lands, *Proceedings of the Prehistoric Society* 57(2): 129–148.

Cullberg, K., J. Nordbladh, J. and J. Sjöberg. 1975. *Hällmalningen i Tumlehed*. Särtryck ur Fynd Rapporter 1975: Rapporter över Göteborgs Arkeologiska Musei undersökningar.

Davidson, I. and W. Noble. 1989. The archaeology of perception: traces of depiction and language, *Current Anthropology* 30(2): 125–156.

Gjessing, G. 1932. *Arktiske halleristninger i Nord-Norge*. Oslo.

Gjessing, G. 1936. *Nordenfjelske ristninger og malinger an den artiske gruppe*. Oslo: Aschehoug. Instituttet for Sammenlignende Kulturforskning Serie B 30.

Hallström, G. 1938. *Monumental art of northern Europe from the Stone Age*, 1: *The Norwegian localities*. Stockholm: Almqvist and Wiksell.

Helskog, K. (1987) Selective depictions. A study of 3,500 years of rock carvings from Arctic Norway and their relationship to the Sami drums, in I. Hodder (ed.) *Archaeology as long-term history*: 18–30. Cambridge: Cambridge University Press.

Lévi-Strauss, C. 1963. *Structural anthropology*. London: Weidenfeld and Nicolson.

Lévi-Strauss, C. 1964. *Mythologiques*. Paris: Plon.

Malmer, M.P. 1981. *A chorological study of north European rock art*. Stockholm: Almquist and Wicksell. Kungliga Vitterhets Historie och Antikvitetsakademiens Handlingar, Antikvariska Serien 31.

Marstrander, S. 1976. Building a hide boat: an archaeological experiment, *International Journal of Nautical Archaeology* 5: 13–22.

Munn, N. 1963. The Walbiri sand story, *Australian Territories* 3: 37–44.

Munn, N. 1973. *Walbirian iconography*. Cambridge: Cambridge University Press.

Munn, N. 1976. The spatiotemporal transformations of Gawa canoes, *Journal de la Société des Océanistes* 3: 39–53.

Munn, N. 1983. Gawan Kula: spatiotemporal control and the symbolism of influence, in J.W. Leach and E.R. Leach (eds), *The Kula: new perspectives on Massin exchange*: 277–307. Cambridge: Cambridge University Press.

Munn, N. 1986. *The fame of Gawa: a symbolic study of value transformation in a Massin society*. Cambridge: Cambridge University Press.

Nash, G.H. 1997a. Symbols in space: rock carvings of the Campo Lameiro region, southern Galicia, Spain, in G.H. Nash (ed.), *Semiotics of landscape: archaeology of mind*: 46–58. Oxford: British Archaeological Reports. International Series S661.

Nash, G.H. 1997b. Experiencing space and symmetry: the use, destruction and abandonment of La Hougue Bie Neolithic passage grave, Jersey, in G.H. Nash (ed.), *Semiotics of landscape: archaeology of mind*: 105–118. Oxford: British Archaeological Reports. International Series S661.

Nash, G.H. 1998. *Exchange, status and mobility: Mesolithic portable art of southern Scandinavia*. Oxford: British Archaeological Reports. International Series S710.

Nash, G.H. 2000. Expressing sexuality, fertility and childbirth in art: engendering south Scandinavian Mesolithic portable artifacts, in L. Bevan (ed.), *Sexuality, society and the archaeological record*. Edinburgh: Cruithne Press: 19–42.

Nash, G.H. 2001 (in press). The use of amber as personal adornment: symbolic exchange during the south Scandinavian Mesolithic, in D. Gheghou (ed.), *The archaeology of fire*. Oxford: British Archaeological Reports. International Series.

Nordbladh, J. 1987. Bird, fish or something in between? The case of the rock paintings of the Swedish west coast, in G. Burenhult *et al.* (eds), *Theoretical approaches, settlement and society: studies in honour of Mats P. Malmer*: 305–20. Oxford: British Archaeological Reports. International Series 366.

Nygaard, S.E. 1989. The Stone Age of northern Scandinavia: a review, *Journal of World Prehistory* 3: 71–116.

Saussure, F. de. 1960. *Course in general linguistics*. London: Peter Owen. [First published 1916.]

Shanks, M. 1992. *Experiencing the past: on the character of archaeology*. London: Routledge.

Shanks, M. and C. Tilley. 1987a. *Re-constructing archaeology: theory and practice*. Cambridge: Cambridge University Press.

Shanks, M. and C. Tilley. 1987b. *Social theory and archaeology*. Cambridge: Polity Press.

Sognnes, K. 1987. Rock art and settlement patterns in the Bronze Age: example from Stjordal, Trøndelag, Norway, *Norwegian Archaeological Review* 20(2): 110–119.

Sognnes, K. 1988. Rock art at the Arctic Circle: Arctic and agrarian rock engravings from Tjøtta and Vevelstad, Nordland, Norway, *Acta Archaeologica* 59: 67–90.

Sognnes, K. 1998. Symbols in a changing world: rock-art and the transition from hunting and farming in mid Norway, in C. Chippindale and P.S.C. Taçon (eds), *The archaeology of rock-art*: 146–162. Cambridge: Cambridge University Press.

Tilley, C. 1991. *Material culture and text: the art of ambiguity*. London: Routledge.

Zubrow, E.B.W. and P.T. Daly. 1999. Symbolic behaviour: the origin of a spatial perspective, in C. Renfrew and C. Scarre (eds), *Cognition and material culture: the archaeology of symbolic storage*: 157–174. Cambridge: McDonald Institute of Archaeology.

Chapter 10

Land of elks – sea of whales

Landscapes of the Stone Age rock-art in central Scandinavia

Kalle Sognnes

Landscape and its perception

During the last decades landscape studies have become an important part of archaeology and of rock-art studies. For some rock-art sites in Scandinavia, topography and subject-matter were the main arguments for identifying sites as made by Stone Age hunters, especially for the site at Vingen in Nordfjord, western Norway in an area especially rich in red deer, which traditionally were chased over the cliffs (Bing 1912). This hunters' rock-art in general has been dated to the Stone Age. Similarly, the location of Bronze Age rock-art in and/or near cultivated land was used in interpreting this rock-art as evidence of fertility rituals (see Marstrander 1963: 256). In the 1970s Gro Mandt Larsen pioneered more profound studies of the location of the Bronze Age rock-art within the landscape (Mandt Larsen 1972; Mandt 1978), followed by other scholars (Bertilsson 1987; Kjellén and Hyenstrand 1977; Sognnes 1983). Later the Stone Age rock-art was brought into this discourse (Ramqvist 1992; Sognnes 1992, 1994).

Recently the term 'landscape' has been much debated in archaeology (Johnston 1998; Tilley 1994), anthropology (Bender 1993; Hirsch and O'Hanlon 1995) and geography (Cosgrove 1984; Livingstone 1992). The term is common to the north European Germanic languages, Dutch *landschap*, German *Landschaft*, Norwegian *landskap* (also *landskapnad*) – it is also known from ancient languages as *landschip* in Old English and *landskapr* in Old Norse (Falk and Torp 1991: 443). The first part of this word, of course, is land; *skap*, still common in modern Norwegian, is used as a suffix only – meaning a group (e.g. *mannskap*, crew) or collection (e.g. *buskap*, cattle) – or the meaning of interest here – character, composition, quality (e.g. *dårskap*, foolishness; *vennskap*, friendship). *Skapnad* leads us to the verb *skape*, which means to shape/create (Aasen 1983: 661). Landscape originally must have been a general term for the characteristics and qualities of a land.

In the sixteenth century Dutch painters started using 'landscape' as a technical term. This new meaning – that the landscape was recognized as such because it reminded the viewer of a painting – has strongly influenced modern Western thinking. People look at landscape, like paintings, from a distance, recognizing foregrounds and backgrounds (Hirsch 1995: 2–3; after Thomas 1984: 265). Because of this distancing from nature, landscape became transformed into a cultural idea, which could be used as an analytical concept. We also have another and more direct relationship with landscape. It is experienced; we live in it, travel through it, and change it. The way we experience landscape includes all our relationship with our surroundings, material culture, architecture, ecology, memories, narratives and cosmologies (Johnston 1998: 317). Landscape is characterized by a duality between nature and culture but also between analytical distance and our experiences from living within it; the landscape is changing and dynamic. This dynamic partly is due to natural and man-made changes in the environment. However, we also alter the landscape through our experiences and interpretations; thus, the landscape can be considered a cultural process (Hirsch 1995: 5).

The background of the landscape often is dominated by verticality, while the foreground to a large extent is horizontal. While moving, we experience that the foreground changes rapidly, while the background for a long time remains virtually the same. We experience this from eye-level, that is, situated between one and a half and two metres above the ground (Gansum *et al.* 1997). When we travel by small boats, the traditional way of travelling in the coastscapes and fjordscapes of Norway, our eye-level may be less than one metre above the water.

Reconstructed landscapes

This chapter concentrates on central Scandinavia, that is, a broad belt across the Scandinavian Peninsula approximately between 62° 30′ and 65° N. This belt comprises parts of two countries, Norway and Sweden, the border between which is less than 350 years old and, of course, had no relevance during prehistory.* The area is quite rich in prehistoric rock-art, both petroglyphs and paintings; it comprises the provinces of Nord-Trøndelag and Sør-Trøndelag as well as parts of Møre og Romsdal in Norway and Jämtland and Västernorrland in Sweden (Figure 10.1).

Many different environments are found within this belt. The North Atlantic coast in the west is dominated by myriad large and small islands, holms and skerries. The dominating geographical feature in this part of Norway is the Trondheim fjord, which leads about 130 kilometres inland; the inner parts of this fjord run parallel with the coast. Numerous smaller fjords, bays and inlets are found at the coast. From the Trondheim fjord, short valleys lead towards the border against Sweden, which here follows the watershed of the Scandinavian Peninsula. On both sides of this border are large mountain plateaux and wide coniferous forests, through which wide and shallow river valleys lead towards the Gulf of Bothnia, often ending in long estuaries. The large Lake Storsjön in Jämtland forms a wide basin virtually halfway between the two coasts. Although the hunters' rock-art in these parts of Sweden and Norway is fairly well known and studied (Gjessing 1936; Hallström 1938, 1960) the modern national border seems to have acted as a mental barrier. With a few exceptions (Lindgaard 1999 and to some extent Hallström 1960), most studies have included only the corpus from one side of the border.

Nature is continuously changing – especially in northern parts of Norway and Sweden experiencing Holocene isostatic land uplift. It is possible to some extent to reconstruct past environments. Palynology and osteology may tell us which species of plants and animals lived in an area at a certain time, and detailed studies may reveal at least the major geomorphological changes. During the Pleistocene the weight of the large ice cap,

---

* I make use of present borders between countries and provinces in Figure 10.1 to make it easier for readers unfamiliar with the investigation area.

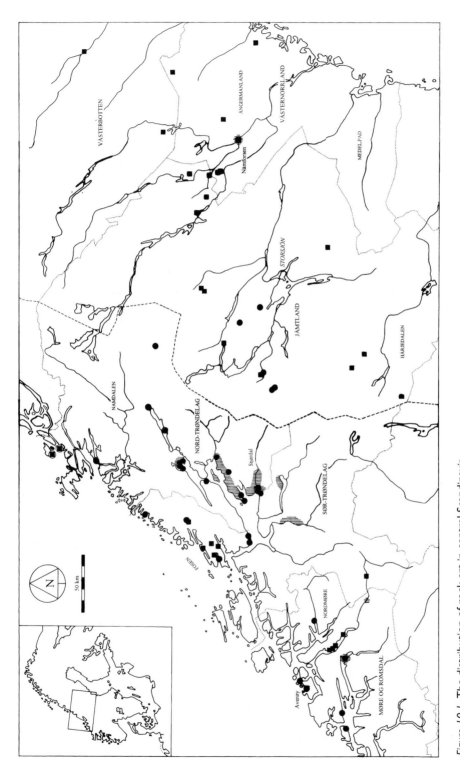

Figure 10.1 The distribution of rock-art in central Scandinavia.
Squares = paintings; squares in rings = cave paintings; dots = Stone Age petroglyphs; hatching = areas with Bronze Age rock-art

up to 3000 metres thick, pressed down the earth's crust. When the ice started melting, the crust began to adjust, trying to regain its equilibrium. This uplift still goes on in central and northern parts of Scandinavia. The late glacial depression was at its greatest at the Gulf of Bothnia; it was much smaller at the west coast of Norway. For this reason the Holocene land uplift has been uneven; on the west coast the eustatic rise of sea level for some time was faster than the isostatic rise of the land, causing a long-lasting transgression (Hafsten 1983).

Modern topographical maps in general are very helpful for our reconstructions. If we manage to identify the heights of the uplift since a certain date we may choose the nearest contour line as contemporary sea level. At the coasts sub-recent and recent changes often are small. Rocky cliffs are little affected; wave action normally creates series of beach bars, which during transgressions may be built on top of older deposits. When steeper slopes emerge the waves start the process of erosion, pushing the slopes inland and destroying older deposits, including traces of human habitation (Sognnes 1976). The situation is more complicated at the river estuaries. Due to the land uplift, the rivers continuously erode deeper into the Late Pleistocene deposits. This vertical erosion is supplemented by horizontal erosion due to meandering. The end result may be topographical and archaeological 'black holes' (see Groube 1981) into which important parts of the ancient landscape have disappeared.

Most archaeological reconstructions of prehistoric landscapes in central and northern Scandinavia have been based on land uplift data alone, ignoring the other Holocene geological processes (Farbregd 1979, 1986). Only for the Stjørdal Valley in Nord-Trøndelag has this problem been seriously discussed (Sognnes 1983; Sveian 1995).

Multilevel studies

The study of rock-art in landscapes may be carried out at several levels: at inter-regional and regional levels, which will be discussed briefly, and at local and site levels, on which I will concentrate. It may also be studied at panel level: when each decorated panel is seen as a miniature landscape with 'foreground' and 'background', 'hills' and 'valleys'; then the location of the images in relation to crevices, grooves, glacial striations and other surface features can be studied in detail. The relevance of such studies is documented for North America (Brody 1989) and southern Africa (Lewis-Williams and Dowson 1990). Numerous micro-topographical features may have been of significance for localizing the images.*

Inter-regional and regional levels

The rock-art of northern Europe frequently is treated as one entity, although it is found within a large area, from the west coast of Norway to Lake Onega and the White Sea in Russia and from south Denmark to northernmost Norway. Preferably, this area should be seen as a network of several rock-art regions, between which contacts must have

---

* Such studies may be flawed by the weathering of the rock. Features that today appear to be of importance may have been of no significance when the petroglyphs or paintings were made.

existed. At this inter-regional level, as well as at regional level, our landscape/rock-art studies are mostly concentrated on horizontality. The sites are plotted on to maps and we search for overall geographical distribution patterns, based on which we may formulate meaningful and relevant interpretations.

Little has been done at the inter-regional level regarding the location of the rock-art sites in the landscape; studies have concentrated on typology and chronology (Malmer 1981). Even a brief glance at the distribution on the Scandinavian Peninsula reveals that most rock-art sites are clustered along the coasts (Sognnes 1988: 28). Studying Figure 10.1, we find that most of the sites in central Scandinavia are not randomly distributed.* They are concentrated within three major drainages, the Lake Storsjön/Indal River drainage in Jämtland, the Ångerman River drainage in Västernorrland and Jämtland, and the Trondheim fjord drainage in Sør-Trøndelag and Nord-Trøndelag. We also find that sites at Nordmøre in Møre og Romsdal are concentrated, mainly into the Tingvoll fjord/Driva River drainage. Other sites in this province are found in the Storfjord drainage. A narrow isthmus, which can be crossed easily, separates this fjord from the Tingvoll fjord. Some sites are also found in the Härjedalen drainage in Jämtland. Real clusters are found only at the Trondheim fjord where virtually all petroglyphs dated to the Bronze Age are found. But also the Stone Age paintings and petroglyphs in this region show a tendency towards clustering.

The Nämforsen site is unique in central Scandinavia, both in its great number of petroglyphs and in the design of most of the animals (mostly elks). For the other sites, morphological similarities can easily be found between images in all the above-mentioned drainages. This has led scholars to postulate close contacts between people living at the west coast and in the interior parts of present-day Sweden (Hallström 1938, 1960). Many sites appear to have been located at major migration routes used by hunter-gatherers (Sognnes 1997). This is most evident for the sites in the Tingvoll fjord/Driva River drainage. That this must have been an important early route between the coast and the mountains is evidenced by the existence of early Mesolithic (Fosna) settlements at the island of Averøy, where two rock-art sites are found. To the east of the upper Driva River, in the Oppdal Mountains, early Mesolithic settlements are found, too (Gustafson 1986). Settlements and rock-art are also found in the area between.

The patterns which we can observe today were not known to Stone Age hunter-gatherers. They knew their own migration routes but not those that belonged to other groups or bands. One question that arises is whether they would have been able to identify migration routes if they entered an unfamiliar landscape. Would rock-art help them to gain such information? And would they recognize sites where this rock art would be located?

Local and site levels

In today's landscape we can quite easily get overviews of the local topography and ways to travel through it. To a large extent this is created by the openness of the landscape, a

---

* The distribution pattern, of course, changes with each new discovery but we can only discuss this question based on the currently available corpus.

Figure 10.2 In the present agricultural landscape horizontal views over fields and pastures are frequent, as at Oppauran in Stjørdal (Nord-Trøndelag). The pre-agricultural landscape in general, however, was dominated by the verticality and density of the forests

Photograph: K. Sognnes

Figure 10.3 Horizontality in the pre-agricultural landscape of central Scandinavia was primarily represented by fjords and lakes. From the Honnhammer rock paintings in Tingvoll (Møre og Romsdal) large parts of the Tingvoll fjord can be seen

Photograph: K. Sognnes

rather recent phenomenon due to farming and modern industrialization. More important is our frequent use of maps. Although we may journey without maps, we carry a cognitive map-imposed image of the landscape in question, in which we emphasize horizontality and spatial relationships between conspicuous topographic and manmade features. As rock-art researchers, we have preconceived conceptions of the locations of the rock-art in the landscape. This makes our experience of the sites very different from that of prehistoric men and women. Therefore, we approach a rock-art site with a strong sense of recognition, but sometimes we also experience surprise when we suddenly discover a hitherto unknown site – especially if this site is found at a place where we had no expectation that rock-art would occur.

While walking in the landscape, our direct experiences are based on visual impressions obtained from eye-level. We may get better views from a hilltop (Figure 10.2) but during prehistory the landscape was less open than today. Most of the land was covered by forests, in which dense rows of trees emphasize verticality, obfuscating the horizontality of the surrounding land. In a landscape like this horizontality and verticality merge. The background disappears. In a pre-agrarian landscape we first and foremost will experience the horizontality of the landscape at the sea (Figure 10.3) and at large lakes and bogs but also at mountain plateaux above the tree limit – and after forest fires.

At a local level we also to a large extent work by means of maps, plotting sites and panels, searching for patterns. In the investigation area discussed here, the Bronze Age petroglyphs, for instance, are strongly clustered, concentrated in a few municipalities at the Trondheim fjord (see Figure 10.1 above). The Stone Age sites are more scattered; we find some minor clusters of petroglyphs at smaller fjord basins and a cluster of paintings at the Fosen Peninsula between the Trondheim fjord and the North Atlantic (Sognnes 1994).

One of these clusters is found at the mouth of the Stjørdal Valley. Around this fjord basin five sites with Stone Age petroglyphs are found (Sognnes 1994). Two sites are found at the south side of this valley at each side of the tributary Leksdal Valley, which leads up towards large forests and mountain areas. In a sense these sites seem to 'guard' the entrance to this area which even today is rich in game, especially elks; during the Stone Age it is likely it was an important hunting ground. In Stjørdal more than 100 panels with Bronze Age petroglyphs are found. Their distribution is distinctly different; they are found in a wider area and most panels are clustered into twenty entities. These entities, which have a fairly regular distribution, may represent Bronze Age/early Iron Age societal (habitation) units (Sognnes 1993). The people making and using the petroglyphs may not have recognized this pattern, discovered by systematic studies of maps.

Most of these Bronze Age or agrarian rock-art panels can only be spotted from within short distances; some from only a few metres, others from several hundred metres distance. Apparently they were known to and could be found only by people who were familiar with this particular landscape, likely still dominated by dense forests. However, at fairly regular intervals the forest was cleared and the land opened up, presenting a new perspective of the landscape, making way for a new perception of the man–nature relationship as well as cosmology.

In contrast, a substantial number of the Stone Age sites are located at conspicuous topographical features, including the sites at the entrance to the Leksdal Valley (at Hell and Lånke; Sognnes 1994). Most of these Stone Age sites today are found near the sea; when they were made, at a time of higher sea level, they were located even closer to the shores. The topographical features chosen for the making of the Stone Age rock-art may not be large, but frequently would be easily spotted by people paddling along sounds and fjords (Figure 10.4). Some sites appear to have been located in the tidal zone, having been covered by beach bars (Bakka 1975). These Stone Age sites clearly have a maritime orientation, to some extent also reflected in the subject-matter.

In our landscape reconstructions we 'remove' the parts of the present landscape that were still submerged when the rock-art was made. In the steep-sided fjords this may be correct; at the coast, which is dominated by a low rim of land – the *strandflat* – this may be wrong. Even today only parts of the *strandflat* are above water; large parts still are submerged. These submerged parts of the *strandflat* create a shallow sea rich in fish and other marine resources; the location of the best catching sites depends on underwater topography. This was the case also during most of the Stone Age.

Sea of whales

For the sites in Norway, I start with those found at the coast. At the island of Averøy in Møre og Romsdal, two sites with Stone Age petroglyphs have been found, at Søbstad (Møllenhus 1968) and at Rødsand (Sognnes 1996a). Whales dominate both sites. At Rødsand, some elks and unidentified quadrupeds are found too. The Søbstad petroglyphs are found on vertical panels on a steep-sided hillock called Søbstadklubben, about ten metres above the present sea level and less than thirty metres from the shore. This hillock forms a promontory at the western side of a narrow north-running fjord, which virtually divides the island into two halves.

Figure 10.4 The rock-art of the Stone Age hunters was frequently located at conspicuous topographical features. The Steinmohaugen hillock at Hell in Stjørdal (Nord-Trøndelag), due to the Holocene land uplift today, is found more than forty metres above sea level. When the rock art at this hillock was made, the panel was probably only a few metres above the contemporary sea level. A small island nearby gives an impression of what this hillock looked like around 6000 years ago

Photograph: K. Sognnes

Søbstadklubben was still an island until the land was less than five metres lower than it is today (Figure 10.5). The land below this level, which constitutes a large part of the fields of the present Søbstad farm, emerged from the sea between 1000 and 2000 BP (interpolated from Møller 1995: 6), that is, in the Iron Age. When the petroglyphs were made, likely rather late in the Neolithic, Søbstadklubben was one of several small islands in a narrow fjord, which opened towards the Atlantic in the north. This topographical situation is almost identical with the rock-art site at Hell (Sognnes 1994), except that the mainland at Hell has a higher relief.

The topographical situation was similar also at the neighbouring site at Rødsand, on the eastern side of Averøy. This site is about twenty metres above the present sea level at the steep eastern side of a dome-shaped hillock. This hillock was on an island of its own; but when the petroglyphs were made, it formed the head of a narrow promontory, similar to that at Lånke. The Rødsand promontory stood out from the surrounding land not only by its shape but also by colour, the rock having a distinct reddish hue. Two phases of petroglyphs appear to exist at this site; a large, strongly weathered cervid, likely an elk, is superimposed by some smaller images. The maximum date for the Rødsand petroglyphs is around 6000 BP. Also at Strand in Osen, Sør-Trøndelag (Gjessing 1936; Petersen 1930), we find a similar situation. A few images, among them a large whale, are found on the vertical south-facing cliff of a hillock, which during the Stone Age was a small island.

Figure 10.5 At Søbstad in Averøy (Møre og Romsdal) petroglyphs are found at a steep-sided hillock around ten metres above shore level. With the sea level less than five metres higher, this hillock was an island

Photograph: K. Sognnes

Common to these coastal sites is their location at steep-sided small islands or at hillocks near the heads of low promontories; they all have depictions of whales and some geometrical patterns. At Strand and Rødsand terrestrial animals are depicted too. Reppen in Fosnes, Nord-Trøndelag, is another coastal site at which whales were depicted. These rather small petroglyphs are found on the sides of a boulder located on a former beach (Sognnes 1981). Engraved boulders are rare. Of several examples found during the last decades, only one remains *in situ*.

Although other animals are also depicted on the coastal sites in this part of Norway, whales dominate (Figure 10.6). These large animals would have been difficult to catch with Stone Age technology. Likely they in general were caught only if they stranded.* Whales are also peculiar animals: they are mammals; they live in water but breathe air; and frequently they leave the sea, jumping into the air. Most of the whale images depict jumping whales as viewed by Stone Age people from the shores or from boats. Fish and seals are represented but the rock-art clearly demonstrates that the coast was primarily a 'sea of whales'.

---

* At Evenhus in Frosta (Nord-Trøndelag) an apparent hunting scene is found. Small whales are found in two boats, within one of which is also a human.

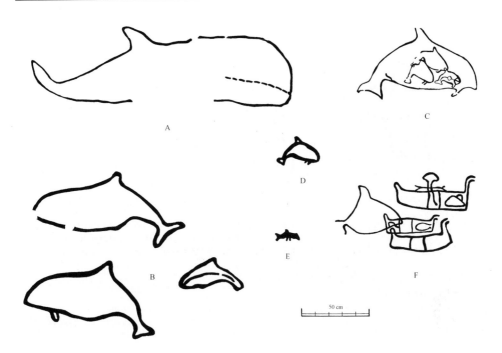

Figure 10.6 A selection of whale petroglyphs from central Scandinavia. A: Strand in Osen (Sør-Trøndelag); B: Søbstad in Averøy (Møre og Romsdal); C: Hammer in Steinkjer (Nord-Trøndelag); Reppen in Fosnes (Nord-Trøndelag); E: Nämforsen in Sollefteå (Västernorrland); F: Evenhus in Frosta (Nord-Trøndelag)

Whales were also depicted at fjord sites, for instance at Lånke (Sognnes 1994). The majority of the whale images are, however, found at two large sites at Evenhus in Frosta (Gjessing 1936; Petersen 1922) and Hammer in Steinkjer (Bakka 1988; Bakka and Gaustad 1974), Nord-Trøndelag. At both sites we find boats together with the whales, at Hammer also birds, at Lånke birds and whales together. At Evenhus some boats look like symbolic birds (Sognnes 1996b). Statistically these three motifs constitute a separate entity. At Hammer and Evenhus the petroglyphs are found at rock outcrops on former beaches. A beach bar covered the panel Hammer VII shortly after the petroglyphs were made (Bakka 1975; Hafsten 1987). It is likely that this happened in the early Neolithic, shortly after 6000 BP. The Evenhus panels, however, did not emerge from the sea until the very end of the Neolithic and this site would have been used mostly during the early Bronze Age. At the end of the Neolithic, the Evenhus site was located at the eastern end of a low island virtually in the middle of the Trondheim fjord. The maritime aspect of this and similar sites is emphasized by the motifs (Figure 10.7). The coastal sites are found at rather small, steep panels with a few petroglyphs, in front of which only small groups of people could come together. The Evenhus and Hammer sites are large with more than 100 petroglyphs; large groups could assemble in front of or around these gently sloping panels.

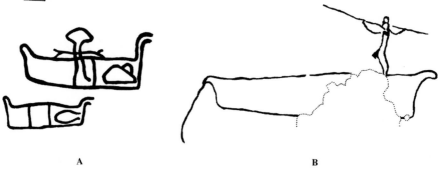

Figure 10.7 The maritime aspect of the petroglyphs at Evenhus in Frosta (Nord-Trøndelag) is emphasized by the presence of both whales and boats (A). Another possible boat hunting scene (B) is found at Vasstrand in Åfjord (Sør-Trøndelag)

Land of elks

Terrestrial animals, above all elks, dominate the other sites (Figure 10.8). Whales do occasionally occur, for instance at Bardal in Steinkjer, where the largest image of all, a whale around six metres long, is found at the top of the large Bardal I panel (Gjessing 1936; Hallström 1938). The elk is the dominating motif at most of the Trondheim fjord sites as well as the sites in Jämtland and Västernorrland. This holds true for both paintings and petroglyphs, including the Nämforsen site (Hallström 1960). Occasionally other cervids – reindeer, for instance at Hell in Stjørdal, and red deer, at Bogge in Nesset (Møre og Romsdal) – substitute for the elk; but there can be no doubt that inland central Scandinavia from a rock-art point of view was a 'land of elks'.

Elks are found together with whales and boats above all at the large beach sites at Evenhus and Hammer; we also find elks (and reindeer) at the conspicuous hillocks at Hell and Lånke (Sognnes 1994). For most of the other fjord sites, the relationship between rock-art and landscape/topography has not yet been studied; some sites appear to be located at or near major promontories.

This question will have to be dealt with at a later date; here I move on to the inland sites, extremely rare on the Norwegian side. Recently two small panels have been found at Nerhol in Oppdal (Sør-Trøndelag) at the Driva River. Between these two panels the river enters a narrow gorge formed by a series of pot-holes or 'giants' kettles' made by meltwater during the early Holocene. Except for their nearness to the river, there apparently are no topographic features that may indicate the existence of a rock-art site. Nerhol I is found under a small rock-shelter only five metres wide and three metres high. It can only be spotted from below. Passing above it in the present pine forest, one may be less than five metres away without realizing its existence. The pot-holes may have been a decisive location factor for the Nerhol panels, especially since they mark the beginning of a series of steep rapids and waterfalls. Likely the noise of the Driva River entering this gorge would lead people to this particular site. It is sound together with the pot-holes, rather than vision alone, that reveals the existence and location of this rock-art site.

Figure 10.8 A selection of elk petroglyphs from central Scandinavia. A from Hammer in Steinkjer (Nord-Trøndelag). B and E from Holte in Levanger (Nord-Trøndelag). C from Evenhus in Frosta (Nord-Trøndelag). D from Nämforsen in Sollefteå (Västernorrland). F from Glösa in Krokom (Jämtland). G from Stykket in Rissa (Sør-Trøndelag)

Most rock-art sites in the Swedish part of central Scandinavia have similar locations. The largest – and most impressive regarding both vision and sound – is Nämforsen, where hundreds of petroglyphs are located at the northern side of the Ångerman River and at three large islands in the middle of this large waterfall (Hallström 1960; Tilley 1991). In the pre-agricultural landscape one could only see the waterfall from below, from the riverbed which could be reached after a walk through the dense forest. The thundering noise from the waterfall, especially during the melting season, would have led people to this spectacular site.

The petroglyphs at Gärde in Krokom (Jämtland) have a similar location. At the first rapids downstream from Lake Gärdesjön, three large elks are found on an island in the middle of the river. At the south-western shore are found some smaller elks together with hoof prints (Hallström 1960). The setting is similar at Glösa in Krokom, where around fifty petroglyphs, mostly depicting elks, are found at the western bank of the Glösa Creek (Hallström 1960). At both Glösa and Gärde the petroglyphs are inundated by spring meltwater; both are located within dense woods and are visible only from short distances.

These river and creek sites are contrasted by a number of sites at lakeshores, where paintings are located at vertical cliffs (Figure 10.9). These settings in many ways are similar to some of the Norwegian fjord sites. The lakes create large open spaces in the

Figure 10.9 At Lake Fångsjön in Strömsund (Jämtland) paintings are found on a vertical cliff facing the lake

Photograph: B.O. Viklund

landscape, but the relief surrounding these lakes is much less steep than in the fjordscapes of Norway. The cliffs in question, which may not be particularly high, appear quite conspicuous when approached by boat or by walking on the ice.

Rapids or waterfalls together with steep cliffs at lakeshores represent the main recognizable distribution patterns at site level in Jämtland and Västernorrland, a pattern hardly found in the adjacent Norwegian provinces. Recently a number of sites have been found which are located neither at lakes nor at rapids. These sites are at small isolated hillocks or large boulders, which still form conspicuous features in this otherwise low-relief landscape (Viklund 1997).

Towards a synthesis: visibility, drainages, contact

Rock-art has been systematically studied for more than 150 years, largely concentrated on motifs (typology) and age (chronology). During the last decades, spatial studies have played a greater role. Still, these studies are in their infancy. Much work remains to be done before we have an adequate knowledge of all relevant variables; some of the work so far clearly will influence future interpretations and our understanding of the relationship between mankind, landscape and rock-art.

At the site level we find that a substantial number of rock-art panels are located at conspicuous topographical features; this mostly demonstrates their conspicuousness in low-relief landscapes. These features often 'disappear' when they still are in the background of the landscape; they become visible while entering the foreground. At the regional and inter-regional levels most of the rock-art known from central Scandinavia is found at major river and fjord drainages. Some differences seem to exist between these drainages, the most significant that between the two large river drainages in Sweden and the Trondheim fjord drainage at which no rock-art has been found in the upper parts – that is, in the valleys adjacent to the fjord.* In the Lake Storsjön/Indal River drainage most of the rock-art is found in the upper part while most of the sites in the Ångerman River drainage are found in the lower part. Across the border from this drainage, the Namdalen drainage in Nord-Trøndelag apparently has no rock-art at all.

Whether there was any contact between people exploiting these drainages is uncertain. Along the Norwegian coast a number of seemingly isolated rock-art sites are found, which emphasize the importance of coastal travel as a major communication agent. In Sweden similar coastal rock-art sites were missing; recently several sites at former river estuaries have been found, among them at the Stornorrfors rapids in Ume River (Baudou 1995). Like Nämforsen, these sites may be interpreted as meeting-places for people exploiting the drainage in question (Forsberg 1993) and between these people and traders from south Scandinavia (Malmer 1981: 107). Interestingly, Nämforsen so far is the southernmost of these Swedish coastal sites; not even at the Lake Storsjön/Indal River drainage, is an estuary rock-art site known.

Contacts between the drainages on both sides of the Norwegian/Swedish border have been postulated by several scholars, especially Hallström (1960). Morphological similarities can be found between the Glösa petroglyphs and those found at Evenhus and Bogge but also between paintings at Flatruet in Härjedal and Honnhammer in Tingvoll (Sognnes 1995; see also Hallström 1960). The apparent void area between the Trondheim fjord and the westernmost sites in Jämtland represents a problem for the proposed existence of hunting trails across this water divide.

The many rock-art sites in central Scandinavia may represent a number of different uses and meanings as well as varying in symbolic importance. Arguably they were located at important migration routes used by hunter-gatherers for millennia – but this does not explain why a particular place was chosen for the making of paintings or petroglyphs. These images may have been made at important resting and/or catching sites; people may also have stopped at these places because they were of special importance, which was signified by the rock-art. Were the rock-art sites of importance for only one group or band, or were they actively sought for and used by people living in a wider area? Further studies of the rock-art and landscape relationship must be conducted at several levels.

Acknowledgements

Bernt Ove Viklund, Härnösand, provided me with updated information on the sites in Sweden. He also kindly let me use one of his photographs for publication.

---

* The two sites at Lake Snåsavatnet (Nord-Trøndelag) apparently deviate from this rule; but the threshold of the moraine that dams this lake lies about thirty metres above the present sea level and did not emerge from the sea until shortly before 4000 BP.

References

Aasen, I. 1983. *Norsk ordbog med dansk forklaring.* Oslo: Fonna. [First published 1873.]

Bakka, E. 1975. Geologically dated Arctic rock carvings at Hammer near Steinkjer in Nord Trøndelag, *Arkeologiske skrifter* 2: 7–48.

Bakka, E. 1988. *Helleristningane på Hammer i Beitstad, Steinkjer, Nord-Trøndelag.* Trondheim: Vitenskapsmuseet. Rapport Arkeologisk Serie 1988: 7.

Bakka, E. and. F. Gaustad. 1974. *Helleristningsundersøkelser på Hammer i Beitstad, Steinkjer, Nord-Trøndelag.* Trondheim: DKNVS Museet. Rapport Arkeologisk Serie 1974: 8.

Baudou, E. 1995. *Norrlands forntid – ett historiskt perspektiv.* Umea: Gewe-förlaget.

Bender, B. (ed.). 1993. *Landscape: politics and perspectives.* Oxford: Berg.

Bertilsson, U. 1987. *The rock carvings of northern Bohuslän: spatial structures and social symbols.* Stockholm. Stockholm Studies in Archaeology 7.

Bing, K. 1912. Helleristningsfund ved gården Vingen i Rugsund, Ytre Nordfjord, *Oldtiden* 2: 25–38.

Brody, J.J. 1989. Site use, pictorial space, and subject matter in Late Prehistoric Rio Grande pueblo art, *Journal of Anthropological Research* 45: 15–28.

Cosgrove, D. 1984. *Social formation and symbolic landscape.* London: Croom Helm.

Falk, H. and A. Torp. 1991. *Etymologisk ordbog over det norske og det danske sprog.* Oslo: Ringstrøms antikvariat. [First published 1903–1906.]

Farbregd, O. 1979. Perspektiv på Namdalens jernalder, *Viking* 42: 20–80.

Farbregd, O. 1986. Elveosar – gamle sentra på vandring, *Spor* 2: 6–12.

Forsberg, L. 1993. En kronologisk analys av ristningarna vid Nämforsen, in L. Forsberg and T.B. Larsson (eds), *Ekonomi och näringsformer i nordisk bronsålder*: 195–246. Umeå. Studia Archaeologica Universitatis Umensis 3.

Gansum, T., G.B. Jerpåsen and C. Keller. 1997. *Arkeologisk landskapsanalyse med visuelle metoder.* Stavanger: Arkeologisk Museum. AmS Skrifter 28.

Gjessing, G. 1936. *Nordenfjelske ristninger og malinger av den arktiske gruppe.* Oslo: Aschehoug. Instituttet for Sammenlignende Kulturforskning Serie B 30.

Groube, L. 1981. Black holes in British prehistory: the analysis of settlement distribution, in I. Hodder, G. Isaac and N. Hammond (eds), *Patterns of the past: studies in honour of David Clarke*: 185–209. Cambridge: Cambridge University Press.

Gustafson, L. 1986. Fangstfolk i fjellet, *Spor* 1: 18–23.

Hafsten, U. 1983. Shore-level changes in South Norway during the last 13,000 years traced by biostratigraphical methods and radiocarbon datings, *Norsk geografisk tidsskrift* 37: 63–79.

Hafsten, U. 1987. Vegetasjon, klima og landskapsutvikling i Trøndelag etter siste istid, *Norsk geografisk tidsskrift* 41: 101–120.

Hallström, G. 1938. *Monumental art of northern Europe from the Stone Age*, 1: *The Norwegian localities.* Stockholm: Thule.

Hallström, G. 1960. *Monumental art of northern Sweden from the Stone Age.* Stockholm: Almqvist and Wicksell.

Hirsch, E. 1995. Landscape: between place and space, in E. Hirsch and M. O'Hanlon (eds), *The anthropology of landscape: perspectives on place and space*: 1–30. Oxford: Clarendon Press.

Hirsch, E. and M. O'Hanlon (eds). 1995. *The anthropology of landscape: perspectives on place and space.* Oxford: Clarendon Press.

Johnston, R. 1998. The paradox of landscape, *European Journal of Archaeology* 1: 313–325.

Kjellén, E. and Å. Hyenstrand. 1977. *Hällristningar och bronsålderssamhälle i sydvästra Uppland.* Uppsala: Upplands Fornminnesförenings Tidskrift 49.

Lewis-Williams, J.D. and T. Dowson. 1990. Through the veil: San rock painting and the rock face, *South African Archaeological Bulletin* 55(151): 5–16.

Lindgaard, E. 1999. Jegerbergkunsten i et øst-vestperspektiv. Cand. philol. thesis at the Norwegian University of Science and Technology (NTNU), Trondheim.

Lindquist, C. 1994. *Fångstfolkets bilder. En studie av de nordfennoskandiska kustanknutna jägarhäll-ristningarna.* Stockholm: Theses and Papers in Archaeology New Series A 5.

Livingstone, D. 1992. *The geographical tradition: episodes in the history of a contested enterprise.* Oxford: Blackwell.

Malmer, M.P. 1981. *A chorological study of north European rock art.* Stockholm: Almqvist and Wicksell. Kungliga Vitterhets Historie och Antikvitets Akademiens Handlingar, Antikvariska Serien 32.

Mandt Larsen, G. 1972. *Bergbilder i Hordaland: en undersøkelse av bildenes sammensetning, deres naturmiljø og kulturmiljø.* Bergen: Universitetsforlaget. Årbok for Universitetet i Bergen, Humanistisk Serie 1970: 2.

Mandt, G. 1978. Is the location of rock pictures an interpretative element?, in S. Marstrander (ed.), *Acts of the international symposium on rock art*: 170–184. Oslo: Universitetsforlaget. Instituttet for Sammenlignende Kulturforskning Serie A 29.

Marstrander, S. 1963. *Østfolds jordbruksristninger: Skjeberg.* Oslo: Universitetsforlaget. Instituttet for Sammenlignende Kulturforskning Serie B 53.

Møllenhus, K.R. 1968. *Nye helleristningsfunn i Romsdal og Nordmøre.* Trondheim: Det Kongelige Norske Videnskabers Selskabs Skrifter 1968: 3.

Møller, J.J. 1995. Isnedsmelting og strandforskyvning i Midt-Norge – metoderedskap i utforskningen av strandnær bosetning gjennom tidene, *Spor* 1: 4–8.

Petersen, T. 1922. Fra hvilken tid stammer de naturalistiske helleristninger?, *Naturen* 1922: 88–108.

Petersen, T. 1930. En nyopdaget helleristning på Strand i Osen, Bjørnør prestegjeld, *Det Kongelige Norske Videnskabers Selskabs forhandlinger* 3: 138–141.

Ramqvist, P.H. 1992. Hällbilder som utgångspunkt vid tolkningar av jägarsamhället, *Fortiden i norr* 3: 31–54.

Sognnes, K. 1976. Comments on 'Two tests of the prehistoric cultural chronology of Varanger, north Norway', *Norwegian Archaeological Review* 9: 56–61.

Sognnes, Kalle. 1981. *Helleristningsundersøkelser i Trøndelag 1979 og 1980.* Trondheim: DKNVS museet. Rapport Arkeologisk Serie 1981: 2.

Sognnes, K. 1983. *Bergkunsten i Stjørdal. Helleristningar og busetjing.* Trondheim: DKNVS Museet. Gunneria 45.

Sognnes, K. 1988. Helleristninger – vitnemål om eldgamle kontakter, *Spor* 2: 26–28.

Sognnes, K. 1992. A spatial approach to the study of rock art in Trøndelag, Norway, in S. Goldsmith *et al.* (eds), *Ancient images, ancient thought: the archaeology of ideology*: 107–120. Calgary: Institute of Archaeology.

Sognnes, K. 1993. The role of rock art in the Bronze Age and early Iron Age in Trøndelag, Norway, *Acta Archaeologica* 63: 157–188.

Sognnes, K. 1994. Ritual landscapes: toward a reinterpretation of Stone Age rock art in Trøndelag, Norway, *Norwegian Archaeological Review* 27: 29–50.

Sognnes, K. 1995. Fra kyst til innland – tidlige kontakter mellom Trøndelag og Jämtland/Härjedalen, *Spor* 2: 4–6.

Sognnes, K. 1996a. Helleristningene på Averøya. Kristiansund, *Årbok for Nordmøre Museum*: 74–85.

Sognnes, K. 1996b. Dyresymbolikk i midt-norsk yngre steinalder, *Viking* 59: 25–44.

Sognnes, K. 1997. Between land and sea: rock art and landscape in Stone Age mid-Norway. Paper presented at the TAG Conference, Bournemouth University.

Sognnes, K. 1999. Rocks, motifs and techniques: a re-evaluation of a 'unique' petroglyph site in Norway, *Rock Art Research* 16: 42–49.

Svean, H. 1995. *Sandsletten blir til: Stjørdal fra fjordbunn til strandsted.* Trondheim: NGU. Norges Geologiske Undersøkelse Skrifter 117.

Thomas, K. 1984. *Man and the natural world: changing attitudes in England 1500–1800.* Harmondsworth: Penguin Books.

Tilley, C. 1991. *Material culture and text: the art of ambiguity*. London: Routledge.
Tilley, C. 1994. *A phenomenology of landscape: places, paths and monuments*. Oxford: Berg.
Viklund, B.O. 1997. Nyupptäckta hällmålningar i Anundsjö, Fjällsjö och Ramsele i Ångermanland, *Oknytt* 3–4: 21–33.

Index